Theory and Evidence

Learning, Development, and Conceptual Change
Lila Gleitman, Susan Carey, Elissa Newport, and
Elizabeth Spelke, editors

Theory and Evidence

The Development of Scientific Reasoning

Barbara Koslowski

A Bradford Book
The MIT Press
Cambridge, Massachusetts
London, England

© 1996 Massachusetts Institute of Technology

All rights reserved. No part of this book may be reproduced in any form by any electronic or mechanical means (including photocopying, recording, and information storage and retrieval) without permission in writing from the publisher.

This book was set in Palatino by Asco Trade Typesetting Ltd., Hong Kong, and was printed and bound in the United States of America.

First printing, 1996.

Library of Congress Cataloging-in-Publication Data

Koslowski, Barbara.
  Theory and evidence : the development of scientific reasoning / Barbara Koslowski.
      p.   cm. — (Learning, development, and conceptual change)
  "A Bradford book."
  Includes bibliographical references and index.
  ISBN 0-262-11209-4 (hc : alk. paper)
  1. Reasoning. 2. Science—Philosophy. I. Title. II. Series.
  Q175.32.R45K67   1996
  501'.9—dc20   95-17409
                                                  CIP

For Richard and Christopher

Contents

Series Foreword

This series in learning, development, and conceptual change will include state-of-the-art reference works, seminal book-length monographs, and texts on the development of concepts and mental structures. It will span learning in all domains of knowledge, from syntax to geometry to the social world, and will be concerned with all phases of development, from infancy through adulthood.

The series intends to engage such fundamental questions as the following:

• *The nature and limits of learning and maturation* The influence of the environment, of initial structures, and of maturational changes in the nervous system on human development; learnability theory; the problem of induction; domain-specific constraints on development.
• *The nature of conceptual change* Conceptual organization and conceptual change in child development, in the acquisition of expertise, and in the history of science.

Lila Gleitman
Susan Carey
Elissa Newport
Elizabeth Spelke

Acknowledgments

When I was a graduate student of his, one of Jerome Bruner's favorite aphorisms was, Given half a chance, eighty percent of the population can score above the mean. In subsequent years, this maxim took on new meaning for me when I began to read the literature on causal reasoning and scientific thinking, because it seemed that in this literature, certain types of reasoning were often dismissed as inadequate when they seemed, to my naive mind, to be rather sensible. Fortunately for my intuitions, I became acquainted with Richard Boyd, who eventually became, among other things, my guide to philosophical approaches to assessing causal and scientific reasoning and who provided me with a framework within which my intuitions could be articulated.

Over the years my thinking about reasoning has benefited tremendously from collaboration with, and feedback from, several exceptionally able students, undergraduate as well as graduate. Those who are not already listed in this book as coauthors of various experiments include Gail Jaquish, Amy Masnick, Joan McLaughlin, Mary Moran, Deborah Olsen, Tina Rosenblum, Melanie Swiderek, and Stephanie Thompson. Susan Barnett's feedback on the first three chapters and the summary was, like her thinking in general, incisive and analytic. The chapters are much better for her having commented on them.

In any institution, the administrative framework can be either a source of obstacles or of facilitating support. While this book was being produced, there were several people who, in their administrative capacities, performed the latter function: Betty Lewis, Irving Lazar, George Suci, and Jerome Zeigler. Until his death, John Condry provided consistent encouragement and a steady stream of New Yorker cartoons. He was a friend as well as a colleague.

In one of his recent books, Frank Keil thanks Susan Carey for having read his manuscript while camping in Yosemite National Park. I thank Susan for having read my manuscript while sitting in Italian cafés. As I am extremely grateful to Susan for her feedback and encouragement as series editor, my wish for her is that she be able, at some point, to enjoy a vacation unencumbered by other authors' manuscripts.

In addition to Susan, Jonathan Baron, Merry Bullock, Richard Canfield, Rochel Gelman, Leona Schauble, and Susan Somerville all read parts of earlier drafts of this manuscript. The book is better because of their comments. (Jon's comments were helpful in a special way because he so frequently saw things differently from how I did.)

The people at the MIT Press were a pleasure to deal with, from Betty Stanton to Amy Pierce and Alan Thwaits. Alan, in particular, did much to improve the clarity of my writing.

When she recently became my secretary, Irene Pytcher did a yeoman's work trying to sort through and make sense of the files left by previous secretaries. Had she been my secretary all along, this book might well have been completed sooner.

Some of the empirical research reported in this book was funded by the National Science Foundation (BNS 8410600). At NSF, Joseph Young was the ideal program officer. I thank him.

Richard Boyd eventually became my husband. I owe him thanks not only for his generosity with his philosophical expertise but also for being nonsexist in deed as well as word. While this book was being completed, Richard not only continued to carry out his childcare and household responsibilities but also took over most of mine. Our son, Christopher, has my thanks for being a delight not only when this book was being written but in general. He is our anchor and puts everything into proper perspective.

Part I
Theory and Evidence

Chapter 1
Introduction

If the prevailing view in the literature is accurate, then both children and adults are poor scientists. They have trouble identifying likely causes. They have difficulty distinguishing between their theoretical commitments and the evidence that supports them. They seek to generate confirmatory evidence rather than to test hypotheses, and when they do encounter disconfirming evidence, they tend to ignore it. They are unable to deal with confounded variables.

However, one's view about whether people are adept at scientific thinking depends heavily on one's view of what scientific inquiry is. In this book, I argue that the view of scientific inquiry that is most heavily relied on in the psychological literature is continuous with the philosophical tradition of logical positivism and its emphasis on covariation. Because of this, the psychological literature largely ignores several crucial principles of scientific inquiry, and one consequence is that it provides either an incomplete or a distorted view of the situations in which people engage in scientific reasoning. I describe several studies whose findings suggest that if one considers aspects of scientific inquiry that are typically ignored, one arrives at a different picture of people's ability to engage in scientific thinking. I suggest that in many of the studies in which people seemed to behave nonscientifically, they did so precisely because they were relying on principles of scientific inquiry that are not typically studied but that nevertheless definitely constitute good scientific practice. Finally, in describing the results of the studies, I attempt to chart, in a preliminary way, the (often tacit) beliefs that people hold about the types of evidence that are important in scientific thinking and I begin to examine the ways in which their beliefs change with age.

The Role of Covariation

Historical Perspective

Research relevant to an understanding of scientific thinking comes from different sources. For example, some of the relevant research consists of studies that were explicitly directed at examining various aspects of scientific thinking such as how people assess evidence (e.g., Kuhn, Amsel, and O'Loughlin 1988; Klahr and Dunbar 1988) or test hypotheses (e.g., Mynatt, Doherty, and Tweney 1977). But because much of science is concerned with identifying causes, studies of causal reasoning are also relevant to the study of scientific thinking. However, studies of scientific thinking and of causal reasoning converge in that they both place a heavy emphasis on the importance of covariation.

For example, in the standard formal-operations experiment, the child's task is to determine which combination of chemicals covaries with the desired effect. Similarly, in Siegler's early work (Siegler and Liebert 1974, Siegler 1975), the child is shown an effect and is asked to decide whether it is caused by one or another of two events. The task is arranged so that one of these events covaries with the effect and the other does not.[1] More recently, in the tasks used by Kuhn, Amsel, and O'Loughlin (1988), subjects were asked to evaluate information about, for example, which sorts of foods did or did not covary with catching cold and about the characteristics of sports balls that either did or did not covary with degree of bounce. Similarly, in the task used by Klahr and Dunbar (1988), subjects were asked to identify which movements of a computer-controlled machine covaried with pushing a particular computer key.

For psychologists as well as for positivist philosophers, the emphasis on the importance of covariation in descriptions of scientific thinking and causal reasoning is rooted in the classic philosophical approach of David Hume. According to Hume, causation is reducible to the priority, contiguity, and covariation of perceptually salient events.

The Humean analysis of causation was, and continues to be, attractive for several reasons. The obvious one is that events that are causally related do in fact covary. All other things being equal, if x causes y, then y is present when x is present and y is absent when x is absent. But the other reason it is attractive is a more subtle one, namely that the Humean approach lends itself to a description of the principles of scientific inquiry that is what philosophers term "theory-independent." As philosophers use the term, a theory-independent principle is one whose application does not depend on the scientist's theories about the phenomena under study. One important consequence of such theory-independence is that principles that are theory-independent in this way are topic-neutral: they can be applied in the same way regardless of content area. On such a view, it would not matter whether one were discussing the causes of secure attachment or the causes of oxidation. The principle would be the same in both cases: to identify the cause(s) of the event, identify what covaries with it.

Identifying theory-independent principles was attractive to early empiricist philosophers because of their explicit desire to describe scientific inquiry in a way that avoided any mention of unobservables such as inferred unobservable forces, fields, and particles. In this way, they reasoned, one could arrive at prescriptions for doing science that were "objective," that is, untainted by theoretical or metaphysical biases.

In the philosophy of science, the logical positivists' original conception of a scientific method independent of theory has been largely abandoned. Social constructivists like Kuhn (1970) and Hanson (1958) and realists like Putnam (1972, 1975a, 1975b), Kitcher (1993), and Boyd (1982, 1983, 1989) have argued that the actual methodological principles of science are deeply theory-dependent. Within the empiricist tradition, there has been widespread acknowledgement of the importance of theory-dependence (see below).

According to critics of theory-independence, the theoretical conceptions on which methodological principles depend include not only general theories about relevant causal factors and the processes by which they operate, but also theoretical explanations of how those factors are methodologically relevant to the design and interpretation of particular experiments. In the psychological literature, the analogous term is "knowledge base." When psychologists write of someone's knowledge base about an area, they have in mind not only relevant facts but also the theories that explain why the facts are relevant.

In the distinction between methodological principles and theories or knowledge base, one can see that the empiricist aim of describing an "objective," "theory-independent" set of scientific principles has not been restricted to philosophy. It is reflected (often only tacitly but nevertheless quite systematically) in psychological research on scientific and causal reasoning.

One of the most salient demonstrations of this aim is the distinction often drawn in the scientific-thinking literature between two approaches to studies of scientific reasoning (e.g., Dunbar and Klahr 1989). As Dunbar and Klahr point out, one approach examines scientific reasoning by describing the structure of the knowledge base (or the structure of one's "theory") about a content area (an approach represented by Carey 1985; Chi, Feltovich, and Glaser 1981; McCloskey 1983a, 1983b, for example). This approach often focuses on knowledge and theories that are relatively domain- or content-specific.

In contrast, the second approach examines scientific thinking by studying strategies people have for reasoning about the world that are not restricted to a particular content area (an approach reflected in the work of, for example, Inhelder and Piaget 1958 and Kuhn, Amsel, and O'Loughlin 1988). As Dunbar and Klahr (1989) note, research in the latter tradition actually aims to minimize the role of knowledge in order to focus on strategy. For example, in Inhelder and Piaget's formal-operational "chemicals" task, the chemicals are both odorless and colorless, preventing the child from identifying them and thus preventing her from relying on her knowledge about them. The aim is not to study the child's knowledge of chemistry but rather to assess whether she relies on the strategy of systematically generating (and testing) all possible combinations. Similarly, in Siegler's early work on causal reasoning, the children were presented with quite unfamiliar events to prevent them from relying on their knowledge of particular causal relations and to assess whether, when presented with stimuli about which they had no (or little) knowledge base, they would rely on Humean principles to identify cause. In short, the aim of the second approach has been to study strategies that can be applied regardless of the content area. Thus psychologists and empiricist philosophers have often had the same aim: to describe a set of strategies for engaging in causal and scientific reasoning that are independent of the content area to which they are applied.

A problem with the convergence of aims is that the shortcomings of the philosophical approach are also the shortcomings of the psychological approach. In philosophy, the classic Humean approach was early on met with a classic criticism, namely that the world is rife with instances of contiguous covariation but that only some of them are taken seriously and judged to be causal (Quine 1969). An approach that reduces cause to nothing more than contiguous covariation (and temporal priority) is not sufficient to explain why it is that some instances of covariation are dismissed while others are not.

Non-Humeans elaborated this criticism by pointing to the crucial methodological role played by considerations of causal mechanism. A causal mechanism is the process by which a cause brings about an effect. A mechanism is a theory or an explanation, and what it explains is how one event causes another. Considerations of causal mechanism would make us take seriously a correlation between treatment with penicillin and death because there is a known process, mechanism, or explanation according to which penicillin can bring about death in a population, namely an allergic reaction to molds. Conversely, considerations of causal mechanism would justify dismissing the correlation between the level of ice cream consumption and the incidence of violent crime as an artifact of their both increasing during warm weather, precisely because there is no known mechanism by which the former can cause the latter. (Of course, if one were to discover that eating lots of fat stimulates, for example, testosterone production, one might reassess one's judgment.) In short, non-Humeans argue that it is considerations of causal mechanism that enable us to decide which of the many correlations in the world are genuinely causal and which are specious. And considerations of mechanism are not theory-independent; they depend heavily on our current knowledge base about the phenomenon, including knowledge of the theories that describe the causal mechanisms that explain the phenomenon.

The early non-Humean emphasis on the importance of mechanism in causal and scientific reasoning was motivated by actual scientific practice. Hume had written that people (presumably including scientists) detect causation by detecting the covariation of perceptually salient events. Empiricist philosophers of science all recognized that this description did not capture the *psychology* of actual scientific practice. They recognized that, in actual practice, scientists group together events not because of perceptual salience but rather because of theoretical (or explanatory) salience, that is, because of the salience of inferred (and unobservable) underlying causal mechanisms such as forces, fields, and particles. Nevertheless, like Hume, early empiricist philosophers of science wanted to avoid any talk of mechanisms such as forces because these mechanisms constituted unobservables and they wanted a science based firmly on only "objective" observable phenomena. That is, in spite of the embarrassing importance of theories to the way scientists actually think, early empiricists wanted somehow to identify the fundamental principles of scientific inference and to portray them as theory-independent, and thus as independent of content area.

The early empiricist way out of this bind was to propose a distinction in science between discovery and confirmation (or justification) and to relegate talk of unobservable mechanisms to the process of discovery. That is, theoretical (content-based) presuppositions were acknowledged to play a psychological role in determining which hypotheses scientists were able to formulate and which methodological approaches they considered fruitful. In contrast, the process of confirmation (of these hypotheses once they were put forward) was seen as one in which there were no theoretical presuppositions and therefore no presuppositions about unobservable mechanisms. On the empiricist view, the process of confirmation consisted of rules that could be applied across content areas.

More recent empiricists have also wanted a description of scientific inquiry that avoided positing knowledge of unobservable phenomena. Unlike their predecessors, however, many recent empiricists acknowledge that in actual scientific practice, during confirmation as well as during discovery, the process of scientific inquiry actually used is theory-dependent: in actual scientific practice, confirmation as well as discovery relies on considerations grounded in previously established theories about causal processes and mechanisms, including unobservable ones.

Thus, modern empiricists must reconcile the role that reasoning about theoretical unobservables plays in actual scientific practice with the empiricist aim of describing a theory-independent scientific process of confirmation. To effect this reconciliation, modern empiricists have offered analyses of the following form: The process of scientific inquiry *appears* to be about unobservables and, from the point of view of an individual scientist's psychology (and in terms of her actual scientific practice), it undoubtedly is. However, from the point of view of a theory of knowledge, the appearance is illusory. Because it is illusory, one of the aims of modern empiricists is to "rationally reconstruct" or translate the methods of science in a way that captures the rationality of science without making a commitment to theoretical unobservables. Furthermore, rational reconstruction is to be applied, not only to considerations of mechanism, but also to considerations of alternative accounts.

Alternative theoretical accounts constitute a special case of the acknowledged theory dependence of confirmation in actual scientific practice. As empiricists (Quine 1969, Goodman 1973), social constructivists (Kuhn 1970, Hanson 1958) and realists (Boyd 1982, 1983, 1989; Kitcher 1993) have remarked, in actual scientific practice, when scientists seek to explain a phenomenon, only a small number of possible explanations are taken seriously. Such accounts, which Goodman (1973) called "projectible," are those that are plausible, given our current information about the phenomenon being explained. Testing a plausible (or projectible) theory consists of testing its predictions or explanations against those of its rivals that are also projectible, and a theory is confirmed to the extent that it fares well in such tests.

Quine's (1969) treatment of theory-dependent projectibility judgments as matters of second-order induction about induction is a paradigm case of such a reconstruction. On his view, when a chemist decides which theoretical answers to a research question are worth taking seriously, she relies on plausibility judgments that depend on previously established theories about atoms, electrons, protons, etc. She will take her practice in this regard to be justified by knowledge previously established by other chemists about the unobservable microconstituents of matter, but she is mistaken about the real justification of her practices. Instead, according to Quine, the real justification is this: Chemists have, for a long time, been employing inductive methods based on the atomic theory of matter as it has been articulated in chemical practice. Of course, because atoms are unobservable, it is impossible to know whether this theory is even approximately true. Nevertheless, the historical record shows that chemists have thus far gotten away with using it: relying on methods that depend on current articulations of the atomic theory of matter, chemists have been able to identify a large number of predictively reliable theories about chemical reactions. From this historical record, we may make an inductive generalization about inductive practices in chemistry, namely, doing chemistry as though the atomic theory were true is a good way to identify predictively reliable chemical theories. It is her tacit knowledge of this inductive generalization about inductive practices in chemistry—and not any knowledge of unobservable atoms—that really justifies the chemist's reliance on theory-dependent methods.

In short, to bring us full circle back to Hume, the modern empiricist aims ultimately, it might be said, to show that one could, in principle, apply a series of rewrite rules to actual scientific practice so as to be able ultimately to reduce scientific methodology (and the consideration of explanatory mechanisms that it involves) to theory-independent Humean considerations of priority, contiguity, and covariation.

In the philosophy of science the empiricist aim of rationally reconstructing the scientific process in a theory-independent way serves as the focus for much current debate between empiricists, who are attempting the reconstruction, and realists, who argue that the effort will ultimately be unsuccessful. Several articles (for example, those in the anthology Boyd, Gaspar, and Trout 1990) can provide the interested reader with an overview of the debate.

Covariation in the Light of Non-Humean Indices

In this book my concern is not with whether, from an epistemological perspective, scientific thinking can ultimately be rationally reconstructed so as to be theory-independent. Rather, the concern is with the strategies that underlie actual scientific practice, and in this regard, the philosophical debate is relevant for the following reason: in terms of actual scientific practice, empiricists and realists alike point out that in causal reasoning and scientific inquiry, strategies are not applied in a theory-independent (that is, knowledge-base-independent) way. As Murphy and Medin (1985) have pointed out, the world is rife with correlations; we use theoretical information to determine which correlations to take seriously. Furthermore, both empiricists and realists point out that in scientific inquiry, this holds for confirmation as well as discovery.

In particular, realists and empiricists alike agree that, in the actual practice of causal or scientific reasoning, Humean strategies (such as, identifying the cause of a phenomenon by finding out what covaries with it) cannot be applied independently of the rest of one's knowledge about the phenomenon (including knowledge that, whatever its philosophical reconstruction, is represented by scientists as knowledge of unobservable causal mechanisms or processes). That is, rather than covariation (along with priority and perhaps contiguity) being a definitive index of causality, it is merely more or less likely to indicate causation, and the likelihood depends on other, knowledge-based information, such as information about mechanism.

Therefore, to study causal reasoning accurately, one must acknowledge that other information—such as information about mechanism—affects which covariations we deem to be worth pursuing as well as the extent to which we treat covariations as indicating causation. Furthermore, to study scientific reasoning, one must acknowledge that relying on causal theories about a phenomenon means that principles of scientific reasoning do not guarantee success; because methods depend on theories, methods are successful only to the extent that the theories about the phenomenon are more or less approximately correct.

But just as covariation does not, by itself, guarantee success, neither do theories by themselves. Rather, theories and methods are interdependent. When there are repeated covariations, then even if there is no mechanism currently known that can explain them, they can nevertheless not only reflect causation but also suggest that there is a mechanism that underlies them but that has not yet been discovered. That is, just as theory can enhance method, so method can lead to new discoveries that can refine and amplify theory.

The Role of Hypothesis Testing in Historical Perspective

Consider again the empiricists' aim of trying to rationally reconstruct scientific inquiry in terms of theory-independent Humean indices. As can be seen from the preceding discussion, this aim goes along with a focus on a fairly circumscribed part of the scientific process, namely hypothesis testing (or what is often referred to as "confirmation"). Because empiricists explicitly acknowledged the role of theory in hypothesis discovery, this part of the scientific process was seen as something that could not be rationally reconstructed in terms of theory-independent principles. Similarly, because hypothesis revision was also seen to be dependent on theory, it too was ignored in attempts to rationally reconstruct scientific inquiry.

When the focus is on testing hypotheses within an empiricist framework, the emphasis is on information about covariation, and the conception of the scientifically rational strategy is clear cut: either covariation obtains, in which case (assuming that constraints of temporal priority and perhaps contiguity are met) the hypothesis continues to be taken seriously, or else it does not obtain, in which case the hypothesis is relinquished. In actual scientific practice, however, strategies for dealing with such situations are more complicated. To be sure, sometimes hypotheses are rejected outright in the light of problematic data. But sometimes theoretical considerations dictate rejecting (or at least questioning) the data themselves, at least tentatively, as resulting from unsuitable measures, especially when the hypothesis in question is especially theoretically plausible and when it provides theoretically plausible explanations for the data that motivated the hypothesis in the first place. In such situations, theoretical considerations suggest that additional supporting data can be discovered in the future if only one uses more appropriate measures.

Furthermore, hypotheses are often not precise, circumscribed propositions that can clearly be rejected in the face of noncongruent data but rather are general working hypotheses that it is appropriate to revise or, to use T. S. Kuhn's (1970) word, "articulate," rather than reject, in the face of noncongruent data. Articulation includes modifying, elaborating, or fine-tuning a hypothesis to make it responsive to additional data (including anomalous data) that have been discovered about a phenomenon. Articulation also includes describing the mechanisms that mediate observed covariation and identifying the limits of an explanation by specifying the situations to which it does not apply. Therefore, decisions about whether to revise or reject as well as decisions about the sorts of revisions that would be seen as warranted are highly theory-dependent and thus take into account much more than merely information about covariation. Because of the theory dependence of decisions about rejection and revision, those aspects of scientific inquiry that dealt with hypothesis revision were largely ignored by empiricists in their accounts of theory testing. Instead of being treated as central components of confirmation and disconfirmation, they were assimilated to the (theory-dependent and thus nonrational) category of discovery or invention.

In short, the empiricist aim of rationally reconstructing scientific inquiry in terms of theory-independent principles went along with an (all but exclusive) emphasis on the role of Humean indices. And this, in turn, brought with it a corresponding emphasis on hypothesis testing rather than hypothesis discovery and revision.

Approach of the Present Book

Omissions and Distortions

As already noted, in the philosophy of science, the empiricist aim of identifying a set of theory-independent principles that form the basis of scientific inquiry has met with many criticisms. I will argue that in psychological research aimed at studying scientific reasoning in lay subjects, the empiricist approach has nevertheless persisted and is reflected in two sorts of tasks. One sort involves asking people to rely on covariation information in situations that are theoretically impoverished, such as the formal-operations task. Because such situations are designed so that considerations of theory or mechanism cannot play a role and because, in scientific reasoning, theory and mechanism information typically plays a crucial role, the tasks provide us with only a very limited picture of how scientific reasoning takes place. They are relevant only to those infrequent situations in which all of the plausible theories to explain a phenomenon have been ruled out and one is left with not even a vague theory to guide further investigation.

The other sort of task that reflects an empiricist approach involves asking subjects to reason about a theoretically rich situation but stipulating, operationally, that correct performance in the task consists of ignoring (or at least overriding) considerations of theory or mechanism and of relying, instead, only on information about covariation. I will suggest a reinterpretation of this research and argue that when scientific reasoning is operationally defined so that correct performance consists of focusing on covariation and ignoring considerations of theory or mechanism, then subjects (who typically do take account of theoretical considerations) are often treated as engaging in flawed reasoning when in fact their reasoning is scientifically legitimate.

In short, relying on theoretically impoverished tasks results in a picture of scientific inquiry that omits a crucial aspect of it; relying on theoretically rich tasks but operationally defining correct performance to consist in relying only on covariation results in a picture of the extent to which people reason scientifically that is distorted.

The Interdependence of Theory and Method, Working Hypotheses, and Bootstrapping

The approach that motivates this book is that neither a reliance on covariation alone nor on theory alone constitutes an algorithm that can guarantee success. The interdependence of theory and method has implications for scientific reasoning in particular cases as well as for scientific progress over time.

For example, the Humean principle according to which one can identify the cause of an event by examining what covaries with it is an important principle of causal reasoning. However, in any particular case, given all the possible covariations in the world, one must rely on a non-Humean index, knowledge of mechanism, to avoid being overwhelmed by irrelevant "noise," that is, to distinguish causal correlations from those that are merely artifactual. The application of the Humean index depends on the interaction of that index with non-Humean considerations. But the converse is also true: the principle of covariation can help us test, refine, and elaborate our knowledge base about the world, including our knowledge of theory and mechanism. For example, if we notice that a particular factor covaries with an event frequently and systematically, then even if there is no known mechanism that can explain how the factor might be causing the event, the frequent and systematic covariation might suggest that there really is an underlying mechanism operating that has yet to be discovered.

Method and theory (or reasoning strategies and knowledge about the world) each enhance the other, as well, in terms of progress over time. Consider again the situation in which, on the basis of covariation, we tentatively propose, as a working hypothesis, a hitherto undiscovered, underlying mechanism. If the working hypothesis turns out to be accurate and the posited mechanism does in fact exist, that mechanism can in turn suggest that we look for additional covariations that might otherwise have gone unnoticed. And these additional covariations (and non-covariations) will help us further refine our working hypothesis by adding to our understanding of how the mechanism operates, which will enable us to make still additional, more refined predictions of the circumstances under which various covariations will obtain. The result, over time, will be an increasingly accurate and complete theory and a set of increasingly accurate and complete reasoning strategies. That is, the knowledge acquired by the mutual enhancement of method and theory will be cumulative.

In short, the principles of scientific inquiry are used in conjunction with (not independently of) knowledge about the world. This means that the success of the principles of scientific inquiry depends on the extent to which our knowledge or theories about the world is approximately accurate and relying on the principles of scientific inquiry helps us discover and refine our knowledge or theories about the world.

The Roles of Causal Mechanism, Alternative Accounts, and Anomalous Information

In the following chapters, the focus will be on how subjects deal with three types of evidentially relevant considerations, in addition to evidence about Humean indices like covariation: evidence about causal mechanism, concerns about rival plausible (i.e., projectible) alternative hypotheses, and anomalous evidence (including disconfirming evidence).

In scientific reasoning, one of the most salient considerations besides information about the Humean indices consists of considerations of causal mechanism. The mechanism in a causal situation explains the process by which a cause brings about an effect. Without the availability of a plausible process, causation is unlikely to be seen as taking place. Covariation is sometimes seen as indicating cause and is at other times seen as merely artifactual precisely because plausible mechanisms are seen as operating in the former instances and as unlikely to be operating in the latter.

But even when the presence of covariation is buttressed by the presence of a plausible mechanism, causation is still not certain. The likelihood of a causal relation also depends on consideration of alternative accounts. Explanations are not evaluated in isolation; they are judged in the context of rival alternative accounts. The fact that alternative accounts play a pivotal role in scientific inquiry can be seen in the importance accorded to control groups. One finds an explanation increasingly compelling to the extent that alternative causes of the effect have been ruled out or controlled for. Conversely, to the extent that alternative causes remain viable, one is less certain that the target cause was at work in the situation in question.

Nevertheless, even when covariation, plausible mechanisms, and appropriate controls all point to a particular causal explanation, one can still have doubts: The context in which an explanation is evaluated includes (in addition to plausible alternative accounts) collateral information about related areas. And collateral information may include information that is anomalous, information that is merely unanticipated, and information that is genuinely disconfirming.

T. S. Kuhn (1970) introduced the term "anomaly" to refer to those sorts of noncongruent data that can, nevertheless, sometimes be reconciled with an explanation or theory, often by modifying the explanation to account for the anomaly. For example, if many cancer patients improve when they are treated with drug x (and do not improve without such treatment), an obvious explanation is that drug x is effective against cancer. If, subsequently, several cancer patients treated with x fail to improve, one might try to reconcile the initial and subsequent findings by modifying the explanation and claiming that drug x is effective but not in all cases. However, not all modifications to accommodate anomalies are seen as being warranted. Some are received as ad hoc attempts to patch up a theory that should, in fact, be rejected. Therefore, while some anomalies are seen as reconcilable with an explanation (or theory), others are seen as calling the explanation fundamentally into question. The option that is chosen depends in part on whether there are mechanisms that can account for why the theory is not applicable to the anomalous situations and on whether there are plausible alternative accounts that can explain the original data as well the anomalies. That is, like evidence about mechanism and alternative accounts, anomalous and disconfirming data affect how we evaluate causal explanations. (The distinctions between rejection and modification, warranted as well as unwarranted, will be amplified in chapters 2 and 3.)

An additional point will also be relevant to examining these types of considerations: For many events, there is a kind of catalogue of standard causes that, all other things being equal, vary in initial likelihood. (Why did John pass the exam? Because the exam was easy; because he studied; because he bribed the professor; etc.) However, the eventual likelihood of a cause might reasonably be expected to depend on the interaction between its initial likelihood (its position in the causal catalogue) and the various types of evidence (or other, rational or methodological considerations). For example, one might expect mechanism information to have a greater effect on initially unlikely causes than on those that are initially likely. That is, to bring us back to questions of plausibility, the extent to which additional evidence is taken into account might depend on the initial plausibility of the explanation to which it is directed.

The Present Experiments

Because neither covariation alone nor theory alone guarantees success, to demonstrate that subjects are reasoning scientifically, it is not sufficient merely to demonstrate that their judgments are based on theoretical considerations. Rather, one must demonstrate as well that the subjects are relying on theoretical considerations in a judicious, methodologically legitimate way. Some of the experiments reported here are a preliminary attempt to do this.

In addition, there is a long, largely Piagetian tradition of seeing early adolescence as a time when the ability to engage in scientific thinking makes rapid developmental progress. The experiments to be reported also examine how subjects' causal judgments change as they move from being college-bound adolescents to being college students.

The research to be reported is of two general sorts. One sort consists, broadly speaking, of studies of hypothesis-testing situations and examines how hypotheses (or potential explanations) are generated and how they vary in credibility as a function of various sorts of evidence and knowledge about the phenomena in question. The second sort focuses more specifically on the way in which people deal with evidence or information that disconfirms or is anomalous to or at least unanticipated by an explanation, that is, this sort focuses on situations in which people have the opportunity to engage in hypothesis revision or what T. S. Kuhn calls "articulation" (or, in some cases, hypothesis rejection.) As will become obvious, the distinction between the two sorts of studies is often a matter of expository convenience rather than substance.

Chapter 2

The Role of Mechanism and Alternative Accounts in Formal-Operational, Causal, and Scientific Reasoning

The rest of this introductory part is divided into three chapters. In the present chapter, I briefly review existing research on formal-operational and causal reasoning, hypothesis testing or rule discovery, and scientific thinking. The aim will be to demonstrate that focusing on covariation to the exclusion of mechanism paints a picture of how people reason that is not merely incomplete but actually distorted. (Brown [1989] has made an analogous point in noting that conclusions about children's ability to transfer are incorrect because transfer studies often ignore the role of mechanism.)

In the following chapter, I discuss research that examines hypothesis articulation, especially in light of disconfirming and anomalous information. This research merits a separate chapter because the question of how people deal with disconfirming or anomalous evidence has been salient in psychology for several decades, and so the research and the issues raised by it are quite extensive. In the last chapter, I describe two experiments that examined how people deal with information other than information about covariation. The findings from these experiments motivated several of the subsequent studies.

A Note about Anomalies, Disconfirming Data, and Terminology

In psychological research, the suppressed assumption that often underlies how researchers evaluate subjects' reasoning is that when subjects generate and test hypotheses, the hypotheses in question are ones that have been precisely formulated (Kuhn et al. 1988, Mynatt et al. 1977). In particular, when subjects generate a hypothesis, such as "Type of juice causes colds" or "Triangles and only triangles repel a moving particle," they are often treated as having generated the precise hypothesis that type of juice *always* causes colds or that all and only triangles repel. The result is that when the subject encounters a *single* instance that does not conform to the hypothesis, the researcher stipulates that correct behavior consists of rejecting the hypothesis on the basis of the single instance.

I will argue below that it is often a mistake to treat subjects as having formulated a hypothesis precisely. But consider first the case of a scientist who has formulated a hypothesis precisely. From the subject's point of view, an instance that does not conform to the hypothesis that some factor always causes an event could mean that the hypothesis should now be modified to account for the data. For example, "Type of juice causes colds but not, for some reason, in this particular case," or "Triangles repel but only if they're near another figure." Alternatively, the nonconforming data could be so numerous that the subject would decide that the hypothesis should be rejected outright—that, for example, the subject should conclude that it is really a type of cereal that causes colds or that it is really gray figures that repel.

What is important to note is that if the hypothesis is treated as claiming that something *always* happens, then, from the point of view of logic, either rejecting the hypothesis outright or modifying it to accommodate the data constitutes treating the data as disconfirming the initial hypothesis: in a strictly logical sense, the hypothesis that type of juice *always* causes colds is incompatible with the hypothesis that type of juice causes colds only in certain cases; it is also incompatible with the hypothesis that it is really type of cereal that causes colds.

Of course, from the point of view of psychology, methodology, and history, one needs to distinguish the two ways of treating hypotheses as having been disconfirmed. Sometimes, for example, rejecting a hypothesis outright in the light of nonconforming data is methodologically unwarranted. For example, if a scientist formulates the hypothesis that drug x always cures disease y and the data are not congruent with this claim but only in those cases in which the victims have already taxed immune systems, then it makes methodological sense to keep the hypothesis in broad outline but to modify it as not applying in this particular case. In other contexts, in contrast, a series of modifications to an initial hypothesis might be seen as consisting of unwarranted ad hoc modifications aimed at salvaging a hypothesis that should, in fact, be rejected outright.

Consider now the fact that subjects do not always entertain precisely formulated hypotheses. For example, imagine a scientist who, in the early stages of an investigation, posits the working hypothesis that drug x cures a particular sort of cancer. Because it is only a tentative, working hypothesis, such a proposal will undoubtedly not be as precise as it could be in principle. It probably would not, for example, specify exactly what sort of dosage is required, whether it will be effective against only some forms of cancer, whether it will be effective in patients whose immune systems are already taxed, etc. Often this sort of information will be discovered when tests of the working hypothesis yield unanticipated data. For example, if the drug works for some patients but not for others, further investigation might uncover the fact that the patients for whom the drug was effective had a different form of cancer than the other patients. With this additional information, the scientist can then elaborate her working hypothesis so that it now specifies that drug x cures only certain types of cancer.

What is important to note here is that when the scientist initially formulated her working hypothesis, she may not have specified anything one way or another about different forms of cancer. Therefore, in this context, the anomalous data enable the scientist to elaborate or augment her initial working hypothesis because the data suggest an additional factor that plays a role and was not considered in the working hypothesis. (Of course, in terms of T. S. Kuhn's terminology, such data are not, strictly speaking, anomalous. They do not call into question a hypothesis or some part of a hypothesis because the hypothesis was formulated imprecisely enough that it made no predictions one way or another about whether such data would obtain.)

When anomalous data are discussed, it will typically be clear from the context whether the experimenter was treating the subject's hypothesis as a precisely formulated statement (for example, that a factor *always* causes an effect). It will also be clear from the context whether the subject might instead have been treating her hypothesis as an imprecisely formulated working hypothesis.

I will use "anomaly" as a generic term that refers to data that lead to the modification, rejection, or elaboration of a hypothesis. It will be clear from the context whether the anomalies are modifying, disconfirming, or elaborating. It will also be clear from the context how researchers are treating the anomalies. It is important to keep the distinctions in mind because they sometimes affect conclusions about whether people are reasoning in a scientifically legitimate way. (For the sake of completeness, it might be worth noting that, unless explicitly noted, "anomaly" will never be used to refer to the kind of data that eventually motivate what T. S. Kuhn referred to as a "paradigm shift"; in this book the hypotheses to which the anomalous data relate are of a much more mundane sort.)

Research on Formal-Operational Reasoning, Causal Reasoning, and Hypothesis Testing or Rule Discovery

Formal-Operational and Causal Reasoning

In the psychological literature, tasks that have been designed to study causal reasoning from an empiricist perspective (in which causation is defined in terms of covariation) are of two general sorts. One sort asks subjects to reason about situations that might be considered theoretically impoverished. The other asks subjects to reason about situations that are theoretically rich but stipulates, operationally, that correct performance consists of ignoring (or at least overriding) theoretical considerations. This section focuses on those situations that are theoretically impoverished.

Studies of formal-operational reasoning and many studies of causal reasoning are obviously relevant to the question of scientific thinking. At least when research is at a fairly advanced stage and the phenomena studied are sufficiently simple, scientists certainly rely on the strategy of varying one thing at a time while holding everything else constant—the same strategy that guarantees success on a formal-operational task. And the motivation for following this strategy is to identify the causes of a phenomenon. However, the paradigm used in formal-operational studies and in most, though not all, studies of causal reasoning is based on a Humean model of causation and focuses almost exclusively on the use of covariation and on hypothesis testing of a fairly circumscribed sort.

Causation is operationalized as covariation

As a prime example of a formal-operational task, consider the "chemicals" task in which the subject has to discover which combination(s) of five odorless, colorless chemicals (one of which acts as a bleach) will produce a yellow liquid. Inhelder and Piaget (1958) explicitly intended that the formal-operational paradigm would model the hypotheticodeductive account of scientific inquiry—an empiricist rational reconstruction in which scientific inquiry is described in terms of the Humean principles of causation. In keeping with Inhelder and Piaget's aim, the formal-operational task is structured so that the causal chemicals are those that covary with the effect. As another example of a causal-reasoning task, consider Shultz and Mendelson's (1974) study in which a child had to decide whether it was pulling one or another lever that caused a light to come on. Again, the task was structured so that the cause was the event that covaried with the effect. That is, in both approaches, causation was operationalized in Humean terms, as being equivalent to covariation.

Because of the emphasis on covariation, these sorts of tasks are structured so that the other types of information relevant to making causal judgments do not play a role. The most salient example of this is that questions of mechanism do not arise. Since the chemicals are all both odorless and colorless, it is not possible to identify them. And even if it were, it would make little difference, as children typically have very little knowledge of mechanisms by which most chemicals operate. Nor do most children at this age have knowledge of mechanisms that might mediate between pulling a lever and having a light come on.

The role of alternative hypotheses is ignored

Furthermore, in both situations, the role of alternative hypotheses is also not explored in any depth. The sense in which alternative accounts or causes are considered is that if one of the factors (one set of chemicals, one of the levers) does not covary with the desired effect, then correct performance consists of checking an alternative factor. There is no attempt to examine whether the subject considers alternatives that are plausible and this relates to the next point.

The actual cause is definitely included in the set

The tasks are contrived so that the actual cause is definitely included in the set of factors presented to the subject. There is thus no way of using this sort of situation to examine how subjects decide, in the first place, whether a particular factor ought to be included in the set of potential causes. When a cancer researcher tries to identify possible cures, for example, there is no one waiting in the wings who tells her that the actual cure can definitely be found in a particular set of possibilities.

Potential causes in the set are stipulated to be equally plausible

Related to the preceding point is the fact that the tasks are structured so that the possible causal factors included in the set of possible causes are all, at the outset, equally likely. Therefore, there is no way of using this paradigm to study how causal judgments are affected by whether the possible causes are plausible or implausible, standard or nonstandard instances. That such considerations do (and should) matter when reasoning about causal situations can be easily seen by thinking about medical diagnosis. Not all possible causes of persistent headaches are (or should be treated as) either standard or plausible. For example, it is usual to investigate brain tumors as a cause of headache only after sinus infections, a need for eyeglasses, stress, etc., have all first been eliminated as possible causes.

In short, many studies of formal-operational and causal reasoning simply bypass questions of mechanism, alternative hypotheses, and the differential plausibility of possible causal factors. This is not to say that the research just discussed tells us nothing about causal reasoning. It is very relevant, for example, to situations in which the mechanisms that are operating are unknown—as happens when one is, for example, trying to figure out the dash knobs of an unfamiliar foreign car or trying to discover which settings of which knobs will improve the picture on a TV screen when any guess is as good as any other guess and even though one does not understand the mechanism by which turning a particular knob will affect the cathode ray tube. Testing the knobs and doing so in a systematic, combinatorial way is a good way of keeping track of which tests have been carried out; it makes for good bookkeeping. Similarly, if all the plausible hypotheses to explain a phenomenon have been ruled out and one is left with no other theoretical considerations to guide further research, then an investigation of whatever factors (however implausible) happen to covary with the phenomenon is often the only option left. (This happens, for example, when the Center for Disease Control has ruled out all plausible known causes of a set of symptoms and must investigate factors that covary with the symptoms in order to discover a disease that has not yet been identified.) However, the limitation of this research is that it does not inform us about causal reasoning in situations in which a subject *does* have beliefs—even incomplete beliefs—about underlying mechanisms or the differential plausibility of possible causal factors. A formal-operational subject, for example, who correctly systematically tests all combinations in the chemicals task might perform very differently (and rightly so) in a task in which there are mechanisms known to be operating for some of the relevant factors but not for others. More on this below.

The tasks emphasize hypothesis rejection rather than modification

Finally, one way of conceptualizing these tasks is as involving a series of hypotheses that the subject tests regarding which of the possible causal factors (or, in the case of the chemicals task, which subset of factors) is the actual causal factor. However, two features of these tasks result in an emphasis on hypotheses testing to the exclusion of hypothesis modification or articulation. One is that, given the way the tasks are designed, the hypotheses can be limited to a fairly small set, and each hypothesis can be formulated in a way that is very precise and thus very circumscribed. Specifically, each hypothesis is that a particular set of chemicals will produce the desired effect. This is in contrast to many noncontrived situations in which it is a fairly imprecise or working hypothesis that one starts out with (for example, that drug x cures infections, without one's specifying the precise dosage required or the particular types of infections and populations for which it is effective).

The second feature of these tasks, in terms of hypothesis testing, is that they are contrived so that there is one factor (for example, a set of chemicals) among a fairly small set of factors with which the data are perfectly congruent. Thus, in formal-operational and causal reasoning tasks, when a hypothesis (for example, that chemicals 1, 2, and 3 produce a yellow liquid) is met with noncongruent or disconfirming data, there is no incentive to treat the data as mere anomalies that warrant modifying the hypothesis in order to accommodate them. Rather, because there is one hypothesis with which all of the data are perfectly congruent, correct performance consists of treating noncongruent data as though they were disconfirming rather than merely anomalous and of continuing to search for that hypothesis (for example, chemicals 1, 2, and 4) with which the data are perfectly in accord. That is, questions about hypothesis modification do not arise, because the tasks are contrived so that correct performance does not require the problem solver to engage in hypothesis modification. Again, by way of contrast, in many noncontrived situations, when a working hypothesis meets with noncongruent data, one can often treat the data as merely anomalous and modify the hypothesis (rather than altogether reject it) to take account of that data. For example, if drug x does not cure colds in the elderly, the working hypothesis that x is effective can be modified to state that drug x is effective but not in the elderly.

Anomalies, modification, and working hypotheses will be discussed in more detail in chapter 3. Briefly, though, I would like to reiterate my earlier point that there certainly are causal situations for which the research paradigm just discussed provides an accurate model of reasoning. In the TV case, for example, there is one set of knob positions that provides the best picture, and the appropriate response to a fuzzy picture is certainly to reject an unsatisfactory set of knob positions and search for a new set. However, in many cases of hypothesis testing, especially when the hypothesis is a working hypothesis, anomalous data call for modification, rather than outright rejection of the hypothesis. And the decision about whether to modify or reject is often influenced by beliefs about what mechanisms are bringing about the anomalies. Therefore, a subject who rejects a hypothesis in the face of anomalous data in the experiments just described might (appropriately) do something quite different in a situation in which there is a mechanism that can explain how the anomalies came to be. Thus, studying causal reasoning in the former situation might provide a distorted picture of what causal reasoning would (and should) look like in the latter situation. More on this in chapter 3.

There is a sense in which hypothesis modification is examined in this research: in some studies of causal reasoning, the factor stipulated to be the causal factor covaries only imperfectly with the effect (for example, Siegler 1975). Therefore, there are some instances that, in a sense, are designed to call for modification rather than rejection because, in these instances, although the causal factor is present, the effect is not. However, the strategy stipulated to be the correct way of dealing with these instances is to conclude that the target factor is necessary but not sufficient, without any concern for identifying what the anomalous instances have in common or what the mechanisms are that make the factor bring about the event in some situations but not in others.

There is certainly a step in scientific problem solving when a judgment that a cause is necessary but not sufficient is the only appropriate response to the data available. When, for example, a new virus is discovered and little is known about it, a probabilistic estimate that it is fatal in a certain percentage of cases might be the best (and only) conclusion possible. However, even in such cases the next response is typically to try to understand *why* the virus is fatal in some cases but not in others. (At the very least, the next response is to try to identify what characteristics distinguish instances in which the virus is fatal from those in which it is not in the hope that doing so will provide a clue to what the underlying mechanism might be that makes it deadly in some cases and not in others.) That is, how probabilistic hypotheses are evaluated—whether they are treated as reflections of random "noise" or as helping to refine our understanding of when the target cause does or does not operate—often depends on information about mechanism. Therefore, studies of how subjects evaluate probabilistic covariation when mechanism information is absent might provide a misleading model of how subjects evaluate anomalies when information about mechanism is available. This point will be addressed in more detail in chapter 3 and in experiment 11.

In short, in many formal-operational and causal reasoning tasks, causation is stipulated to be equivalent to covariation with little attention paid to the roles of mechanism, anomalies, and alternative theories or hypotheses. Indeed, the tasks are designed to present situations that are theoretically impoverished so that questions of theory or mechanism cannot arise. In addition, a limited number of fairly circumscribed hypotheses are designed to be either conclusively confirmed or disconfirmed because anomalous data are designed to be disconfirming; the tasks are not designed so that anomalous data call for working hypotheses to be modified rather than rejected. The result is that there is a focus on hypothesis testing to the exclusion of hypothesis modification or articulation. These tasks undoubtedly provide us with information about causal reasoning in situations in which plausible hypotheses to explain a phenomenon either do not exist or have been ruled out. However, they might well provide misleading expectations of how people reason in situations in which information about mechanism is available.

Hypothesis Testing or Rule Discovery

The literature on hypothesis testing or rule discovery is also relevant to the issue of scientific thinking because the tasks used in such research typically involve identifying the properties of a set of stimuli or discovering what the effects are that covary with a particular cause. However, neither type of task is aimed at examining subjects' beliefs about mechanism. For example, Wason's (1960) task asks subjects to identify the rule exemplified by the series 2, 4, 6. Questions of mechanism do not arise in this sort of task. Tasks used by Klahr and his associates (e.g., Klahr and Dunbar 1988; Klahr, Dunbar, and Fay 1990) require the subject to discover what the function is of a particular key or command on a computer device. Again, since the subjects are expected to know not how the key brings about a particular outcome but merely what the outcome is, these tasks also do not examine the role of mechanism. (However, some of Klahr's tasks do examine the role of alternative hypotheses, and this aspect of his tasks will be discussed below. In addition, rule-discovery tasks do, in some sense, deal with the issue of subjects' alternative hypotheses. This feature of the tasks will be discussed in chapter 3.)

Existing Research on Information about Causal Mechanism and Alternative Accounts

As mentioned earlier, there have been some exceptions in the causal-reasoning literature that did examine young children's beliefs about causal mechanism.

Recent research has taken as its starting point Piaget's (1972) work with young children. Using as data children's verbal explanations for various natural phenomena (such as the phases of the moon) and mechanical events (such as the working of bicycles and steam engines), Piaget concluded that young children were either indifferent to causal mechanism or actually held the false belief that intervening mechanisms were not necessary, that is, that action at a distance is possible.

Using less complicated tasks than the ones Piaget had used, several researchers (Bullock et al. 1982; Koslowski, Spilton, and Snipper 1981; Shultz 1982) have found that, contrary to what Piaget had concluded, even four- and five-year-olds spontaneously invoke possible causal mechanisms when explaining how an apparatus works. That is, in at least some situations, children are neither indifferent to considerations of mechanism nor do they hold a false belief in action at a distance.

For obvious reasons, the tasks used to study the causal reasoning of children have been fairly simple and concrete. In contrast, the research on college students and adolescents reported in this book studies situations involving more abstract, verbal problems. Furthermore, in much recent research, because the emphasis was on considerations of whether mechanism information played any role at all in the causal reasoning of children, there was little attention to how mechanism information was evaluated when it was combined with (or pitted against) other causal information (in contrast to the present experiments). However, there are two studies relevant to this question.

One, by Mendelson and Shultz (1976), found that when a visible connection was absent between a putative causal agent and its effect, children were likely to rely on temporal contiguity rather than on regularity of co-occurrence. However, when a visible connection was present, regularity played a greater role. The authors suggested that a visible connection provides a rationale for (or, in terms of the present discussion, a mechanism that can explain) a fairly long temporal delay so that when the connection is present, children are more likely to take regularity into account. The other study, by Shultz (1982), found that when mechanism information conflicts with information about covariation, even children as young as three years of age accord more importance to the former than to the latter.

Studies of causal reasoning among adults have used more abstract, verbal problems and have also found that considerations based on mechanism often override or interfere with the conclusions suggested by a strict reliance on covariation. For example, in their classic study of illusory correlations, Chapman and Chapman showed undergraduates a series of "drawings, each drawing being arbitrarily paired with contrived statements about the symptoms of the alleged patient who drew it" (1967, 194). The subjects' task was to discover which kinds of drawings were made by patients with each symptom. Even when there was no correlation, subjects reported having observed one, and their "observations" of "illusory correlations" corresponded to (independently assessed) prior beliefs (or, in terms of the present discussion, rudimentary theories), such as that a man worried about how manly he is would draw a picture of a muscular, manly male.

Similarly, Murphy and Medin (1985) make an analogous argument when they discuss the role of covariation in concepts. They point out that the world is rife with correlations, many of which are artifactual or based on an arbitrary cutting up of the world. To account for why we look only for some correlations and take them seriously when we find them, an account of concepts and categories must acknowledge the role that theories play. We search for and take seriously only some correlations precisely because it is these correlations that we have theoretical (or causal mechanistic) reasons for believing to be important.

Finally, Tversky and Kahneman (1974), as well as Nisbett and Ross (1980), demonstrate that our ability to apply various statistical principles can be overridden by prior beliefs in the form of causal theories. For example, if told that Steve is shy and withdrawn, invariably helpful, but with little interest in people or the world, and that he has a need for order and structure and a passion for detail, we infer that he is more likely to be a librarian than a salesman, even if given the base-rate information that the group he is in consists of 30 librarians and 70 salesmen. Presumably, we override the base-rate information because we believe that certain personality variables are one of the causal mechanisms by which various career choices are made.

Worth noting at this point is that in some of the work just discussed (for example, Chapman and Chapman 1967 and Kahneman and Tversky

1974), the reliance on explanation or theory is treated as a flaw in the reasoning process. In contrast, one of the arguments being made here is that a reliance on explanation or theory is legitimate. By way of illustration, consider a variant of the Kahneman and Tversky example. Imagine learning that 1 percent of the U.S. population is infected with the AIDS virus. Imagine now being told that John has, for some time, been a casual user of intravenous drugs and frequently shares needles, lives in the Hell's Kitchen section of New York, and often works as a male prostitute. I would suspect that most of us would ignore national base-rate information in this case as well and infer that John is more likely than members of the general U.S. population to be infected precisely because we have some beliefs about the mechanism by which AIDS is transmitted. And I would also argue that in this case, overriding base-rate information with background beliefs is scientifically legitimate. A public health officer who inferred, on the basis of the base-rate information, that there was a 1 percent chance that John had AIDS would be medically irresponsible. The background beliefs make a causal suggestion that John was drawn from a different population than the one for which the base-rate data are appropriate. Similarly, in Kahneman and Tversky's example concerning whether John is a librarian or a salesman, I would argue that the problem is not that subjects were ignoring or overriding base-rate information because of their causal theories. The problem *may* have been that the subjects were not sufficiently skeptical about the causal theories they held, but this is a separate issue. And in any case, the base-rate information that subjects were presented with did not actually call their theories into question.

The question of whether reliance on theory is legitimate or mistaken is not trivial, because it is relevant to how one can teach people to be more rigorous in their thinking. If the problem is that people are ignoring the principles of statistical inference in favor of causal theories, then the solution should be to teach them more statistics. However, if, as I have argued, the problem is not that people are relying on causal theories but rather that people are not being sufficiently skeptical of or informed about whether their theories are correct, then the solution is to teach them more about their theories, such as its limitations, alternatives to it, etc.

The possible advantages of skepticism aside, the point I am making is that the practice of ignoring causal theories in favor of base-rate information about a general population is not always a reasonable approach; tasks that stipulate that such an approach should be used may provide us with an inaccurate picture of how people reason in situations in which theoretical information should be taken into account. (Of course, the illusory correlations observed by Chapman and Chapman's subjects are, indeed, a reflection of flawed thinking. More on this in chapter 3.)

Scientific Reasoning

Scientific Reasoning as Conceptual Change

In terms of recent research, there have been two major approaches to the study of scientific reasoning. One has looked at the sort of conceptual reorganization that takes place (historically as well as ontogenetically) as people acquire more knowledge about a scientific construct such as aliveness (Carey 1985), heat and temperature (Wiser 1987), dinosaurs (Chi and Koeske 1983), physics (Chi 1992; Chi, Feltovich, and Glaser 1981; McCloskey 1983a, 1983b; etc.).

In this approach, one of the issues is whether or not the kind of reorganization that takes place involves the sort of radical restructuring analogous to what T. S. Kuhn has called a "paradigm shift." A second issue is the related one of the extent to which people's naive conceptions parallel the conceptions that were held in earlier historical time periods. In short, the issues addressed in the conceptual-change literature complement the questions addressed here. However, they intersect with my questions in several ways. First, they emphasize the importance of theoretical frameworks in organizing data, and this is continuous with my interest in the importance of causal mechanism in scientific reasoning. Second, in drawing attention to the role of knowledge in scientific reasoning, the research on conceptual change makes the same point made in experiments 3, 4, and 5, namely that one's knowledge about a domain may affect the methodological import of the principles one uses to reason about it. For example, consider the principle that x becomes less likely to have caused y if one can find no evidence for any of the mechanisms by which x might (plausibly) have brought y about. This principle might be difficult to rely on if one does not have the knowledge base to identify what the plausible mechanisms are likely to include. Finally, just as one can ask about conceptual change whether it involves radical restructuring, one can also ask whether the standards of evidence that people employ undergoes an analogous shift with age. That is, one can ask whether people of different ages employ qualitatively distinct strategies for generating, testing, and refining hypotheses.

Scientific Reasoning as the Application of Principles for Assessing Evidence

The second major approach to the study of scientific reasoning has examined the principles or strategies that people use in generating and testing hypotheses. The formal-operational approach of Inhelder and Piaget (1958), explicitly intended to model the hypotheticodeductive account of scientific inquiry, is based on the role of Humean indices and has already been discussed. Recall that this research examined scientific reasoning by relying on task situations that might be described as theoretically impoverished. In this section my focus will be on tasks that are theoretically rich but in which correct performance has been stipulated to consist of ignoring or overriding considerations of theory or mechanism.

The work of D. Kuhn et al.

In recent work, one of the most significant contributions to research on scientific thinking has been made by Kuhn, Amsel, and O'Loughlin (1988). Their research is significant in two respects: It is a systematic body of research that addresses in a clear and precise way the important question of how a subject's existing theories are reconciled with new evidence. Furthermore, like all thoughtful research, Kuhn et al.'s work raises at least as many questions as it answers and is therefore significant in this respect as well.

Research and conclusions   Kuhn and her colleagues used several tasks to study subjects' ability to coordinate theory and evidence. In one of the tasks, Kuhn et al. began with hypotheses that they had asked subjects to generate about, for example, whether eating one type of food rather than another would make children more or less likely to catch cold. Kuhn et al.'s emphasis was on the way in which subjects would deal with subsequent information that either confirmed or disconfirmed one of their hypotheses. (In describing their research, I will use the terms "confirmed" and "disconfirmed" because these are the terms the researchers themselves used in describing the data they presented to their subjects. However, I will later argue that in many cases subjects were behaving in a scientifically legitimate way when they treated the "disconfirming" evidence as merely anomalous data that called for modification, not rejection, of the hypotheses they were evaluating.)

For each subject, the experimenters identified two causal variables, for example, type of potato (fried versus baked) and type of cereal (granola versus Special K) that the subject believed would have an effect on colds and two noncausal variables that the subject believed would not affect childrens' likelihood of catching cold. Then the subject's beliefs about one causal variable (for example, type of potato) and one noncausal variable (for example, type of juice) were confirmed, while her beliefs about the other causal and the other noncausal variable were disconfirmed.

In all cases, confirmation and disconfirmation consisted of presenting the subject with evidence that, in a particular school population, the target variable either did or did not covary with the effect. (For example, in the disconfirm condition, a subject who believed that eating chocolate cake rather than carrot cake caused more colds would be shown evidence that children who ate carrot cake were just as likely to get colds as children who ate chocolate cake.) In short, the only type of information presented to the subject was information that a variable did or did not covary with an effect.

In another task, subjects were asked to identify what it was that made some sports balls bounceable and others not. Subjects were presented with four variables (size, color, texture, and presence or absence of ridges). The focus of the study was on two variables: the one the subject had identified as making the most difference and the one the subject had identified as making the least (or no) difference. (For future reference, it is worth noting that color was explicitly included to make it likely that one of the variables would be seen as noncausal, and in fact "most" subjects selected color as the variable least likely to make a difference.) In one section of the task, subjects were asked to generate evidence that would support their own theory and also to generate evidence that would support someone else's conflicting theory. Subjects did this by arranging the sports balls in two baskets (labeled "good serve" and "bad serve"). That is, they demonstrated how the factors would covary with type of serve if each of the two theories were true. Subjects were also asked to justify the arrangements they proposed. In another part of the task, half the subjects were presented with evidence that the two variables (the one chosen as most likely, and the one chosen as least likely, to be causal) did covary with the effect, and half were shown evidence that the two variables and the effect did not covary. Again they were asked to evaluate the evidence.

In yet another task, subjects were asked to articulate their causal theories about, for example, why children fail in school or why prisoners return to crime upon being released from prison. Subjects were then asked various questions ("If you were trying to convince someone that your view is right, what evidence would you give to try to show this?") designed to tap their beliefs about what would constitute evidence for their theories.

Because many of Kuhn et al.'s tasks dealt with disconfirming information (or, on my view, anomalous information), their research will also be discussed, again in chapter 3. Yet it is relevant to this chapter for several reasons: One is that it illustrates my claim that in most studies of scientific thinking (as in most studies of causal reasoning), causation is operationalized as equivalent to covariation and correct performance consists of ignoring, or at least overriding, considerations of theory or mechanism. Another reason it is relevant to this chapter is that it provides an example supporting the argument, made earlier, that an empiricist emphasis that operationally reduces causation to covariation (often to the exclusion of other information) can lead to a distorted picture of subjects' reasoning in situations in which mechanism information is available. A third reason is that Kuhn and her colleagues have drawn many conclusions about people's ability to engage in scientific thinking, and these conclusions have provoked studies designed to examine the extent to which the conclusions can be generalized.

The most basic conclusion is that at all ages, but especially among younger subjects, there is a fairly robust inability to coordinate theory and evidence. Furthermore, this inability is intertwined with a metacognitive inability to think *about* theories rather than *with* them. According to Kuhn et al., the general inability to distinguish theory and evidence is reflected in several ways in the tasks just described.

For example, after subjects generated evidence to support either their own or a conflicting theory, they frequently provided a theory-based response, rather than a response based on covariation evidence, to explain why the evidence supported the theory. Indeed, this was true even when subjects were justifying an arrangement generated to support a theory that conflicted with theirs. For example, when a ninth-grader was asked to generate evidence to show that her theory (that texture affects bounceability) was correct, she (correctly) placed smooth balls in the "good serve" basket and rough balls in the "bad serve" basket. When asked to explain how this evidence supported the theory, she responded, "The rough texture will make the ball heavier, so it won't go so far when hit" (Kuhn et al. 1988, 170). In explaining why this subject mentioned only theory and not evidence in her justification, Kuhn et al. note, "We can assume that it is her lack of a firm differentiation between theory and evidence that prevented her from acknowledging explicitly the meaning of covariation evidence, though she obviously had some appreciation of its meaning" (1988, 270).

In the "foods" task also, subjects' justifications often made no reference to evidence, by which D. Kuhn et al. meant information about covariation. For example, many of the theory-based responses, instead of citing evidence of covariation (or noncovariation) cited evidence based on, among other things, "some mechanism connecting cause and effect" or on "intuition." An example of evidence based on mechanism was provided by a subject who explained that type of cake makes a difference: "Carrot cake has ... is made with carrots, and chocolate cake is made with a lot of sugar. But this [carrot cake] is made with some sugar too, but it's made with less sugar.... Less sugar means you don't ... your blood pressure doesn't go up. It makes a difference" (Kuhn et al. 1988, 78–79). An example of intuition occurred when a subject explained that the kind of breakfast roll does not make a difference "because the breakfast rolls are pretty much the same thing. The only thing, they taste differently, but they are made the same way, they have the same thing—dough; they have to mix" (Kuhn et al. 1988, 73). (If this example is representative, I would argue that some examples of intuition might also have been based on considerations of mechanism: One could interpret this example as reflecting the idea that, since the rolls have the same ingredients, there is no mechanism by which the different rolls could have produced different outcomes.) In short, according to Kuhn et al., in many cases, subjects' justifications were based on theory, not evidence, because subjects could not distinguish theory and evidence.

In contrast, consider some of the examples that Kuhn et al. cite of valid reasoning: "No, because the tomato soup is with healthy children here and sick children here." "Some children with colds had tap water, and some had bottled water, so it makes no difference" (Kuhn et al. 1988, 58). Kuhn et al. argue that in examples of valid reasoning, theory and evidence were treated as independent, and evidence was used to evaluate theory. As can be seen from the examples, this meant that in examples of valid reasoning, subjects cited covariation evidence to support their theories or to call them into question.

Furthermore, in Kuhn et al.'s tasks, in most cases, there were no evidence-based responses (that is, justifications that mentioned covariation), and there were theory-based responses, even when the instructions explicitly called for the former. For example, in one of the studies, subjects were explicitly told "to consider only the information that the scientists collected," "to answer the question not from what you know about foods, but based only on the scientists' findings" (Kuhn et al. 1988, 51). And although such instructions made the sixth-graders produce more evidence-based responses, the difference was not statistically significant.

According to Kuhn (1989), another example of people's inability to distinguish theory from evidence is that, when asked explicitly to provide evidence for a belief, even adults often merely elaborated the belief, providing a causal script of "how it happens." For example, asked to answer the question of what causes prisoners to return to a life of crime, one subject cited a combination of leniency in the judicial system and overcrowding: "I think some of our laws today are really not strict enough.... And let's face it, today some of them even commit murder, and they are out on the street the next day. Plus, they've got the overcrowding in the prisons, and I don't think—well, in some places, they are letting them out before their time" (Kuhn 1989, 683). When asked to provide evidence, this subject merely elaborated his script: "The judges and a lot of them, I don't think they give them the full amount in sentencing" (Kuhn 1989, 683). After further probing, the subject suggested that a survey of prisons could be taken to show that they were indeed overcrowded. Even here, the proposed-survey evidence was directed toward supporting the script of how it happens, rather than toward providing evidence that certain factors such as overcrowding covary with returning to a life of crime.

According to D. Kuhn et al., people's inability to distinguish theory from evidence is also reflected in the fact that people are not troubled by confounded data. For example, in the sports-balls study, one subject who had antecedently identified texture as likely to affect a ball's bounce and color as likely to be irrelevant was then shown a situation in which texture and color were confounded so that both covaried with bounceability. When this happened, the subject was quite content to identify texture as the cause and to ignore color. According to D. Kuhn et al., the subject did not realize that, given that texture and color both covaried, the actual cause was indeterminate. In a word, according to Kuhn et al., subjects failed to consider (and rule out) alternative hypotheses.

Furthermore, according to Kuhn et al., the lack of attention to issues of confounding and control was also apparent when subjects generated evidence on their own. They write, for example, "The major source of error in the generation of covariation evidence, however, was the failure to recognize the potential effects of other variables and the need to control them in order to produce a valid demonstration" (1988, 181).

The inability to distinguish theory and evidence also meant, according to Kuhn et al., that "subjects had less difficulty generating covariation evidence to demonstrate the correctness of a causal theory than they did generating noncovariation evidence to demonstrate the incorrectness of a causal theory" (1988, 180–181).

Kuhn et al. also note two additional ways in which the inability to distinguish theory and evidence makes it difficult for subjects to deal with disconfirming or anomalous data. One is that, even when subjects did refer to evidence, to preserve theory they often adjusted the evidence to fit the theory, pointing out the number of times that, for example, mustard did co-occur with colds but ignoring the instances in which mustard co-occurred with no colds. Conversely, subjects also often adjusted their theory to fit the data, claiming that the theory in question "was right with respect to those instances that conformed to the covariation pattern but was wrong with respect to those instances that did not" (Kuhn et al., 1988, 126).

According to Kuhn et al., the second way in which an inability to distinguish theory and evidence affects the evaluation of disconfirming data is that, in the face of disconfirming evidence, subjects have more difficulty relinquishing a causal than a noncausal belief. Presumably, when the disconfirming evidence is directed toward a causal belief, the subject cannot distinguish the disconfirming evidence (which shows that the causal relation is absent) from the theoretical belief that the causal relation ought to be present.

In short, according to D. Kuhn et al., flawed scientific reasoning is present at all ages (although it is more pronounced in younger subjects and is also affected by educational level) and is realized in a number of situations.

An alternative interpretation

In light of the conclusions just described, consider three of the points raised earlier.

First, it is clear that Kuhn et al.'s work exemplifies an approach in which causation is operationally defined in terms of covariation. This is not to say that causation is explicitly stated to be equivalent to covariation (or not equivalent, for that matter); it is to note that the operational measures that subjects are to use when assessing causation consist of assessing covariation. The tasks are structured so that what it means for type of cake to cause colds is that type of cake covaries with colds.

The second point is that when subjects cite mechanism or theory rather than covariation as evidence, their answer is treated as flawed, as a way in which "theoretical belief compromises both generation and evaluation of evidence" (Kuhn et al. 1988, 183), and this relates to the third point.

The third point I will defend is that reducing causation to covariation provides a misleading description of the situations in which subjects' judgments deviate from good scientific practice. In the present section, I will discuss some of the specific findings in Kuhn et al.'s work by way of arguing that very often the subjects' behavior was scientifically reasonable, because relying on mechanism or theory is reasonable. I will then consider a possible rejoinder, namely that the subjects' reliance on their beliefs about mechanism was not reasonable, because the subjects were not sufficiently skeptical of their beliefs about theory or mechanism and, in particular, did not use covariation information to test those beliefs, even when told explicitly "to answer the question ... based only on the scientists' findings." Next I will suggest some flaws that were present in the subjects' thinking but that did not involve relying on theory in a way that interfered with the coordination of theory and evidence. I will then argue that, although it is reasonable to take some correlations more seriously than others, it does not always make sense to ignore correlations that are implausible.

Briefly, my argument is this: Subjects' behavior in many of Kuhn et al.'s tasks was reasonable because theory or mechanism can be evidential; the presence of a plausible mechanism that could have mediated between a factor and a correlated event actually functions as some evidence that the correlation might be causal. (It counts as some evidence that Jones died from being treated with penicillin that she had an allergy to molds, because the allergy demonstrates that there was a mechanism by which the penicillin could have been fatal.) In addition, in the face of anomalous data, it is sometimes reasonable to treat a theory as a working hypothesis to be revised rather than rejected, and it is reasonable precisely because of considerations of theory or mechanism. In the Kuhn et al.'s tasks, subjects treated theory and data as mutually interdependent; they brought their theories to the experimental situation and relied on them in assessing covariation evidence. And Kuhn et al. point this out. However, there are two differences between their approach and the approach defended here. One is that Kuhn et al. treat theory or mechanism information as being quite distinct from, and inferior to, evidence that consists of covariation. The other is that Kuhn et al. treat subjects' reliance on theory to evaluate data as an example of flawed reasoning; it is citing covariation information that is treated as good thinking. In contrast, my approach is that treating background theory or mechanism information as evidentially relevant is scientifically legitimate (as is interpreting either in the light of the other). On my view, the subjects' reasoning may well have been flawed, but the flaw was not that subjects relied on theory or mechanism as well as on covariation. Indeed, rational scientific standards for taking covariation information into account *require* that one consider mechanism or theory when possible. The contrast between the approaches provides an alternative interpretation of some of Kuhn et al.'s results.

Consider first cases in which the subject was asked to arrange covariation evidence and then to justify the arrangement. For example, consider the ninth-grader who responded to the request for evidence that texture affects bouncability by explicitly putting all the smooth balls in the "good serve" basket and all the rough ones in the "bad serve" basket and who then justified her arrangement with the theory-based explanation that the rough texture makes the balls heavier. Admittedly, the subject did not explicitly describe the covariation evidence, but rather than showing a lack of metacognitive awareness, the subject's justification may instead have reflected the view that since she had already provided the covariation evidence (by putting the balls in the appropriate baskets), she would now provide additional evidence by describing the mechanism by which the covariation might be causal. (Note also that on this view there is a sense in which the subjects in the sports-balls study had a remarkably robust understanding of how to evaluate causal relations: not only were they able to generate the appropriate covariation to support a theory that conflicted with their own, but they were also able to provide theory-based explanations for theories that conflicted with theirs. Again, this will be discussed, in the following chapter on disconfirmation.)

Conversely, when a subject points out that two types of "breakfast rolls are pretty much the same thing," she could easily be construed as voicing the belief that there is no mechanism that could account for how bread could make a difference. (Indeed, in experiment 13 below, several of our subjects gave the explanation that "milk is just milk" and therefore couldn't affect sleep. However, they frequently elaborated this by pointing out that "there's no difference between types of milk except for fat, and fat doesn't make it hard to sleep," that is, does not constitute a causal mechanism.)

In a word, subjects were relying on beliefs about mechanism, which they had acquired before entering the experimental situation, just as scientists (appropriately) continue to rely on their accumulated knowledge when they enter their own laboratories.

In evaluating Kuhn et al.'s work, it is important to note that they claim not that subjects do not cite evidence but rather that subjects do not cite covariation evidence. However, what is also clear is that the tendency not to cite covariation evidence is treated as flawed reasoning. What I am arguing is that, at least in this regard, the subjects' reasoning is not flawed, because what subjects are doing is relying on information about mechanism to explain why they are taking some covariations seriously while dismissing others and this is a scientifically legitimate thing to do. (It is worth noting that graduate students were less likely than other subjects to provide theory-based responses. I suggest that this is because they were more test-wise in realizing that the rules of the experimental situation called for them to suspend their beliefs about mechanism, which they certainly would have relied on in a noncontrived situation.)

A skeptical rebuttal and a rejoinder   Turn now to the question of subjects' skepticism. The obvious rebuttal to the argument that subjects were reasonable in treating mechanism information as evidential is that, had the subjects been engaging in good scientific thinking, they would have been more skeptical about their own theory-based beliefs. On this view, they either would have relied on covariation information to assess whether their beliefs were supported or, at the very least, would have cited both covariation and mechanism information as evidence. Consider this rebuttal with respect to four sets of results. (The question of skepticism with respect to anomalous evidence will be dealt with again in chapter 3.)

Arranging evidence for rival theories   Consider first the sports-balls study in which subjects were asked to arrange high-bounce and low-bounce balls in the appropriate baskets in order to provide evidence to support a theory about which variables caused bounceability. It is important to note that subjects were able to arrange the appropriate covariation evidence and were able to provide theory-based explanations not only for their own theories but also for theories that conflicted with theirs. That is, if subjects did lack skepticism, it did not prevent them from being able to describe what both types of support for a rival theory would look like.

Not citing covariation as evidence   Consider next subjects like the one who proposed that it is judicial leniency and overcrowding in the prisons that causes prisoners to return to a life of crime. When asked to provide evidence for his belief, the subject merely elaborated his causal script by suggesting that judges give criminals less than the full sentence and by proposing a survey of prisons to document that overcrowding is indeed a problem. That is, the subject did not propose gathering covariation evidence to determine whether leniency and overcrowding did in fact covary with returning to a life of crime. However, when asked, "What evidence would you give to convince someone that your view is right?" such a subject might have understood the question to mean, "What is your justification for saying that *now*?" rather than as meaning, "What sort of evidence could you gather *in the future* to support your argument?" And, in terms of providing a justification for saying now that leniency might be a source of recidivism, it is reasonable to say, roughly, "The reason I'm suggesting leniency as a cause is because of my perception that many judges don't give maximum sentences," or, "I've suggested early release as a cause of overcrowding and I would justify having said that by taking a survey to show that prisons are indeed overcrowded." (In experiment 16, below, when it was made clear to subjects that they were being asked to gather evidence that did not now exist, all subjects at all ages did propose a treatment/control contrast to see whether the target factor would covary with the effect.) (In chapters 3 and 13, I discuss reasons why, even when subjects do want to gather covariation evidence, they may lack the technical knowledge to be able to do so. This does not mean that they do not see covariation evidence as important, but rather it simply means that they do not know how to arrange a controlled design, especially when the data are naturally occurring or correlational.)

Evaluating confounded data   The objection that subjects should have been more skeptical of their theory-based beliefs could also be leveled against their behavior when evaluating confounded data. But here too acknowledging the importance of mechanism information suggests an alternative interpretation. Recall that, in the task that involved the bounciness of sports balls, one of the possible causal factors was color. Color was included specifically to make it likely that one of the variables would be seen as noncausal, and in fact it was color "which most subjects selected as the variable they believed least likely to make a difference." In this task, even when it was clear that color (or whatever variable a subject had chosen as noncausal) and the variable that had been chosen as causal

both covaried with the effect, subjects frequently ignored the confounding data and maintained their view that only the latter factor was causal.
For Kuhn et al., this reflected an inability to take account of covariation
evidence. However, on an alternative view, it reflected the fact that subjects were being thorough in that they were taking account of *all* of the
evidence available to them—including evidence about mechanism—and
were using mechanism evidence to decide that one of the covariates was
likely to be irrelevant noise. Before entering the experimental situation,
subjects had already learned that, with respect to bouncability, color has
very few causal properties. As a causal factor, it is simply not plausible.
(Color may be used as an index of something causal, but this is a separate issue.) Subjects bring this information to the experimental situation
and, in consequence, ignore the covariation of color with bouncability
precisely because, in taking account of *all* available evidence, they can
think of no mechanism that could render the covariation causal rather
than coincidental.

As for whether this is good scientific thinking, consider the following
thought experiment: Imagine learning of a study done on two wards of
a single hospital in which infants who were frequently held developed
better than infants who were not. Imagine also learning that the infants
who were frequently held were from the ward that happened to be blue
and those not held were from the ward that happened to be yellow. I suspect that few people would be tempted to conclude that since developmental outcomes covaried with ward color as well as with the amount of
holding, it would not be possible to decide which of the two variables
was the causal one. In experiment 6, chapter 6, I describe a study in which
the factor that covaried with an effect was sometimes confounded with
another factor that is causally relevant in the real world. When both confounded factors were causally relevant, even sixth-graders concluded that
confounded data were more likely than controlled data to be indeterminate. (These results are also congruent with the findings of Bullock [1991],
described below.)

Responding to anomalous data   Perhaps the most striking example of the
objection that subjects should have been more skeptical of their theory-
based beliefs might be found in the colds study. Here as well one could
argue that a more skeptical approach would have been to reject the theory
when the covariation evidence was not congruent with it, especially when
subjects were explicitly told "to answer the question not from what you
know about foods, but based only on the scientists' findings." However,
rejecting the theory was something subjects seemed reluctant to do, as
evidenced by the following two results: subjects often tried to preserve
the theory by adjusting it to fit the anomalous data or by adjusting the

anomalous data to fit the theory, and anomalous data had a smaller effect on causal than on noncausal theories. Both results will be discussed in chapter 3 because they are relevant to the literature on disconfirming evidence. However, it is worth briefly mentioning them briefly now in order to note that an analogous point applies: an emphasis on covariation underestimates the extent to which subjects deal with disconfirming evidence in a scientifically reasonable way.

As a first step, my rejoinder to this skeptical rebuttal is to note that it is misleading to study scientific reasoning by studying whether subjects can follow instructions to ignore information that they have already acquired. As Keating notes in his discussion of causal reasoning, including scientific reasoning, "There is little point in trying to explain reasoning independent of a knowledge of content" (1990, 66). In evaluating evidence, scientists do not, nor should they, ignore what they know (including the theories they know). A cancer researcher, for example, who somehow managed to do this would not be very productive. As Boyd (personal communication) has pointed out, to study scientific reasoning by asking subjects to evaluate covariation evidence while ignoring what they already know about theory or mechanism is analogous to studying verbal memory by studying memory for *meaningless* nonsense syllables in order to control for the effects of meaning: there is no reason to think that one would learn about verbal memory, since verbal memory almost certainly relies on meaning-dependent strategies. Similarly, studying scientific reasoning by ignoring what we know about theory or mechanism might tell us something about the subject's ability to follow experimental instructions but not about scientific reasoning.

Nevertheless, what a critical skeptic could argue is that in the colds study, even if the subjects did not ignore (and possibly should not have ignored) what they already knew, they nevertheless been skeptical enough about their own theories that they rejected rather than modified them in the face of the anomalous evidence. To this I offer a three-part rejoinder:

First, the anomalous evidence was incomplete. In the colds task, subjects' beliefs about which foods caused colds were based on considerations of mechanism (however rudimentary or incorrect) as well as on covariation. However, what Kuhn, et al. called "disconfirming" evidence called into question only subjects' beliefs about covariation, leaving their beliefs about mechanism intact. Therefore, when subjects were explicitly told "to answer the question not from what you know about foods, but based only on the scientists' findings," the subjects changed their behavior only to a negligeable extent. (Experiment 13, chapter 10, presents some evidence suggesting that disconfirming or anomalous evidence that deals with the mechanism component, as well as the covariation component, of a belief is more compelling than disconfirming or anomalous evidence that deals with covariation alone.)

Second, even when disconfirming or anomalous evidence is compelling, it is often scientifically legitimate to modify one's belief by restricting its scope. For example, if one discovered a strep infection for which penicillin was not effective, it would make sense not to abandon the general belief in the efficacy of penicillin against strep but rather to treat it as a working hypothesis that can be modified and to conclude that the theory that penicillin cures strep infections was right with respect to only some strep infections. That is, we would be tempted to conclude (though perhaps in a more articulate way) exactly what Kuhn et al.'s subjects had concluded, namely, that it "was right with respect to those instances that conformed to the covariation pattern but was wrong with respect to those instances that did not" (Kuhn et al. 1988, 126). Yet this conclusion was treated as reflecting flawed thinking. In short, one of the effects of ignoring the legitimate role of mechanism in scientific reasoning is that reasonable hypothesis modification or articulation is treated as reflecting flawed thinking.

Similarly, it is also sometimes scientifically legitimate to question data that do not accord with a theory especially if the theory includes a mechanism that explains why the problematic data should not have obtained and why the data anticipated by the theory should have obtained. For example, suppose that scientists are testing the hypothesis that a broad-spectrum antibiotic of well established efficacy will actually be effective at doses much lower than those currently employed (which would be important for economic reasons as well as to minimize side effects). Suppose further that scientists treat a number of patients suffering from diseases for which the drug has been effective in the past, giving them doses ranging from the currently standard dosage down (by increments) to 1 percent of the standard dose. If *none* of the patients improved, it would be rational to begin by questioning the data, that is, by tentatively adopting an explanation of the data that did not require any change in their attitude towards the test hypothesis at all, since it would be rational to suppose that the drug samples were defective. As already noted, these issues will be discussed in more detail in chapter 3. (Note that this is not to argue that subjects' beliefs about what causes colds were correct; clearly, many of them were quite erroneous. It is simply to point out that the disconfirming covariation evidence dealt with only one component of their beliefs and that in the face of disconfirming evidence, hypothesis modification rather than rejection, is often scientifically legitimate and not an example of flawed thinking.)

Third, Kuhn et al. (1988), as well as Schauble (1990), found that as disconfirming or anomalous evidence accumulated, subjects *did* become increasingly likely to reject their theories. (These findings will be relevant, again, in chapter 3.) That is, subjects did not frivolously reject their theories at the first sign of anomalous evidence, but they also did not ignore anomalous data when repeated occurrence made it clear that the data were not accidental.

In short, maintaining a certain skepticism about one's own beliefs is often an admirable thing to do. However, skepticism that is unconstrained by, among other things, considerations of theory or mechanism can be counterproductive; without some way of deciding which correlations or beliefs should be taken seriously (at least at the outset), one would be overwhelmed. In the same vein, to reject theories at the first sign of anomalous evidence might be to reject them when modification would instead be appropriate.

Note also the point about terminology made in the beginning of this chapter. If we understand a hypothesis tested by Kuhn et al.'s subjects to have been "Variable x *always* causes colds," then changing the hypothesis to be "Variable x causes colds only in certain instances but not in the ones we were presented with here" would, in a logician's sense, be a rejection of the initial hypothesis. Thus a subject who made this modification would not have failed to understand (and apply) the logic of confirmation and disconfirmation. Of course, the question could still be raised of whether the modification in question was well motivated, as opposed to ad hoc. But if the subject's initial hypothesis is instead treated as an imprecise working hypothesis, then its refinement would be a case of what I have been calling elaboration rather than one of modification. Here too there would be the question of whether the elaboration in question was well motivated or ad hoc, but there would be no question of whether the subject appreciated the necessity for making some revision in the light of the data. It is not clear from the reported data which interpretation of the subjects' hypotheses is appropriate or (more important) whether or not their revisions to them were well motivated. In experiment 11 there is some evidence that subjects do prefer theoretically motivated to ad hoc hypotheses.

The flaws there were   Returning to the question of whether Kuhn et al.'s subjects engaged in flawed thinking, I suggest that in some cases they certainly did but the flaws had to do with information-processing limitations rather than with an inability to coordinate theory and evidence. One example of flawed thinking was that subjects were better able to generate covariation evidence to support a causal theory than they were to generate noncovariation evidence to demonstrate the incorrectness of a causal theory. However, as Kuhn et al. themselves point out, "Non-covariation evidence could be of three types: (1) a selection of balls of a single variable level distributed across two outcomes, (2) a selection of balls of both levels of the variable yielding the same outcome, and (3) a combination of the two preceding types, that is, a selection of balls of both levels of the variable distributed across both outcomes" (1988. 175–176). I suggest that the three types might have been conflated in the subjects' thinking so that, although the subjects understood conceptually what it meant that a variable made no difference, they might have been unable to sort through and disambiguate the three ways of demonstrating operationally that the variable made no difference, and the reason they might have been unable to disambiguate is that either they lacked the information-processing capacity to be able to do so or else they lacked a strategy that would have enabled them to do this kind of sorting with the information-processing capacity that they did have.

Another flaw that may have reflected information-processing limitations is that the major source of error in generating covariation evidence was the failure to recognize the potential confounding effects of other variables and the need to control for them. As already noted, one reason for the subjects' lack of attention to control may have been that they, like many practicing scientists, did not feel the need to control for a variable that they believed to be causally irrelevant. (This may, of course, have reflected a mistaken belief about which variables were irrelevant, but it did not necessarily reflect the belief that a control is not important.) However, information-processing limitations might also have played a role. For example, if the target variable were size, then one strategy for testing its effect would be to put a large ball in one basket and a small in the other while holding all other variables constant. However, another would be to put large balls in one basket and small ones in the other and to have each pair of balls matched on the other three variables. In terms of information processing, and for the subject who had no prior training in experimental-design strategies, it might be difficult to disentangle the two approaches, and in cases in which more than two balls were used, it might be difficult to keep track of the other three variables. (Some evidence that information processing might be have been playing a role can be found in Bullock's [1991] study, discussed below.) In short, then, one possibility is that information-processing limitations (rather than subjects' reluctance to reject their theory-based beliefs) made the generation of noncovariation evidence more difficult than the generation of covariation evidence and, when covariation evidence was generated, made it difficult to keep track of (and therefore difficult to control for) confounding variables.

A caveat about theories   I have been arguing that relying on theory or mechanism considerations is scientifically legitimate and, in particular, that it is reasonable to do so in deciding which correlated factors are likely to be causal rather than artifactual. However, in making this argument, I am not suggesting that variables that seem to be causally irrelevant should never be taken into account. Sometimes factors that are in fact causal seem nevertheless to be causally irrelevant simply because the operative underlying mechanism has not yet been discovered. In terms of the earlier example regarding the color of hospital wards and developmental outcomes, if the two wards differed only in color and not also in terms of amount of holding the infants received, and especially if other hospitals also found a systematic correlation of developmental outcome with ward color, then color would be worth a second look because it might indicate as yet undiscovered effects of color on, for example, the infants' moods, irritability, etc. However, note that when seemingly irrelevant correlations are given a second look, the second look is typically motivated by information other than covariation: typically, in such cases, the usual causes of the phenomenon have all been ruled out and the covariation is observed more than once. What I am suggesting is that without this other information, and given the large number of correlations in the world, it is reasonable that some instances of covariation should be dismissed as artifactual in order to avoid being overwhelmed by irrelevant noise. In this regard, recall that when the subjects of Kuhn et al. (1988) and Schauble (1990) were repeatedly exposed to disconfirming covariation evidence (that is, in terms of the present suggestion, when they were shown that the anomalous covariation was systematic), they did indeed become increasingly likely to reject theory-based beliefs. (This point is developed in experiments 9 and 10, below.)

In short, the guideline that implausible alternative hypotheses ought to be ignored and the qualifier that implausible alternative hypotheses should sometimes be taken seriously both ought to be followed, but at different points during scientific investigation. It is resonable to slight seemingly irrelevant correlations and implausible alternative hypotheses in the early steps of data collection. If, as evidence accumulates, a seemingly irrelevant correlation continues to obtain, then the implausible correlation ought to be pursued, especially if more plausible possibilities have been ruled out. In a word, skepticism about seemingly irrelevant causes needs to be constrained. (These issues are examined in experiments 7 through 10, below.)

The notion of constrained skepticism is also related to the suggestion, mentioned in chapter 1 and to be elaborated in subsequent chapters, that scientific reasoning can be described as a bootstrapping operation. Briefly, the argument is as follows: Principles of scientific inquiry (such as, identify the cause of an event by identifying its correlates) function as rules of thumb rather than algorithms because they do not guarantee success. The success of the principles depends on the accuracy of the background information (such as information about mechanism) that the principles are used in conjunction with. However, principles of scientific inquiry can help in the discovery of relevant background information not now known. That is, we are more likely to identify a genuinely causal correlation if we are already approximately correct about what the mechanism is that distinguishes it from specious correlations, but pursuing apparently specious but systematic correlations might enable us to discover an underlying mechanism not now known.

Related work

Turn now to the third point regarding Kuhn et al.'s (1988) work, namely, that it has provoked studies designed to examine the extent to which its conclusions can be generalized. Consider two conclusions in particular. In Kuhn et al. 1988 one of the ways in which people are said to have difficulty distinguishing theory from evidence is that they have trouble testing hypotheses. The other is that they are said to have difficulty dealing with confounded variables. Recent work by other researchers has examined both of these claims.

Sodian, Zaitchik, and Carey designed their experiments to test the claim that, when asked to determine the causes of a phenomenon, young children "act as if their goal were simply to produce or repeat the effect, rather than to discover its causes" (1991, 753). They presented their first- and second-grade subjects with a problem in which two brothers were trying to find out whether the mouse living in their house was large or small. Two boxes were described: one with a large opening and one with a small opening. The subjects were then asked which box the brothers should put out if they wanted to tell, according to whether the food was gone in the morning, what size the mouse was. If a subject wanted to test the hypothesis about size, she would suggest the box with the small opening should be used, since only the small mouse could fit through it. However, a subject could fail on this test because she interpreted the task of testing the hypothesis about the size of the mouse as the task of feeding the mouse (that is, of producing a desirable effect). To assess whether children could distinguish these two goals, Sodian et al. also gave children a second task in which they had to choose which box to put out to make sure that the mouse got some food no matter what its size. Subjects were also asked questions about conclusive and inconclusive tests: they were asked what conclusions would follow if the food were removed from the box with the large opening or from the box with the small opening. Most of the first-graders and all of the second-graders gave evidence that they were distinguishing the goal of testing a hypothesis from the goal of producing an effect. The most frequent pattern (observed in 55 percent of the first-graders and 86 percent of the second-graders) consisted of correctly choosing the box with the large opening to feed the mouse and the box

with the small opening to find out the size of the mouse, correctly justifying both choices, and correctly answering questions about conclusive
and inconclusive tests. In the second study, the same children were told
that two brothers wanted to find out if aardvarks have a good or a poor
sense of smell. First the subjects were simply asked what they could do to
find this out, in order to see what subjects would spontaneously propose.
Then they were asked whether, to distinguish between the two hypotheses, they should put out a strong-smelling or weak-smelling piece of
food, in order to see whether subjects could choose the conclusive test.
While few children in either age group were able spontaneously to propose a conclusive test, the majority of children, when presented with the
two possible options, did suggest using the conclusive weak-smelling
food rather than the inconclusive strong-smelling food.

Sodian et al. are careful to point out the many differences between their
task and tasks in which subjects have engaged in less sophisticated behaviors. Nevertheless, what their work demonstrates is that, at least in some
situations, very young children are able to distinguish testing a hypothesis from merely producing an effect.

The results of their study are also relevant to the claim that children
have difficulty understanding that some data are inconclusive. In Sodian
et al.'s study, subjects were able to choose a conclusive test by drawing
inferences about what additional things would be true (about animals'
behavior) if each of two hypotheses were true. Although this does not
mean that subjects can recognize inconclusive data (or design conclusive
tests) in all situations, it does suggest that subjects' understanding of an
inconclusive test is more complex than it might appear to be and that
analyzing their understanding in more detail might be necessary to paint a
more fine-grained picture of how it develops.

Some recent work by Bullock (1991) also concerned inconclusive tests,
but her task was one more directly comparable to the sports-balls task.
Like Kuhn et al. (1988), Bullock presented her subjects (second through
fourth graders) with a problem that involved identifying a causal factor.
Specifically, subjects were told that a young boy wanted to make some
lanterns that would not go out in the wind. The lanterns could be made
with many small holes or a few large ones, with short wide candles or tall
thin ones, and with or without a roof. Subjects were then told that the
boy wanted to find out whether having a roof makes a difference to how
well a lantern burns in the wind. There were two measures: One was what
the subjects spontaneously proposed. The other was what choices they
made when presented with a set of eight cards, with each card depicting
one of the eight possible types of lanterns (for example, a lantern with a
few large holes, a short wide candle, and no roof).

The large majority of third and fourth graders (74 percent and 84 percent) spontaneously proposed a contrastive test (one lantern with a roof and another without). Only a small percentage also added that one would have to hold one or both of the other variables constant. However, when subjects were choosing which of the eight cards would provide a good test of whether a roof makes a difference, a third of the third-graders and most of the fourth-graders chose cards that held everything constant and varied only whether or not a roof was present.

In a word, in Bullock's task, subjects were able to choose the sorts of tests that avoided confounding, whereas in Kuhn et al.'s bounce task, subjects were not able to recognize indeterminacy when presented with a confounded design. I suggest that the difference can be understood in terms of the argument offered earlier in this chapter: In Kuhn et al.'s task, one of the confounded variables had already been identified by the subject as being causally irrelevant (and when the variable was color, which it was for "most" subjects, then it actually was causally irrelevant). Thus there was a rationale for ignoring it. In contast, in Bullock's task, the various factors that could be confounded all made causal sense. One could imagine a mechanism by which the factor could affect whether the lanterns blew out in the wind. (Large holes, for example, could admit large gusts of wind.) And because subjects could see the relevance, they controlled for confounding. Related results are reported in experiments 6 and 16, below.

In addition, the fact that subjects found it difficult to propose tests that controlled for nontarget variables but found it easier to choose an arrangement of cards that enabled nontarget variables to be controlled for supports my earlier suggestion that information-processing limitations also play a role in how subjects deal with confounding: choosing an arrangement of cards may have been less cognitively demanding than designing a test from scratch.

General Summary

In summary, I have argued that the research on formal-operational reasoning and on causal reasoning has, for the most part, examined scientific reasoning by asking subjects to reason about a theoretically impoverished environment and by stipulating that correct performance consists of equating causation with covariation. Although these sorts of situations approximate the kind of predicament that exists when plausible hypotheses either do not exist or have been ruled out, such tasks provide a picture of causal reasoning that is, at best, incomplete. In most circumstances, people do not (nor should they nor can they) treat all covariations as equally indicative of plausible causes. And distinguishing correlations that are genuinely causal from those that are merely artifactual is done, in part, by relying on considerations of theory or mechanism. Therefore, asking subjects to reason about theoretically impoverished situations describes subjects' scientific reasoning in a way that omits many of its most important aspects.

But this is not simply an argument that a lack of attention to the role of theory or mechanism is an omission that produces an incomplete picture of scientific reasoning and nothing more. When experimental tasks consist of having subjects reason about situations that are theoretically rich but in which correct responses are stipulated to consist of ignoring considerations of theory or mechanism, then the resulting picture of scientific reasoning is not merely incomplete but is actually distorted. When laboratory tasks are contrived so that correct performance consists of ignoring mechanism and treating covariations as roughly equivalent to one another, then subjects who ignore certain covariations while taking others seriously or who treat mechanism as evidential will be treated as engaging in flawed reasoning when they are, in fact, reasoning in a way that is scientifically legitimate.

This chapter has focused on hypothesis testing. The following chapter will deal with the kind of hypothesis articulation or modification that takes place in response to disconfirming or anomalous data. (Although there is a distinction between these two activities, the distinction is not at all a sharp one. It is often very difficult to tell when hypothesis testing ends and hypothesis modification begins.) I will argue that here too an undue emphasis on covariation underestimates people's ability to think scientifically.

Chapter 3
Disconfirming and Anomalous Evidence

The previous chapter focused on the way in which people identify causes or formulate at least preliminary causal explanations for various events. But one of the hallmarks of scientific inquiry is that explanations in general, and especially preliminary ones, are not always perfect. The result is that subsequent data may be anomalous to the explanation.

Conclusions about Disconfirming Evidence

In the social-psychological literature, the question of how people evaluate explanations in light of disconfirming data has been examined in studies of attitude change. Although there are certainly exceptions, Gleitman's summary of the findings is representative: "The overall picture is one of attitude stability rather than of attitude change. Attitudes can be altered, but it takes some doing. By and large, there seems to be a tendency to hold on to the attitudes one already has" (1983, 343). In many of these studies, the attitudes in question concerned beliefs about politics, abortion, capital punishment, race, personal efficacy or worth, etc. The typical conclusion about the stability of such attitudes makes intuitive sense. It is easy to imagine that they would be quite resistant to change for two reasons. One is that such attitudes are often emotion-laden, and it would hardly be surprising if the emotional component of the beliefs served to filter out or somehow distort disconfirming evidence. Another reason is that these sorts of beliefs, far from being circumscribed, are typically interwoven with much broader beliefs (including beliefs about what can count as evidence) that define a kind of worldview. Thus arguments that run counter to the circumscribed belief may do little to change it, because they may have little to do with the broader web of beliefs within which the target belief is imbedded and by which it is buttressed. (This is not to say that worldviews are never changed. Clearly they sometimes are, but usually over a period of time longer than the typical experiment.)

In short, the claim that the beliefs just discussed are tenacious seems to have a certain face validity. However, what seems less intuitively obvious are analogous results from the cognitive literature on how people deal with disconfirming evidence. Here too the conclusions drawn from the research have been quite uniform and consist of two main points. The first is that, by and large, people do not seek disconfirming evidence and only sometimes take it into account when it is presented to them. That is, people are said to exhibit a confirmation bias (e.g., Bruner, Goodnow, and Austin 1956; Wason 1960). The second is that when people fail to take account of disconfirming evidence, their behavior is parallel to the behavior of scientists, as described by T. S. Kuhn (1970), who cling to their theories in the face of disconfirming data that call for the theories to be rejected (Mynatt, Doherty, and Tweney 1977; Kuhn, Amsel, and O'Loughlin 1988; Wason 1977).

There are two reasons for questioning these conclusions. One is that there are other results, also in the cognitive literature, that suggest the exact opposite. The other is that it is initially implausible that nonscientists' behavior in the cognitive experiments would resemble the scientists' behavior as described by T. S. Kuhn.

Questioning the Conclusions

Cognitive Research on Hypothesis Testing

Consider first empirical work from a related cognitive area not directly aimed at studying how people deal with disconfirming evidence: the body of research on hypothesis testing in which relinquishing hypotheses is precisely what people (children as well as adults) do (Stevenson 1972). In the bulk of these tasks, subjects generate and test a series of specific hypotheses, and each time a hypothesis proves not to be correct (that is, each time a hypothesis is disconfirmed), the subject moves on to generate and test a different hypothesis. Indeed, people frequently adopt a win-stay/lose-shift strategy for relinquishing a disconfirmed hypothesis with maximum efficiency. That is, standard behavior in these studies consists of doing precisely what subjects are often said, in studies of disconfirming evidence, to be reluctant to do.

Normal versus Crisis Science

Consider next whether it is initially plausible that nonscientists' behavior in the experiments in question resembles the scientists' behavior as described by T. S. Kuhn. When T. S. Kuhn drew attention to scientists unwilling to relinquish their theories in the face of disconfirming evidence, he was describing situations that occur during what he termed periods of "crisis" as opposed to "normal" science. Crisis situations involve paradigm shifts that affect not only the content of the beliefs in a discipline but also the very methodology that the discipline is based on. For many of the scientists practicing during a crisis period, the paradigm shift calls into question the work of a lifetime. In this context, a tendency to cling to their old paradigms in the face of disconfirming evidence has strong emotional as well as cognitive roots. In a very real sense, the scientists' careers are at stake.

Now consider the sorts of psychological tasks in which nonscientists are said to be clinging to their theories. These tasks involve hypotheses such as whether one rather than another geometric figure repels a moving dot on a computer display (Mynatt et al. 1977), whether drinking apple juice versus orange juice causes more colds (D. Kuhn et al. 1988), whether the rule that defines a number sequence is "any increasing series" (Wason 1960), etc. These tasks do not involve beliefs that define whole careers or even worldviews about a particular area. They are of little consequence, and therefore of little emotional import. True, some of the beliefs are ones that the subjects themselves have generated, and thus they undoubtedly reflect a certain amount of ego involvement but presumably only a pale copy of the kind of ego involvement that occurs when a career's worth of work is at risk. Nevertheless, the conclusions are parallel: the subjects are said to have a confirmation (or verification) bias; they avoid searching for and taking account of disconfirming evidence.

How, then, to explain data that lead to conclusions that seem, on the face of things, to be implausible? Of course, one explanation is that even when beliefs are inconsequential, people nevertheless hold on to them and ignore disconfirming evidence. However, there are other explanations, as well.

An Alternative Account of the Data

One reason the conclusions may have been unwarranted is that in some cases they were based on measures that were either confounded or ambiguous. Another reason is that the many different readings of "confirmation bias" are not always adequately distinguished, the result being that behavior that would be genuine confirmation bias on one reading would not be on another. A third reason is that many studies of confirmation bias are based on misleading descriptions of scientific inquiry that ignore the importance of considerations based on theory or mechanism.

Inconclusive Measures

Clinging to an initial theory versus being unable—if only temporarily—to generate an alternative
Clinging to one's initial theory need not reflect a preference for the familiar over the new. Instead, it may reflect the temporary inability to generate

an alternative, and therefore a preference for some explanation (however defective) over no explanation at all. That is, there are two senses in which measures of confirmation bias have been flawed. One is that, although the term "confirmation bias" connotes a fairly long-term disposition, the measures have assessed what may be merely temporary states. The other is that the measures have confounded clinging to the old explanation with being unable to generate an alternative to replace it.

As a case in point, consider the series of studies carried out by Karmiloff-Smith (1984). Karmiloff-Smith has identified three phases that children go through in solving a problem. The first, a procedural data-driven phase, is one in which each behavioral unit is successful in the sense that it achieves its goal but in which the individual units are not linked to one another in a consistent whole. For example, in her classic block-balancing task (Karmiloff-Smith and Inhelder 1974/1975), in which the task is to balance ordinary blocks as well as blocks that contain either conspicuous or hidden weights, children in phase 1 balance each block successfully by relying on proprioceptive feedback, but they treat each block as an isolated problem. Therefore, once a child has succeeded in balancing a conspicuously weighted block, she does not then try another block of that type in order to make use of her newly acquired knowledge. Blocks are simply taken up in the order in which they lie on the table.

Phase 2 behavior is described as being top-down or theory-driven. The child generates a metaprocedural rule, that is, a simplified procedure that allows the child to link the previously isolated problems into a single problem. For example, in the block task, the child generates the rule that blocks balance at their geometric center. The cost of this top-down procedure is fewer successes than in phase 1, because the weighted blocks in fact do not balance at their geometric center. Furthermore, what is striking is that in phase 2 the children actually ignore noncongruent data by, for example, dismissing the weighted blocks as being "impossible to balance."

Finally, in phase 3 the children integrate the data-driven procedure with the top-down strategy, trying first a geometric-center theory but rapidly adjusting the position of the weighted blocks in accord with proprioceptive feedback.

The data from phase 2 clearly demonstrate that frequent counterexamples alone do not induce a change in the child's theory. In fact, in phase 2 the counterexamples are typically dismissed as being "impossible." This has lead at least one researcher to conclude, "Children hold on to their initial theory for as long as they can" (Wason 1977).

However, it would be mistaken to conclude from these findings that ignoring disconfirming data is a general feature of the child's cognitive life. It would be equally mistaken to conclude that in holding on to their theories, the children were choosing between competing theories and were basing their choice on comfortable familiarity rather than explanatory value.

As Karmiloff-Smith (1984) points out, one of the salient features of the children's behavior was that ignoring "impossible" data was only a temporary strategy. It was adopted to rule out anomalous noise just long enough to permit the initial theory to be consolidated. Once consolidation took place, then the children did begin to deal with the "impossible" instances, first by trying to generate a separate theory independent of the initial one and then by aiming at a single unifying theory that could account for both types of blocks. That is, ignoring disconfirming data was a temporary strategy rather than a general dispositional state.

In addition, dismissing noncongruent data need not mean that the children viewed the data as unproblematic for the explanation. It could mean instead that they were simply unable to generate an alternative explanation to take account of the data. Being dissatisfied with an explanation and having the wherewithal to generate a replacement for it are two separate processes that ought to be treated as independent. Yet when Wason (1977) was inferring that children cling to their theories, his conclusion was based on their not having generated an alternative. One can easily be dissatisfied with an existing explanation without necessarily having the resources to generate a replacement for it.

Karmiloff-Smith (1984) also notes that practicing scientists often simplify the data they are dealing with by temporarilly ignoring evidence that does not quite fit. Minerologists, for example, sometimes assume, as a temporary working hypothesis, a symmetrical crystalline structure even when they know that the structure is, in fact, asymmetrical. Such an oversimplified working hypothesis not only reduces information-processing demands (as does, for example, the focus-gambling strategy of Bruner et al. 1956) but also serves as a framework within which the anomalous data can be organized and against which they can form a pattern that suggests either a systematic modification or an alternative.

Preferring an explanation—however flawed—over no explanation

Furthermore, in Karmiloff-Smith's studies, the temporary inability to generate an alternative also had another consequence. When the initial theory was generated in phase 2, it did in fact explain some of the data. More to the point, perhaps, it was the only theory available to the child; the child had not yet been able to generate a theory that could account for all of the data. Thus, clinging to the old theory did not reflect the rejection of a new theory of better (or even equal) explanatory value in favor of the old theory, *because there was no new theory*. Instead, it might have reflected a preference for an explanation that did account for some of the data (albeit in an imperfect way) over a state of affairs in which there was no explanation for any of the data.

Preferring a theory because its competitors have been found wanting

Klahr and his colleagues found that subjects were less skeptical of self-generated hypotheses rather than other-generated hypotheses—which would seem, on the surface at least, to reflect a confirmation or belief bias. However, this conclusion also is open to question.

In one of the tasks, Schunn and Klahr (1992, 1993) asked subjects to discover the function of an unknown command (delta) in a computer device that directed a "milk truck" to execute a sequence of actions associated with a dairy delivery route. Subjects generated and ran programs to test hypotheses about how the delta command worked.

Another task consisted of a computer-controlled robot tank called "BigTrak" that could be programmed to do several things, including going forward and backward and rotating left and right (Klahr, Fay, and Dunbar 1993). Programming was done by entering the instructions with various keys. The subjects' task was to discover how the repeat key (RPT) worked. There were two global hypotheses: The correct "N-role: selector" hypothesis was that a command of RPT N repeated the previous N instructions once. However, most subjects generated the "N-role: counter" hypothesis according to which RPT N meant that either the entire program or the single instruction preceding RPT would be repeated N times.

Klahr et al. (1993) represent the subjects' hypothesis space in terms of frames. The two major frames that corresponded to the two *global* hypotheses were the "N-role: counter" frame and the "N-role: selector" frame. In terms of the earlier discussion, a frame might be thought of as analogous to a working hypothesis. (Recall that the "N-role: selector" hypothesis was the correct one.) Each major frame consisted of a *local* hypothesis about four attributes (such as the type of element to be repeated, the boundaries of the repeated element, etc.). The experiment space included the results of various experiments.

Using the milk-truck task, Schunn and Klahr (1993) found that when subjects tested hypotheses generated by someone else rather than by themselves, they tested more programs and did so over significantly more time even though they rated self-generated and other-generated hypotheses as being comparably plausible. That is, they tested self-generated hypotheses less rigorously—a finding compatible with a confirmation bias. However, Schunn and Klahr (1993) also report that Koehler found that self-generated hypotheses were given lower confidence ratings than other-generated hypotheses because, Koehler argued, the process of hypothesis generation forces the individual to consider more alternative hypotheses.

In a word, whether subjects are more rigorous in assessing self- rather than other-generated hypotheses is not clear.

Using the BigTrak task, Klahr, Dunbar, and Fay (1990) found that subjects were more likely to retain self-generated hypotheses rather than other-generated hypotheses in the face of negative evidence—a finding that would seem also to reflect a belief bias. However, "belief bias" connotes a situation in which a subject's belief leads her to ignore or distort disconfirming data, and there is an alternative explanation for Klahr et al's. finding that turns on Koehler's point: It may be that to produce a self-generated hypothesis, a subject contrasts various possible hypotheses and evaluates them in the context of the evidence to be explained. The hypothesis that is then presented as self-generated is one that has already been evaluated favorably with respect to its competitors. Therefore, when a self-generated hypothesis is confronted with anomalous evidence, the evidence has diminished effect because to take it seriously would mean to impugn the target hypothesis in favor of one of its competitors when the competitors have already been evaluated and found wanting. In contrast, an other-generated hypothesis may be one that the subject has not previously evaluated with respect to its competitors; it may not have already been chosen as being more compelling than its competitors. Therefore, when the target is other-generated, the subsequent presentation of disconfirming evidence might make it easier to reject the target because the subject has not already decided that it is more convincing than its competitors. In short, the stronger commitment to a self-generated theory might reflect a prior (favorable) assessment of it in relation to the alternatives rather than the sort of commitment that simply prevents the subject from questioning something that she herself has generated.

Dunbar and Klahr (1989) also observed third- to sixth-graders learning how the RPT key worked and concluded that there were several developmental differences. The first is that children and adults proposed different hypotheses: children were more likely to propose partially specified (ambiguous) hypotheses rather than fully specified hypotheses. "Second, the children did not abandon their current frame and search the Hypothesis space for a new frame, or use the results of experiment space search to induce a new frame. Third, the children did not attempt to check whether their hypotheses were consistent with prior data. Even when children knew that there was earlier evidence against their current hypothesis, they said that the device *usually* worked according to their theory" (Dunbar and Klahr 1989, 132). However, the second conclusion needs to be qualified. Karmiloff-Smith (1984) found that children did eventually do the analog of abandoning their current frame and either searching for or inducing a new frame. The difference is that in Karmiloff-Smith's studies, the tasks were less esoteric and the mechanisms (for example, hidden weights, balance beams, physical forces, etc.) could be apprehended proprioceptively. In addition, the third conclusion suggests the sort of reluctance to relinquish a current hypothesis that is compatible with a confirmation bias. However, it could have been instead that the children found their current hypotheses less compelling than it had been in the light of anomalous evidence but that they were unable (at least temporarily) to generate an alternative that would account for the initial data as well as the anomalous data.

In short, in the absence of a competing theory of equal or better explanatory value, clinging to one's initial theory may reflect either or both of two things: a preference for a flawed explanation over no explanation at all and a temporary inability to formulate a new competing theory. In the same vein, a commitment to a self-generated theory might reflect the fact that it has already been evaluated with respect to its competitors and found to be more compelling than them. In a word, although a standard conclusion in the cognitive literature is that people, including children, exhibit a confirmation bias, the data thought to demonstrate such a bias are open to alternative interpretations.

In the studies reported here, when subjects were presented with anomalous or disconfirming data, direct measures were used to assess whether such data made subjects less committed to the existing theory. In addition, when subjects were asked to choose between an old theory and its replacement, they were typically provided with the replacement; they did not have to generate it on their own.

A Conflated Term

The second reason why conclusions about confirmation bias in cognitive tasks may not have been warranted is that the various referents of "confirmation bias" are not always clearly distinguished, so what might be genuine confirmation bias on one reading would not be on another. The term "confirmation bias" has been used to account for several different conclusions, including the following:

• People often do not accurately perceive data unless their theory predicts that the data should be there (e.g., Chapman and Chapman's [1967, 1969] work on illussory correlations).
• People cannot describe what disconfirming results would look like (D. Kuhn et al. 1988).
• People cannot (or do not) generate or seek disconfirming rather than confirming tests or evidence (Mynatt et al. 1977; Bruner, Goodnow, and Austin 1956; Wason 1960).

• When faced with disconfirming data, instead of relinquishing their theories, people continue to maintain them by modifying them to take account of the disconfirming results (D. Kuhn et al. 1988).

• In testing their hypotheses, people do not adequately consider alternative hypotheses (D. Kuhn et al. 1988, Mynatt et al. 1977, Dunbar and Klahr 1989).

By way of illustrating the sort of problem that the conflation of referents can result in, consider a subject who, in response to disconfirming data, modifies her explanation to take account of the data. If by "confirmation bias" one means that disconfirming data are filtered out, then the subject's behavior would not reflect a confirmation bias; she would have discerned the disconfirming data. However, if "confirmation bias" is taken to mean modifying rather than rejecting a hypothesis in the face of disconfirming data, then such behavior would be treated as reflecting a confirmation bias.

This chapter does not deal with situations in which theoretical commitments cause one to filter out or distort data that do exist or to "see" data that are merely illusory. Such situations are indeed examples of something that genuinely deserves to be called "confirmation bias." Rather, my discussion will focus on situations in which people are treated as reasoning in a flawed way when (I would argue) they are in fact merely relying on theory or mechanism information in a way that is scientifically legitimate.

An Incomplete Account of Scientific Inquiry

Finally, the third reason why conclusions about confirmation bias in cognitive tasks might not be warranted is that many studies of confirmation bias are based on incomplete or misleading descriptions of scientific inquiry and, in consequence, ignore the importance of considerations that involve theory or mechanism information. They therefore label as "confirmation bias" behavior that is in fact congruent with sound scientific practice.

Much of the psychological research relevant to the question of confirmation bias was influenced by the approach of sir Karl Popper (1959). Psychologists have often interpreted Popper as having argued that the strategies or tests for confirming a theory are distinct from the strategies for disconfirming or falsifying it, and further that in testing a theory, disconfirming strategies provide conclusive evidence whereas confirming strategies do not. Therefore, when testing a theory, scientists ought to generate tests that disconfirm it rather than tests that confirm it. Central to Popper's falsificationist position is that disconfirmation is an all or nothing affair: a particular result either disconfirms the hypothesis or else it does not.

Relevant Research

Some of the research relevant to the issue of disconfirmation (for example, D. Kuhn et al. 1988, Klahr and Dunbar 1988, Karmiloff-Smith and Inhelder 1974/1975) has already been described. Additional relevant research is the work of Mynatt et al. (1977, 1978) and of Wason (1960).

Mynatt et al.'s (1977) work was motivated explicitly by Popper's approach. They asked whether "subjects tend to select situations for testing their hypotheses which allow only confirmatory observations rather than selecting situations which allow alternative hypotheses to be tested" and whether "subjects who obtain direct falsifying evidence change hypotheses." To answer their questions, Mynatt et al. presented undergraduates with two computer screens on which were displayed figures of various shapes (triangle, square, or disk) and levels of brightness (I will refer to these levels as black versus gray). A particle could be "fired" at any of the figures from a fixed point. The subject's task was to generate a hypothesis to describe the motion of the particle. In fact, all gray figures repelled the particle because a circular, nonvisible boundary extended 4.2 cm. from the geometric center of the gray figures. However, the task was contrived to suggest that it was shape that mattered by having a black triangle located within the nonvisible boundary surrounding a gray disk. Thus the gray triangle and the black triangle both repelled the particle, but the gray triangle did so because it was gray, while the black triangle did so because it was within the boundary of a gray disk. The analysis focused on those subjects who hypothesized that triangularity was the cause.

After generating their hypotheses, subjects were presented with ten pairs of screens and told to choose one member of each pair to have the particle fired at. The particle was not actually fired, however. For some pairs Mynatt et al. identified certain pair members as "confirmatory," "disconfirmatory," or "providing evidence for an alternative" to a triangle hypothesis. The three terms were treated as mutually exclusive. In terms of this discussion, it is important to note that, within Mynatt et al.'s framework, confirmatory and disconfirmatory choices were stipulated to involve different screens. A free response phase followed in which the particle was actually fired. Table 3.1 shows the ten pairs of screens along with the symbols that designated various pair members as "confirming," etc., a triangle hypothesis. (Recall that I am substituting the terms "gray" and "black" for the brightness designations 0.5 and 1.0.)

Mynatt et al.'s results were straightforward. For the paired-screen choices, the tendency to choose screens stipulated to be "confirmatory" rather than screens that "suggested an alternative" was significantly greater than chance and was present early on: 15 of the 20 subjects chose the confirmatory rather than the alternative screen in pair 1. Fur-

Table 3.1
Paired-screen descriptions

Pair no.	Screen A	Screen B
1	Gray disk, black square[b]	Gray triangle, black square[a]
2	Gray triangle[a]	Gray square[b]
3	Black square, black disk	Black square, black square
4	Gray disk, gray disk[b]	Gray disk, gray triangle[a]
5	Gray triangle	Black triangle[c]
6	Black square	Black disk
7	Black triangle, gray square[a]	Black disk, gray square[b]
8	Black square	Black disk, black disk
9	Gray triangle[a]	Gray disk[b]
10	Black disk, gray disk[b]	Gray triangle, black disk[a]

a. Confirmatory choices for subjects with triangle hypotheses.
b. A particle fired at the figures on this screen would stop, providing evidence for an alternative to a triangle hypothesis.
c. A particle fired at the triangle on this screen would not stop, logically disconfirming a triangle hypothesis.

thermore, during the free-response phase of the study, those subjects who chose the "falsifying" screen (5B) were more likely than those who did not to have a final hypothesis that was correct or partially correct.

From the data on paired-screen choices, Mynatt et al. concluded that "subjects failed to consider alternative hypotheses" and instead showed a preference for "confirmatory" screens, which, they said, indicated that "confirmation bias ... may be a general cognitive process" (1977, 93). From the free-response data, they concluded that subjects could use falsifying data once they obtained it.

In a subsequent study (Mynatt et al. 1978), subjects were shown 27 objects, only some of which repelled the particle. The angle of deflection was determined by angle of incidence, brightness, and size. Subjects reasoned out loud. Almost always, subjects seemed to be seeking confirmation (for example, "My pet hypothesis is ..., so I'm going to start trying to figure out if that's feasible") (Mynatt et al. 1978, 401). Furthermore, when tests yielded disconfirming data, the hypothesis was rejected only 30 percent of the time but modified 37 percent of the time. Mynatt et al. see the small number of hypothesis rejections as additional evidence of confirmation bias.

Wason's (1960) rule-learning task illustrates similar points. Wason gave his subjects three numbers (2, 4, 6) and told them to identify the rule to which the numbers conformed (Wason 1977). To do this, subjects were to generate (and receive feedback on) other three-number series that might or might not be instances of the rule. The correct rule was "numbers in increasing order of magnitude," and few subjects generated it. But what was more interesting was the way subjects tested their hypotheses. The overwhelming tendency was to test series that were consistent with the particular hypothesis subjects were considering and to avoid generating series that ran counter to their own hypotheses. For example, one subject tested the series 8, 10, 12 in order to test the hypothesis that the rule was "even numbers increasing in twos." That is, as did Mynatt et al., so Wason found little evidence for testing incompatible alternative hypotheses. Furthermore, when subjects received feedback that their rule was incorrect, in more than half the cases, the rule was maintained, "even though some other attribute, e.g., order" may have been tested (Wason 1977, 309). As in Mynatt et al.'s task, subjects responded to disconfirming data by maintaining (albeit in modified form) their initial, disconfirmed hypothesis.

An Alternative Analysis of Scientific Inquiry and Confirmation Bias

Return now to the general claim that the view of scientific inquiry reflected in many studies of confirmation bias describes scientific inquiry in a way that is misleading as well as incomplete. Given a misleading description of scientific inquiry, it is difficult to decide whether laymen—or even scientists, for that matter—do in fact demonstrate a confirmation bias.

In discussing this claim, it is important to distinguish among four phenomena relevant to the assessment of confirmation bias: the strategies or tests carried out to evaluate a hypothesis, the actual results generated by the tests, what the subject's hope or motivation is for carrying out a particular test, and how the subject deals with anomalous results.

Confirmation versus disconfirmation: a false distinction

In cognitive psychology, one of Popper's legacies is that confirmation and disconfirmation are often treated as involving distinct strategies; tests are said to be either confirming or disconfirming. Furthermore, disconfirming strategies are treated as being preferable to the "biased" strategies of confirmation (see, e.g., Evans 1982, Gilhooly 1982). In Mynatt et al.'s task, this is reflected by the fact that the three types of pair members that subjects could choose to test (stipulated to be confirmatory, disconfirmatory, and suggestive of an alternative) were treated as being mutually exclusive.

However, more recent work by philosophers of science (Boyd 1985; T. S. Kuhn 1970; Putnam 1962, 1974) has demonstrated that these strategies are *not* mutually exclusive; that confirmation, disconfirmation, and generating evidence for alternatives all involve carrying out the same sorts of tests. The same point is central to any Bayesian account of confirmation.

Briefly, the argument is this: When scientists seek to confirm a hypothesis, if they are well-trained, they typically take into account plausible alternative hypotheses in order to rule them out by way of making the target hypothesis more convincing. Similarly, when scientists seek to disconfirm a hypothesis, they again take into account plausible alternative hypotheses in order to demonstrate that it is in fact one of the alternatives rather than the target hypothesis that provides the better account. That is, the formal aspects of confirmation and disconfirmation are the same; both involve taking into account plausible alternative hypotheses. I will illustrate this point with two sorts of examples because both occur in the literature on disconfirmation. The first involves a causal claim. In terms of the terminology from the previous chapters, this example represents theoretically rich situations. The second example involves a claim about the properties of a set, and thus constitutes an example of a theoretically impoverished situation.

Testing a causal claim   Consider first research designed to confirm the causal hypothesis that drug x cures colds. To amass confirmatory evidence for the hypothesis, one would need to rule out (at least) the plausible alternative hypothesis that it is the body's own immune system that eventually gets rid of the virus. Therefore, to test this hypothesis, one would need two groups of subjects: generally healthy and generally rundown. Then, within each group, some subjects would receive drug x and some would not. One could then establish whether it was general health or treatment with drug x that was affecting the course of colds.

If general health were found to have a negligible effect, then it would be ruled out as a serious alternative hypothesis. That is, the results would help confirm the target hypothesis. But notice that the same test could also yield results that disconfirmed the target hypothesis: If general health were found to have an effect and drug x not, then the hypothesis that drug x cures colds would be disconfirmed. In short, the test generated to confirm the hypothesis could potentially yield results that were either confirmatory or disconfirmatory.

Turn now to a test designed to *dis*confirm the hypothesis. To disconfirm the hypothesis that drug x cures colds, one would need to examine cases in which the hypothesis is likely to go wrong, that is, cases suggested by a plausible alternative, such as the operation of the body's own immune system. To do this, one would use the same design and systematically vary both general health and treatment with drug x in order to measure which of the variables was affecting the course of colds. If general health were found to have a substantial effect and drug x not, then the results would disconfirm the target hypothesis. But if drug x did have an effect and general health did not, then the results would tend to confirm the hypothesis that drug x is effective. That is, tests to confirm and tests to disconfirm both would involve taking into account plausible alternative hypotheses.

At first glance it might seem that one would *not* need to consider alernative hypotheses in order to test a target hypothesis—at least if one could rely on direct experimental intervention rather than naturally occurring or correlational data. For example, for testing the effectiveness of drug x, one could, if circumstances permitted, simply give the drug to half the afflicted population and withold it from the other half, without controlling for the subjects' general health. However, when this contrastive strategy is carried out well, it is combined with random assignment of a representative sample, in this case random assignment of afflicted subjects to the treatment and control groups. And the reason random assignment is so crucial is precisely because of the assumption that, with a large enough sample, random assignment will *control for alternative hypotheses and thus permit them to be ruled out*. For example, one assumes that with random assignment from a representative sample, the proportion of subjects in good general health will be roughly comparable in both treatment and control groups. (Indeed, with random sampling, one assumes that the two groups will be roughly comparable on all sorts of variables, including even those that have not yet been identified as being relevant.) However, as soon as random assignment is not possible, then the issue of matching arises, and the question of which variables to match on (that is, the question of alternative hypotheses) again becomes a concern that has to be explicitly dealt with.

Even when random sampling is possible, the question of alternative, or at least additional, explanatory causal variables is also a concern in deciding the more basic question of which population is the representative one from which a random sample should be drawn. The question of whether to test the effectiveness of drug x by drawing a sample from a population in which all the subjects have roughly the same level of general health or by sampling without controlling for level of health depends on one's beliefs about whether general health provides an alternative interpretation for the effects of the drug (or at least interacts with the effects of the drug) and depends as well on the samples to which one wants to generalize the results.

Testing a claim about properties of a set   The drug example dealt with two possible causes because the general point had to do with scientific inquiry and so much of science is concerned with identifying causes. However, in many studies of disconfirmation, the hypothesis in question concerns the properties of a set of stimuli; the hypotheses are of the form "*As* are *Bs*." For example, all triangles repel (Mynatt et al. 1978), "members of the target category are red circles" (Bruner et al. 1956), and "instances that follow the rule are any increasing series" (Wason 1960). Nevertheless, with this sort of statement as well the same points apply: good confirmation and disconfirmation strategies require the same test strategies, and each test strategy can yield potentially confirming or disconfirming results.

Recall that in Mynatt et al.'s (1977) task, the "triangularity hypothesis" that the task was contrived to suggest "included hypotheses with at least some mention of triangularity but no mention of brightness." To test this hypothesis (whether to confirm or disconfirm), one would have to test two sorts of shapes: nontriangles and triangles. And any such test could potentially yield either confirming or disconfirming results. For example, if one tested a square and found that it too repelled, then the hypothesis that *only* triangles repel would be disconfirmed. But if the square did *not* repel, then one would be closer to having tested all the nontriangles, thereby getting additional confirmatory evidence. Analogously, if a subject were testing the rule that the series 2, 4, 6 exemplified the rule "increasing intervals of two," then the series 3, 5, 7 could yield either confirmatory results or disconfirmatory results, depending on which rule the experimenter had stipulated to be correct. These issues will be relevant in experiments 14 and 15.

Tests versus results   If tests to confirm and tests to disconfirm do not involve distinct, mutually exclusive strategies, then what distinguishes hypotheses that are confirmed from those that are disconfirmed? It is the results of tests, not the tests themselves, that distinguish hypotheses that are confirmed from those that are not, and any test can potentially yield either confirmatory or disconfirmatory results. A triangle can either repel (confirming the triangle hypothesis) or not repel (disconfirming the hypothesis). A nontriangle can either repel (disconfirming the triangle hypothesis) or not repel (thereby providing confirmatory evidence). (Similarly, either drug x or the body's own immune system can have the greater effect on colds.)

Working from the perspective of decision theory, Klayman and Ha (1987) have made an argument compatible with the present one that turns on the distinction between tests and results. They argue that many behaviors thought to reflect confirmation bias are better understood as reflecting a general "positive-test strategy," according to which one tests those instances that are expected to fit the hypothesized rule rather than those expected not to fit. For example, in Mynatt et al.'s (1977) task, if one held the hypothesis that triangles repel, then a positive test strategy would consist of firing the particle only at triangles. That is, Klayman & Ha's positive-test strategy is an example of confirmation bias in that it involves seeking only data expected to be congruent with one's hypothesis; it is only part of an appropriate test because it does not include a test of nontriangles as well as triangles. However, Klayman and Ha demonstrate that even the biased positive-test *strategy* does not always yield confirmatory *results*. Specifically, they demonstrate that when one is investigating a relatively rare phenomenon, then the positive-test strategy is likely to discover instances that are expected to conform to the hypothesized rule but do not, and thus that falsify the hypothesis.

Consider Klayman and Ha's example: if very few students do well in a graduate program, then carrying out a positive-test strategy (that is, sampling students who have the characteristics thought to predict success in the program and who have already been admitted) is very likely to detect students who have the characteristics *thought* to lead to success but who in fact do *not* do well in the program. That is, a positive test strategy can detect instances that disconfirm the rule. (Furthermore, in this case a positive-test strategy is a more efficient way of disconfirming the hypothesized rule than is sampling the much larger number of students who are never admitted to the program because they do not have the characteristics thought to predict success.) Baron was also invoking the distinction between tests and results when he noted that "when we choose a question, ... we do not know in advance what the answer will be" (1985, 131).

However, it is worth noting that, even if one thinks in terms of Klayman and Ha's positive-test strategy, considering alternative hypotheses will still improve the liklihood of detecting instances that disconfirm the target rule. To return to the example above, imagine that the characteristics thought to predict a student's success in a graduate program include undergraduate grades and quality of letters of reference. Now imagine that in reality these characteristics matter only if the student also received her undergraduate training in a good undergraduate program. If one has this alternative hypothesis in mind, one will be even more likely to detect a disconfirming instance than if one does not, because one will probably be more likely than otherwise to focus the positive-test strategy, that is, to examine the records of students who have good undergraduate grades and letters of reference but who were trained in poor undergraduate programs. Because these students are especially likely to do poorly, choosing to examine their records will make it more likely that one will disconfirm the target rule that it is only undergraduate grades and letters of reference that predict success. (Of course, the suppresseed premise here is that efficiency is desirable, so testing all graduate students is not an option.)

Consider the issue of disconfirming results with respect to another finding from Mynatt et al.'s (1977) research: how can one reconcile the argument that confirmation and disconfirmation involve the same tests with the finding that subjects who chose the "falsifying" screen (5B, a black triangle) during the free-response phase (when feedback was provided) were more likely than those who did not choose it to have a final hypothesis that was correct or partially correct?

Note first that the result of choosing the black triangle (which does not repel) does not merely disconfirm the triangle hypothesis; it also suggests an alternative based on shade. That is, data that falsify and data that suggest an alternative are not mutually exclusive, although they were treated as such in Mynatt et al.'s studies.

Second, testing the black triangle is useful not because of the test itself but because of its results. Testing a black triangle yields evidence that disconfirms the triangle hypothesis, but testing a gray square or a gray disk would also have yielded disconfirming results because both gray figures, though not triangles, would also have repelled the particle. In short, although the black triangle is stipulated to be a disconfirming test while the gray square and gray disk are described as merely providing evidence for an alternative, in fact all three tests would have disconfirmed the triangle hypothesis and would have suggested the alternative of shade. Again, data that falsify and data that suggest an alternative are not mutually exclusive.

Why, then, did subjects who chose screen 5B perform better than those who did not? To answer this question, it is important to recall that the black triangle, though stipulated to be merely disconfirmatory, also in fact suggested the alternative shade hypothesis. Therefore, an important question (not addressed in the study) would be whether subjects who chose the black triangle (5B) (stipulated to be disconfirmatory) performed any better than subjects who chose either the gray square (2B) or the gray disk (9B) (which also suggested an alternative). That is, was there something special about a test stipulated to be "disconfirmatory"; or was it useful simply because it suggested an alternative?

In addition, consider that, because of the way the task was contrived, the results of testing a black triangle disconfirmed the initial hypothesis (and added confirmatory evidence to an alternative) only if the subject generated an initial hypothesis based on triangles *and also* considered an alternative based on shade. If a subject considered a different ("incorrect") alternative, then choosing the same black triangle might not have confirmed her alternative. This means that the black triangle suggests the alternative of shade only if the subject is already considering the shade alternative before she chooses the screen (or else is astute enough to realize, after choosing the screen, that the results suggest the alternative of shade). In short, these data show that if a subject happens to be considering the correct alternative, either at the outset or after the data suggest

it, then she can make use of data that confirm that the alternative is correct. This finding certainly demonstrates that subjects do take account of
data. However, this finding does not demonstrate that there is a special
kind of falsifying test nor does it demonstrate that it is this test (rather
than the results of the test and the astuteness of the subject in recognizing what the results suggest) that propels a subject toward the correct
hypothesis.

In short, because tests to confirm and tests to disconfirm involve the
same strategies, the real measure of whether subjects are open to having
their hypothesis disconfirmed is not whether they choose a disconfirming
as opposed to a confirming test. The real measure is whether they take
into account plausible alternative hypotheses (either by controlling for
them or by recognizing them when they are suggested by the results of
the tests). However, because of the way many hypothesis-testing tasks
are structured, it is not possible to determine from the data whether
subjects were considering plausible alternatives because the tasks were
designed so that questions of plausibility did not arise: in Mynatt et al.'s
task, because genuinely causal relations were not at issue, the correct
hypothesis that gray figures repelled was just as plausible as, for example,
that figures repelled only if they were in close proximity to another
figure. This is in marked contrast to causal claims, in which questions of
plausibility play a big role (an issue to be discussed in the next section).

Klahr and Dunbar's (1988) work is also relevant to the question of what
an appropriate test is and to the distinction between tests and results.
Klahr and Dunbar found that in their study, subjects sought confirming
rather than disconfirming evidence. However, they make two important
points about this. One is that in terms of the framework suggested by
Klayman and Ha (1987), this was a reasonable strategy. The other is that
although subjects often searched for confirming evidence, their search frequently yielded results that were disconfirming and "although adults did
not abandon their hypothesis on the basis of a single disconfirming
instance, they did attempt to understand inconsistencies" (1987, 137).
That is, the subjects did not simply ignore the disconfirming data.

Critical confirmation versus straw-person confirmation[1]
Finally, it is important to note that although confirmation, disconfirmation, and controlling for an alternative hypothesis all involve the same
strategies or predictive tests, nevertheless there are certainly several senses
in which someone might be said to have a confirmation bias. In the motivational sense, one might carry out a particular test in the fervent hope
that the actual results of the test will constitute confirmatory evidence.
Furthermore, a motivation to confirm can make it more difficult to gen-

erate plausible alternative hypotheses and can make it easier to filter out or distort those test results that happen to be disconfirming.

However, a confirmation bias might also consist, not in choosing a "confirmatory" testing strategy (since genuinely "confirmatory" and genuinely "disconfirmatory" strategies are the same), but rather in testing the target hypothesis against alternative hypotheses that are implausible and therefore unlikely to be true, that is, in testing a target hypothesis against an alternative that is in fact a straw person. True confirmation bias depends not on formal strategies but rather on estimates of the plausibility of the alternative hypotheses that are seen as potential rivals. And plausibility estimates ordinarily depend on information about theory or causal mechanism.

Consider an extreme example: Imagine that on the basis of school records from several large cities in the Northeast, a researcher formulates the hypothesis that boys from father-absent homes do not do well in school because they lack a male role model. A plausible alternative hypothesis would be that the causal factor is not the absence of a male role model but rather the poverty that results from growing up in a single-parent family headed by a female. Imagine further that, instead of testing the plausible alternative hypothesis, the researcher tries to muster supporting data by documenting that the same relation (between absence of a father and poor school performance) also obtains in several large cities in the Midwest. This test would be an example of straw-person confirmation: it would rule out the unlikely alternative that absence of a father produces poor school performance *only in large cities in the Northeast*, but it would leave untested the plausible alternative that it is really poverty rather than the absence of a role model that is the culprit.

In many studies of disconfirmation, it is impossible to tell whether subjects were engaging in straw-person confirmation, because the tasks were designed so that issues of plausibility did not arise. For example, in Mynatt et al.'s task the tacit premise is that there is only one alternative to the triangle hypothesis that subjects consider, namely shade. But, of course, subjects could easily have considered others (for example, that whether a figure would repel would depend on whether it was physically close to another of a different shade, etc.). In Mynatt et al.'s task, unless a subject was prescient, there was no way of deciding that some alternatives were plausible and others not. The objects that repelled the particle had nothing to do with genuinely causal relations, such as electromagnetic forces. They were arbitrarily chosen, noncausal figures. The experimenters could just as reasonably have stipulated that black rather than gray objects would be the repellers or that an object would repel only if it were close to another of the same shade. Similarly, the rule of "numbers in increasing order of magnitude" was equally arbitrary and therefore no more or less plausible than the alternatives the subjects themselves generated. I mention this to point out that because these sorts of tasks were theoretically impoverished, there was no opportunity to study a very important way in which true confirmation bias operates, namely, by leading one to test a target hypothesis against implausible rather than plausible alternatives. Because there was no information about causal mechanism, there was no basis for distinguishing hypotheses that subjects considered plausible from those that they considered implausible in the way in which plausible hypotheses are typically identified in scientific inquiry.

(Of course, there is a way in which uncritical confirmation could have occurred even in this task: the alternative hypotheses could have been irrelevant to the task as it is usually construed. For example, "I want to see whether it matters if the window in the interview room is open or closed." However, this sort of construal is probably rare.)

In Klahr and Dunbar's task, there was a sense in which issues of plausibility were dealt with. Given how programming tasks are usually structured, there were only two reasonable hypotheses: the "N-role: counter" frame and the "N-role: selector" frame. Of these, the "N-role: counter" frame was the more plausible hypothesis. And in fact this is the working hypothesis that subjects typically chose first.

A Corollary about Inferring Motive

Some of the points made in this section involve subjects' possible motivations in various cognitive tasks. However, recall that any particular test can yield results that are potentially confirmatory or disconfirmatory. Thus in carrying out any particular test, one can fervently hope for confirmatory rather than disconfirmatory results. However, irrespective of one's hopes, the tests for confirmation and for disconfirmation are the same. Therefore, if the only information the researcher has is that a particular test was carried out, one cannot infer whether, in carrying out the test, the subject's motivational aim (or hope) was to gather confirmatory or disconfirmatory results. In many of the tasks described above, the subjects were not asked to verbalize whether their motivation was to acquire confirmatory results that ruled out an alternative or disconfirmatory results in favor of an alternative. Therefore, in these tasks, conclusions about whether or not subjects held a confirmation bias (in the sense of hoping for confirmatory results) could not be drawn.

As an example of how inferring motivation on the basis of testing strategy can be problematic, consider again the Mynatt, Doherty, and Tweney study. In that study the authors draw a sharp distinction between "disconfirming a triangle hypothesis" and "providing evidence for an alternative to a triangle hypothesis." And they treat the former as being the more scientifically sophisticated of the two strategies. However, in terms of my earlier argument, seeking evidence for an alternative hypothesis is in fact exactly one of the strategies that scientists rely on when they aim to disconfirm a target hypothesis. That is, these two activities need not reflect two different motivational aims. And in terms of the information sought, the different activities converge.

Articulating or Modifying Working Hypotheses

The following sections discuss another reason why it is sometimes difficult to decide whether subjects are exhibiting a confirmation bias, namely that often, though not always, it is scientifically legitimate to deal with anomalous evidence not by rejecting the hypothesis but by treating it as a working hypothesis to be modified in order to accommodate the evidence.

As already noted in chapter 2, in the literature on disconfirming evidence, tasks are often structured so that hypotheses are supposed to be tested in an all-or-nothing way: the hypothesis is supposed to be treated as having been either confirmed or (outright) disconfirmed. The result is that correct performance consists of treating the anomalous evidence as warranting outright rejection of the target hypothesis rather than as calling merely for its modification or elaboration to take account of new data. That is, because of the way the tasks are structured, this approach ignores a crucial aspect of scientific inquiry: the ways in which scientists learn about a phenomenon by successive approximation. Often, when a precisely formulated hypothesis is refuted by data or a less precisely formulated one is faced with unanticipated data, it is rational for scientists to adopt a version of the hypothesis reformulated to account for those data rather than to reject the hypothesis as altogether a mistake. Recall as well that in the case of precisely formulated hypotheses, interpreting anomalous data as requiring theory modification in this way *is* a special case of treating the data as *disconfirmatory*.

The rest of this section develops these themes of chapter 2 and presents the following argument: Hypothesis modification can be scientifically legitimate because it can involve specifying more precisely which of the many variables operating in a situation might be constraining the effectiveness of the target cause. Viewed from a different perspective, it can involve specifying more precisely the situations in which a mechanism will produce an expected covariation. However, some modifications are more likely to be scientifically legitimate than others: some preserve the real insights of the original hypothesis; others are ad hoc attempts to save it from outright disconfirmation. Therefore, the question of when theory modification is scientifically legitimate has implications for the question of confirmation bias.

Causal relations involve many variables, some unspecified

In many cognitive tasks, part of the reason anomalous evidence can be treated as outright disconfirming rather than as modifying or elaborating is that the hypotheses (or at least the ones the experimenter, if not necessarily the subject, has in mind) involve a small number of variables and can therefore be specified in a very circumscribed way. For example, in Mynatt et al.'s task, the hypothesis that the experimenters aim to induce is a simple one: all and only triangles repel. (And the "correct" alternative—that all and only gray figures repel—is equally simple.) That is, because each hypothesis is based on only one variable, a single triangle that does not repel is a sufficient reason for rejecting the triangle hypothesis.

The problem with this sort of approach is that, although the experimenter may have it in mind that only shape and shade are important, the subject can be (and often is) thinking of several other variables (location on the screen, proximity to other figures, etc.) that might also be playing a role (and in addition, the hypotheses they consider are often less precise working hypotheses) (Koslowski and Maqueda 1993; see experiments 14 and 15, chapter 11). The result is that a single anomalous instance need not call for outright rejection of the subject's hypothesis. For example, if the subject is considering screen location as well as shape, a single triangle that does not repel might indicate not that triangles in general do not repel but that triangles do not repel when they are located in that quadrant of the screen. And this mimics real life in the empirical, rather than the logical, world.

Hypotheses are almost never as precise as they could be in principle because, for any hypothesis, there are, in principle numerous conditions that could be specified (but typically are not) as being either relevant or irrelevant to the hypothesis. That is, even when they are formulated in an apparently precise way, many hypotheses are working hypotheses in which numerous potentially relevant and irrelevant variables are not specified and may not even be known. For example, a working hypothesis might be that drug x cures colds. Such a hypothesis would not (and possibly could not) specify that drug x might cure colds only in certain doses, only if administered intravenously rather than orally, etc.; or that its effectiveness might be not at all affected by type of virus, nutritional status, or phases of the moon. Although some of these variables can be identified as likely to be relevant (or irrelevant) beforehand by relying on the results of previous research and existing theoretical expectations, some can be discovered to be relevant (or irrelevant) only after additional evidence (including anomalous evidence) has been gathered. For example, if drug x is found to be ineffective in people below a certain age, this suggests that the patient's age is a relevant variable. Conversely, if it is found to be effective at all ages, this suggests that the patient's age is not relevant.

What this means in practice is that it is very easy (and often appropriate) to elaborate an imprecise theory or to modify (rather than to reject outright) a more precise theory by invoking an additional variable as a constraint on the target factor (drug x works but not for certain age groups). Thus, although any particular, very specific hypothesis (a local hypothesis, in Klahr and Dunbar's [1988] terminology) can be either significantly confirmed or disconfirmed by a particular plausible test, in many cases (and probably the cases employed in psychological studies) the appropriate response to anomalous data is modification rather than outright rejection. Such modifications allow one to maintain the basic working hypothesis (Klahr and Dunbar's global hypothesis) but they also enable one to further articulate the working hypothesis, that is, to specify it more precisely in a way that takes account of the anomalies. Therefore, to focus only on confirmation and outright disconfirmation is to ignore the important activity of modification or articulation. Unless there is an alternative theory that can explain not only the instances in which drug x does not cure colds but *also* the instances in which it does (and which suggested the hypothesis in the first place), then it may make sense to keep the theory that drug x does cure colds but to treat it as a working hypothesis to be modified so that it is seen as applying in only certain situations. (By way of underlining the importance of modification rather than outright rejection in many situations, consider the mistake an early astronomer would have made had she posited, as a working hypothesis, a perfectly spherical earth, found some disconfirming measurements, and in consequence rejected rather than modified the perfect-sphere hypothesis in favor of the flat alternative.)

Within Klahr and Dunbar's (1988) system, hypothesis change can occur either within a frame or by changing frames. When hypothesis change occurs within a frame, there are only minor differences between adjacent hypotheses; subjects change the values of only one or a few of the attributes. However, when a subject generates a different frame, there are large differences between two hypotheses; subjects change the values of all four attributes in the frame. Klahr and Dunbar use this finding to reinterpret Mynatt et al.'s (1978) data. They suggest that Mynatt et al.'s "subjects were exploring frames and switching frames after they had exhausted all possible values of the frame. In fact, Mynatt et al. (1978) note that many hypotheses were minor variations on a previous hypothesis—which is congruent with investigation of a frame—and that there were also occasional large differences in adjacent hypotheses—indicating a switch to a new frame" (Klahr and Dunbar 1988, 41). Klahr and Dunbar's description of Mynatt et al.'s subjects as exploring hypotheses within a frame is analogous to my suggestion that Mynatt et al.'s subjects could be construed not as mechanically seeking confirming evidence but rather as refining and testing the limits of the working hypothesis (the frame) that they were currently considering and as relying on the disconfirming evidence to explain the exceptions and in some cases to suggest an alternative.

Finally, to elaborate a point suggested in the preceding chapter, rejecting an explanation (even an incorrect explanation) when there is no viable alternative with which to replace it is to leave oneself with no framework within which to organize the data—be it the "confirming" data that suggested the hypothesis in the first place or the anomalous data calling it into question. If nothing else, such a framework, by providing a way of organizing data, might reduce the information-pocessing load. But it might also make it easier to detect a situation in which the anomalous data suggest an alternative because they form a pattern (as such data did in the Karmiloff-Smith and Inhelder [1974/1975] study.)

In short, rejecting a hypothesis (especially a global hypothesis) outright at the first sign of anomalous data is not always efficient. Rejecting it might be methodologically unwise because the hypothesis might be basically correct. And rejecting it in the absence of an alternative might make it harder to apprehend a pattern in the anomalous data that could suggest an alternative.

Disconfirming covariation but ignoring mechanism

The fact that there are often many causal variables operating in a situation is also relevant to the suggestion, mentioned briefly in chapter 2, that it is often reasonable to maintain an explanation in the face of disconfirming evidence if the evidence disconfirms the covariation component of the explanation but leaves the mechanism component intact.

In this regard, consider the finding of Kuhn et al. (1988) that it was more difficult to disconfirm subjects' causal beliefs than to disconfirm their noncausal beliefs. Might the difference in difficulty have indicated that subjects were allowing their theoretical beliefs to override information about covariation? If so, might this have reflected a confirmation bias? I suggest that the results are ambiguous, because of the nature of the anomalous evidence that subjects were presented with.

Kuhn et al. disconfirmed (and confirmed) subjects' beliefs about which foods did and did not covary with colds. However, as Kuhn et al. note, there is some evidence from subjects' justifications that their beliefs about covariation were accompanied by beliefs about mechanism (sometimes explicitly referred to by Kuhn et al. as beliefs about mechanism and some-times, I argued in chapter 2, coded as "intuition"). This is important because it is beliefs about mechanism that in part determine assessments of plausibility. Subjects found their beliefs about covariation plausible because, in many cases, the beliefs were accompanied by a belief in a mechanism that explained how the covariation was brought about. ("Orange juice makes you healthier because it has lots of vitamins.")

However, when Kuhn et al. disconfirmed subjects' beliefs, the anoma-lous or disconfirming evidence dealt only with the covariation component of the subject's belief. For example, if the subject's belief was that type of juice covaries with colds, the disconfirming evidence was simply that the two did *not* always covary. Thus the disconfirming evidence left intact the belief about the mechanism ("lots of vitamins") that had been expected to bring about covariation. This left subjects with the possibility that the mechanism would continue to operate and that the expected covariations would continue to obtain but not, for some reason, in the particular sit-uation described in the experiment. And given the many variables that can be causally relevant to a situation, this was not unreasonable. One can imagine thinking, for example, that there might be something about the children at this particular school that made it difficult for type of juice to have the expected effect but that in other schools or for other groups of children, type of juice would indeed covary with colds.

What this means with regard to D. Kuhn et al.'s finding that it is harder to disconfirm a causal belief than a noncausal belief is that in the former case two components need to be replaced: a belief about covariation and a belief about the mechanism that accounts for the covariation. However, in the latter case, when the belief in the covariation is undermined, there is no additional belief about mechanism to be dealt with. Kuhn et al. make roughly the same point when they conclude that when evaluating data that disconfirm a causal belief, subjects do not distinguish the disconfirm-ing evidence that shows that covariation does not obtain from the theo-retical belief according to which the covariation ought to obtain. The dif-ference between their approach and the approach taken here is that Kuhn et al. treat subjects' concern with mechanism as an obstacle that interferes with their ability to assess anomalous covariation (or noncovariation) data. In contrast, on the approach taken here, taking account of the mech-anism is reasonable; it means taking account of all, rather than only some, of the information available. Furthermore, in terms of the point made in the preceding section, this is often reasonable.

By way of analogy, consider what would happen if data came to light that, on the surface, seemed to disconfirm the hypothesis that penicillin cures bacterial infections. Imagine, for example, that several (even hun-dreds of) people with bacterial infections were treated with penicillin and nevertheless failed to improve. I suggest that, even if the number of such subjects was very large, one would nevertheless be reluctant to reject the hypothesis that penicillin cures bacterial infections. As a first step, one might question the validity of the data by asking about some of the many variables that could have interfered with the operation of the penicillin. (Could that particular batch of penicillin have been defective, improperly stored? Could the dosage have been inadequate?)

But, even if the data were judged to be valid, I suggest that, again like T. S. Kuhn's (1970) scientists, one would not leap to reject the hypothesis outright; rather, one would try to treat the hypothesis as a working hypothesis to be modified to take account of the disconfirming data, and one would cast about for possible variables that might have prevented the penicillin from bringing about the expected covariation in this situation. One might wonder, for example, whether the subjects were afflicted with a new strain of bacteria that is resistant to penicillin or whether their general nutritional status was so poor that even penicillin could not be effective. That is, one would certainly not accept the hypothesis in its current form, but one would also not altogether reject it in light of the disconfirming data; one would modify it. In a word, as noted in chapter 2, one might well conclude, as Kuhn et al.'s subjects did, that the hypothesis "was right with respect to those instances that conformed to the covariation pattern but was wrong with respect to those instances that did not" (1988, 126). As we have seen earlier, there are often so many variables that can affect whether a mechanism will operate that learning about one situation in which it does not still leaves the possibility that it will operate in other situations. (However, as I argue below, one would also probably try to specify what it was about the various instances that made the hypothesis not applicable to them.)

More to the point, I would argue that such an approach is reasonable. For most people, a belief in the efficacy of penicillin includes some notion, however rudimentary, that the mechanism by which penicillin works is that it makes it difficult for germs to survive and reproduce. Without data that suggest that this mechanism is incorrect and ought to be relinquished, it is reasonable to expect that the mechanism would continue to operate, that is, that penicillin would continue to kill germs, though perhaps not bacteria of this particular sort or in these particular patients. Such an approach would be especially reasonable given the many variables that can operate in a situation to limit the effectiveness of medication (for example, dosage, nutritional status of patients, etc.).

Consider this point also in relation to Kuhn et al.'s finding that some subjects in the colds study did not acknowledge the disconfirming evidence until after they had articulated a modified theory to account for the evidence. For example, after having first claimed that type of condiment would make no difference, a ninth-grader responded to the evidence that type of condiment did covary with colds by suggesting, in one of his early responses, that mustard has more ingredients than catsup and this makes it good for one's health and then that mustard is used on things that are either hot or cold while catsup is used only on hot things. Only after doing this did the subject make reference to the covariation evidence. As Kuhn et al. note, "It appears almost as if they are not willing to acknowledge the implications of the evidence unless they have a compatible theory in place that can provide an explanation of this evidence" (1988, 83). I would argue that when subjects adopt this strategy, it is because the anomalous evidence undermines only the covariation component, and not the mechanism component, of their beliefs and they see no reason to relinquish their beliefs because the mechanism component has not been replaced. When they are finally able, on their own, to generate a replacement for their intially proposed mechanism that enables them to treat the anomalous data as more than a fluke, then they treat those data as being harder to dismiss. (However, I would also argue that the very fact that they were trying to generate a modified replacement for the mechanism component indicates that they were, at least tacitly, acknowledging the disconfirming evidence all along and treating it as cause for concern. The fact that they did not explicitly mention it until they were able to generate their own replacement mechanism does not necessarilly mean that they were thinking neither about it nor about its problematic implications for the explanation.)

I am not arguing here that even sixth-graders have a precise understanding of how it is that different types of foods cure colds. I am arguing that they have some rudimentary understanding or expectation that *some* sort of mechanism is involved and that the mechanism probably has something to do with the immune system or with an undifferentiated notion of general health. And some support for this is that when Kuhn et al. (1988) used material that was more neutral, namely sports balls, subjects were more likely to treat anomalous covariation evidence as calling the hypothesis into question.

(Note also that this argument is analogous to the point made in chapter 2 regarding Kuhn et al.'s sports-balls study. "Most" subjects identified color as causally irrelevant to bounce and did not suspend this belief when presented with data in which color and, for example, texture were confounded so that both covaried with bounce. In terms of the present argument and in light of some of the justifications given by the subjects, such as that rough texture makes the balls heavier, I would suggest that subjects did not suspend their belief that color was irrelevant, because, although the anomalous evidence demonstrated that color was one of the factors that covaried with bounce, it did not provide any mechanism to explain the process by which differences in color could produce differences in bounce.)

As already noted, experiment 13, chapter 10, suggests that disconfirming evidence that deals with the mechanism component as well as the covariation component of a belief is more compelling than disconfirming evidence that deals with covariation alone.

To return to the question of theory modification and elaboration, if additional possible causes are likely to exist that might restrict the application of, and therefore provide a way of modifying or elaborating an explanation, then an obvious problem arises: how does one decide when modification or elaboration is warranted or when, instead, outright rejection would be more appropriate? This question is addressed in the following section.

Theoretically motivated modifications versus ad hoc modifications

The question of when theory modification rather than outright rejection is appropriate is not trivial: in noncontrived situations, there are often so many potentially causal variables that can restrict a belief that, in the face of anomalous data, an explanation can invariably be modified by invoking one of the variables to account for why the target factor does not operate as expected in a particular situation. (Similarly, there are often so many situations in which a mechanism is expected to produce an effect that learning about one situation in which the effect does not obtain still leaves the possibility that the mechanism will operate in other situations.) The result is that in principle one can always respond to anomalous data simply by modifying a hypothesis to account for it. However, in practice there are limits on the extent to which some modifications are seen as warranted; there is no question that explanations sometimes ought to be altogether rejected rather than merely modified, given the evidence.

The tension between modifications that are seen as warranted and those that are not is reflected in the distinction between theory modification, which is treated as a legitimate response to anomalous data, and what is often pejoratively called "ad hoc theorizing," which is seen as an unwarranted attempt to "patch up" a theory in the face of anomalous data when the theory in fact ought to be discarded.

The decision about whether anomalous data call for modifying or rejecting an explanation is based on several factors. Many of these have to do with the explanation itself, such as the nature and amount of evidence that supports it and the extent to which one's commitment to it has emotional components. However, the decision to modify rather than to reject is also often based on the structure of the anomalous data itself and on one's (sometimes only tacit) theory about how this structure makes it more or less difficult for a variation of the explanation to accommodate the anomalies.

An important consideration that distinguishes warranted from unwarranted modifications (though by no means the only one) involves information about mechanism. Briefly, modifications are theoretically motivated rather than ad hoc when there are plausible mechanisms to explain the anomalous data while maintaining the basic explanatory strategy of the original hypothesis. For example, if one learns that a drug aimed at curing colds is not effective for the elderly and that there is a mechanism that might account for this (namely that the elderly metabolize it too slowly), then it might make sense to maintain the hypothesis that it is effective but to modify it by explaining how the drug's effectiveness is constrained by metabolism. That is, the mechanism that accounts for the anomaly also refines our understanding of how the target factor operates by explaining why it will not operate in certain situations.

As an extension of this point, if the anomalies seem to form a pattern (for example, if the patients for whom drug x is not effective all share a common feature, such as a chronic illness like diabetes or high blood pressure), then even if there is no plausible mechanism currently known that can explain the anomalies, the pattern formed by the common feature might suggest that one will eventually be discovered. (One can imagine discovering, for example, that the stress on the body induced by chronic illness interferes with the way the drug is absorbed.) That is, a pattern in the anomalies might refine our understanding of how the drug works by helping us discover one of the mechanisms that constrains the drug's effectiveness.

The reason why common features and causal mechanisms motivate modification rather than outright rejection of a theory illustrates a point familiar from the philosophy of science concerning the distinction between justified and ad hoc modifications to a theory in the face of anomalous data. Theoretically motivated modifications are seen as appropriate because they represent a strategy for "fine-tuning" or amplifying our understanding of the relevant causal factor(s). Because they add to our understanding of when a relevant causal factor fails to operate, they tell us something about the conditions that must be being satisfied when the causal factor does operate. A modification based either on a hypothesis about the causal mechanisms that brought the anomalies about or on a pattern in the anomalies (which might suggest an underlying, undiscovered mechanism) would be seen as more likely to be warranted in that it would add to our understanding of when and how the operation of the causal factor is affected by other variables.

In contrast, modification would be seen as less likely to be warranted when the anomalies do not form a pattern, that is, when attempts to make sense of them can discover only idiosyncratic rather than common features and/or when there is no causal mechanism that can account for the anomalies. For example, suppose that there were three sizable groups for whom the drug did not work. The obvious next step would be to try to identify what the members of the groups had in common that distinguished them from the people for whom the drug did work.

Next suppose it was discovered that, relative to the people for whom the drug was effective, the only differences were that one group consisted of people who were more likely to drive Chryslers than Fords, another group consisted of people more likely to own IBMs than Macs, and the third group consisted of people more likely to wear single-breasted coats than double-breasted coats. Suppose also that there are no known mechanisms that could explain how these three factors could interfere with the drug's effectiveness. In such a situation, the lack of a common pattern among the three groups and the lack of mechanisms to explain the anomalous groups would make it difficult to refine the theory. The fact that some (but only some) of the anomalous individuals happened, for example, to be more likely to wear single-breasted rather than double-breasted coats could easily be merely a fluke.

Of course, if the three groups for whom the drug was not effective were all discovered to have some fourth factor in common or if mechanisms came to be discovered that could explain how each of these factors could have interfered with the drug's effectiveness, then that would be a different story. However, without a systematic pattern (that is, a commonality) among the anomalous instances, the anomalies do little to help us refine our theory. Instead, they detract from the theory's overall credibility rather than help to specify it more precisely. They suggest that in those cases in which the drug seemed to cure colds, perhaps it was really the body's own immune system that was working.

This in turn might lead one to discover that the anomalies actually did have something in common (namely a poorly functioning immune system), but the discovery of such a pattern would go along with rejecting the hypothesis that the drug cured colds in favor of the hypothesis that it was the body's own immune system that was responsible. In this case, insofar as we discerned a pattern or commonality in the anomalious groups, our discovery would call the target account into question. (And, as suggested earlier, such a pattern might be easier to detect with the original hypothesis in place as a framework within which to organize the anomalous data.) As we will see in experiment 11, chapter 9, in evaluating anomalies to an explanation, subjects do rely on information both about mechanism and about patterns formed by common features.

The importance of theoretically motivated hypothesis modification is related to the notion that science involves bootstrapping. The strategy of modifying a hypothesis if anomalies to it form a pattern or if there are mechanisms to explain them is a strategy that can be used to discover additional variables that can add to our knowledge of the phenomenon by articulating more precisely the situations in which it obtains. However, such a strategy is effective only to the extent that the patterns actually do reflect mechanisms rather than coincidence and only if the mechanisms invoked to explain the anomalies are approximately correct. Furthermore, in the case of complex phenomena, one can imagine that even if the anomalies have nothing in common, it might still make sense to preserve the explanation by modifying it because if a large number of variables are causally related to the phenomenon, it might well be that there are many different restrictions that constrain the target and that each restriction produces a distinct type of anomaly. That is, the strategy in question is not an algorithm; it is at best a first step. Subsequent steps must examine additional evidence.

In light of the above discussion, consider again the frequent conclusion that one type of evidence for a confirmation bias is that in the face of some anomalous data, subjects modify rather than reject their theories. On the view being taken here, such a modification strategy would constitute a confirmation bias only if the modification were nontheoretically motivated or ad hoc, that is, only if it neither identified a pattern to the anomalies nor proposed a mechanism to account for them.

However, in the typical study of how subjects respond to anomalous evidence, the distinction between theoretically motivated and nontheoretically motivated modification does not arise, and as a result, such studies may provide a misleading picture of the situations in which subjects are reasoning in a scientifically legitimate way. To return to Mynatt et al.'s (1978) task, the premise was that there were basically two viable hypotheses that the subject would consider: the target triangle hypothesis and the alternative based on shade. Thus the assumption was that reasonable behavior would consist of treating anomalous evidence as warranting rejecting the hypothesis in favor of the alternative rather than as calling for its modification or elaboraion. However, in this task, subjects do consider hypotheses other than simple shape and shade (Koslowski and Maqueda 1993; see experiments 14 and 15, chapter 11). Furthermore, since the task does not involve genuine causal relations, there is no reason for subjects to think that any single hypothesis is more or less plausible than any other one. And in consequence, there is also no reason to believe that hypothesis modification or elaboration, rather than rejection, would be inappropriate. For example, if a particular triangle did not repel and that triangle were near a gray circle, then given the structure of the task, there would be no reason to assume it would be inappropriate to modify the triangle hypothesis so that triangles were construed as repelling but only if they were not near other figures.

In short, then, not all cases of theory modification in the face of anomalous data reflect a confirmation bias in favor of the existing explanation. Sometimes they constitute a reasonable way of taking a (probably) basically correct working hypothesis and fine-tuning it to take account of new empirical information. However, a confirmation bias could nevertheless exist in such cases if the modifications were ad hoc rather than theoretically motivated. Existing research on disconfirmation does not typically address this distinction.

The skeptical rebuttal, a rejoinder, and a caveat about theories

Recall that chapter 2 already addressed several possible ways in which subjects were not being sufficiently skeptical of their theories and also presented a rejoinder to this skeptical rebuttal. This section deals specifically with the question of subjects' skepticism as it relates to the research discussed in the present chapter.

Consider again Kuhn et al.'s finding that it is harder to disconfirm a causal belief than a noncausal belief. I have argued that one reason might be that the anomalous evidence disconfirmed the covariation component of the belief but left the mechanism component intact, and furthermore that continued belief in the mechanism might have been reasonable, that without evidence disconfirming the mechanism (by replacing it with an alternative mechanism, for example), it might have been reasonable to expect that the mechanism would continue to bring about the predicted covariation, but not in all situations. I further argued that this option might have been attractive because in many circumstances there are many causal factors that can interfere with the operation of the target cause in a particular situation, making hypothesis modification rather than rejection quite reasonable.

However, in making this argument, I am not suggesting that evidence that disconfirms only the covariation component of a belief ought never to be treated as sufficient reason for outright rejection of the belief. Clearly, subjects should be skeptical enough about their theories that at some point it should not matter whether the mechanism has been disconfirmed or replaced; if the covariations predicted by the mechanism fail to obtain in a wide enough range of situations, then this in itself ought to be grounds for rejecting the belief. Evidence that could call the target mechanism into question might not yet have been discovered, but the repeated nonoccurrence of the expected covariation might suggest that such evidence does nevertheless exist. Also, even if there are many additional causal factors that *could* have interfered with the target cause, this is no guarantee that they did.

If subjects are being appropriately skeptical about their own beliefs, then as the disconfirming evidence accumulates (even if it consists only of additional situations in which x and y fail to covary and the mechanism is left unchallenged and unreplaced), subjects should find their causal beliefs increasingly untenable and the difference between disconfirmed causal beliefs and disconfirmed noncausal beliefs should diminish. And in fact this is exactly what Schauble (1990) found.

Schauble designed a task in which subjects investigated their causal beliefs that engine size and tailfin would affect the speed of a car and their noncausal beliefs that color and muffler would not. Subjects manipulated the different factors and watched the effect of their manipulations on a computer-simulated car. The task was designed so that one causal belief was confirmed and one disconfirmed and one noncausal belief was confirmed and one disconfirmed. Like Kuhn et al., Schauble also found that in the face of disconfirming evidence, children were more likely to cling to causal beliefs than to noncausal beliefs. On the view I am defending, this made sense. The children's beliefs about the features certainly included beliefs about which factors would and would not covary with speed, but their beliefs also included mechanisms to explain why the covariation would or would not obtain. The disconfirming evidence that Schauble's subjects encountered included only evidence about covariation, leaving the mechanism component intact.

However, it is important to note that "although the children displayed the typical belief bias, it was not altogether resistant to the cumulative weight of the evidence" (Schauble 1990, 54). Schauble's "study also replicates findings (e.g., Kuhn et al. 1988) that people tend to interpret identical patterns of evidence differently, depending on whether that evidence confirms or disconfirms their prior beliefs, but demonstrates how those effects can be somewhat mitigated over time and with experience" (1990, 54). What this suggests is that if Kuhn et al.'s subjects had been interviewed over a longer period of time, their behavior might have changed in a comparable way.

In short, when Schauble's subjects initially maintained their belief in the face of disconfirming evidence, their behavior need not have reflected a nonrational commitment to a theory faced with anomalous data. Instead, it could have reflected the fact that, although the covariation component had been disconfirmed, the mechanism component had been left intact, and the fact that the evidence that disconfirmed the covariation component had not been very extensive. When the disconfirming covariation evidence mounted, subjects' commitment to their causal belief diminished.

Furthermore, as already noted, to reject outright an explanation (especially a global hypothesis) at the first sign of disconfirming evidence is not always efficient: First, the explanation might be basically correct, and rejecting it in favor of an alternative would lead one astray. Second, rejecting it before an alternative can be articulated might leave one with no framework within which to organize the data—either the data that suggested the explanation in the first place or the disconfirming data, which, by forming a pattern, might suggest the correct alternative.

Note that here too the point being discussed is related to the notion that science involves bootstrapping: The argument that it might be reasonable to maintain a belief that has had only its covariation component disconfirmed is based on the assumption that the belief can be modified so that the mechanism is still expected to bring about the predicted covariation, but not in some situations. But the fact that scientific methodology does not consist of algorithms that guarantee success means that sometimes such modifications will be mistaken and it will turn out that rejection would have been more appropriate.

One might also argue that yet another way in which the subjects who modified rather than rejected their theories were not being appropriately skeptical is that they assumed, in the first place, that their initial explanations and expectations were fairly plausible and thus not the sort to be rejected on the basis of one piece (or even a few pieces) of anomalous data. For example, to return to the hypothetical early astronomer, her working hypothesis of a perfectly spherical earth would have been plausible because of a host of observations and measurements that suggested the hypothesis. In contrast, the subjects in question did not have this sort of background data. Their theories were based, and only loosely at that, on what their parents had told them ("My mother says orange juice is better for you") or on personal experience ("When I eat pork, I get sick") as well as on possible mechanisms that could have connected cause and effect. (Furthermore, given what subjects reported in experiment 13, chapter 10, even when subjects do mention mechanisms, they are often based on what parents and teachers have said or on personal experience.) Therefore, one could argue that subjects, in modifying their theories in the face of anomalous evidence, were not being appropriately skeptical about whether their theories were warranted in the first place. However, as many philosophers of science have pointed out, scientific inquiry is an essentially social enterprise, one of whose features is that scientists defer to the knowledge of experts. (Biochemists rely on the findings of X-ray crystalographers; meteorologists on the findings of geologists; etc.) Admittedly, the "expert knowledge" that the children were deferring to included that of their parents as well as their own personal experience. As a result, the knowledge was undoubtedly incomplete at best. However, though the knowledge itself may have been either incomplete or flawed, the strategy of deferring to experts is a strategy that scientists also rely on.

(Of course, to come full circle, one could argue that hypotheses should be assessed, by scientists as well as nonscientists, without concern for their initial plausibility, so the first bit of disconfirming evidence should result in rejection. However, as already noted, it is not possible to do this, because plausibility assessments are the basis for deciding which hypotheses to take seriously in the first place. And since some hypotheses are approximately correct, modifying rather than rejecting them is often appropriate. Relying on plausibility considerations is essential, even when applying Humean indices of causation, since it is such considerations that permit discrimination between specious and informative correlations.)

Modifying hypotheses and ignoring evidence
Finally, the methodological role of modification and elaboration also has consequences for how one answers the question of whether people ignore anomalous or disconfirming evidence. If "ignore" means that people are actually not aware of such evidence (that they somehow filter it out), then the finding that people use anomalous evidence to modify a hypothesis is just as much evidence that they are not ignoring it as is the finding that they are rejecting the hypothesis because of it. In both cases the anomalous data are getting past the confirmatory filter. (This is not to say that anomalous data are never ignored; it is merely to note that when such data are used to modify a hypothesis, this is extremely good evidence that the disconfirming data are not being filtered out in this particular case.)

However, more relevant to the present discussion, "ignore" could also mean that people cling to a theory by modifying it in order to accommodate the anomalous data (for example, D. Kuhn et al., 1988) even when the evidence dictates that they should be rejecting the theory outright. If a theory in fact ought to be rejected, then modifying it is certainly one way of ignoring disconfirming data—or at least dismissing such data as unproblematic. However, I have argued that in some cases modification is treated as an example of flawed reasoning when it is in fact scientifically legitimate—especially when there are data that suggested the hypothesis in the first place. Taking an initial working hypothesis, based on preliminary evidence, that drug x cures colds and, in light of anomalous evidence, modifying it to claim that x works under only certain conditions need not be an instance of clinging to a faulty hypothesis that should instead be relinquished. Rather, it may be an example of having discovered more about how x works and making one's working hypothesis responsive enough to take account of this important empirical discovery. The modification may well be methodologically legitimate rather than ad hoc.

In their second study, Mynatt et al. (1978) note that of the tests that resulted in what they coded as disconfirming evidence (but what, on my view, would be treated as anomalous), only 30 percent led to the permanent rejection of the hypothesis, while 37 percent led only to a revision of the hypothesis. The small percentage of rejections was, of course, seen as further evidence of confirmation bias, that is, of less than reasonable behavior. On my view, the modifications were evidence that subjects were both aware of the problematic evidence and taking it seriously enough to modify their hypotheses to take account of it. And though the modifications may not have been in accord with the experimenters' understanding of the range of reasonable alternative hypotheses that they had stipulated to be correct, it is not clear that the modifications were unwarranted, given the subjects' hypotheses and the data they were presented with.

What Confirmation Bias Is and What It Is Not

It follows from the points just made that confirmation bias does *not* consist of using a confirming test strategy. There is no such thing as a confirming test strategy. Tests that are potentially confirming or that are potentially disconfirming or that take into account alternative hypotheses are not mutually exclusive, and any single test potentially can yield either confirming or disconfirming results. Clinging to an initial hypothesis rather than adopting an alternative when the initial hypothesis encounters anomalous evidence is not necessarily evidence of a confirmation bias. It could reflect either not having the wherewithal to generate an alternative or else a temporary strategy of holding a hypothesis in abeyance while sorting out the implications of anomalous data. Finally, confirmation bias is not necessarily reflected in attempts to modify a hypothesis in light of anomalous data. Such attempts could reflect legitimate refinements of a well-motivated working hypothesis in order to make it appropriately responsive to new data.

Although there are many things that confirmation bias is not, there are also many things that confirmation bias can be. It can be the motivational hope that a test will yield confirmatory rather than disconfirmatory results, or it can be the filter that makes one ignore or distort anomalous results or "see" as confirming results that are merely illusory. Confirmation bias can also consist of not testing negative instances (that is, of using Klayman and Ha's [1987] positive-test strategy) when testing negative instances would be likely to detect disconfirming data, or of considering only those alternatives that are implausible straw persons and thus unlikely to discover disconfirming results. Finally, a confirmation bias can consist of modifying an initial hypothesis to take account of anomalous data where the modification is ad hoc rather than theoretically motivated or when an alternative hypothesis can explain not only the data that suggested the initial hypothesis but also the data that disconfirm it. That is, it can consist of clinging to an initial hypothesis even when an alternative provides a better explanatory account.

General Summary

In summary, I have argued in this chapter that one of the problems in deciding whether subjects are exhibiting a confirmation or belief bias is that confirmation and disconfirmation are often treated as involving test strategies that are mutually exclusive with each other and with tests that explore alternative accounts. However, the three sorts of tests are not mutually exclusive, because tests to confirm and tests to disconfirm a hypothesis both involve taking account of competing alternative hypotheses. It is the results of the tests, not the tests themselves, that distinguish hypotheses as confirmed or disconfirmed, and any test can potentially yield either confirmatory or disconfirmatory results. Furthermore, as Klayman and Ha (1987) have demonstrated, even using positive-test strategies can, in certain circumstances, uncover disconfirmatory data. And, either appropriate tests or positive test strategies can yield disconfirmatory data, even if the subject's motivational hope is to confirm the hypothesis. Therefore, in trying to decide whether a subject is exhibiting confirmation or belief bias, the real question is whether she is using test strategies that adequately take account of alternative hypotheses and whether the alternative hypotheses are actually plausible rivals or are instead merely implausible straw persons. However, in many studies of disconfirmation, it was not possible to tell whether subjects were engaging in straw-person confirmation, because the tasks were designed so that issues of the plausibility of alternatives did not arise. The target rule as well as the alternatives were arbitrarily chosen.

An additional problem with deciding whether subjects are exhibiting a confirmation bias is that sometimes maintaining an explanation by modifying it to accommodate new data (even anomalous data) is methodologically legitimate. However, in principle, a hypothesis can invariably be modified to take account of potentially disconfirming evidence. Therefore, in deciding whether hypothesis modification rather than rejection indicates a confirmation bias, the important question is whether the modification is ad hoc rather than theoretically motivated.

A Note about Scientific Reasoning and the Reasoning of Scientists

In this book I refer to scientific reasoning or the principles of scientific inquiry. There is certainly a literature (often controversial) on the extent to which working scientists themselves reason scientifically. This literature is not my concern here. However, it is certainly the case that to some extent what is counted as scientific reasoning depends in part on what scientists actually do. Therefore, in examining various principles of scientific reasoning, my focus in this book is on principles that are fairly noncontroversial (for example, confounded data are inconclusive) or that illustrate the framework that motivated this book (for example, the presence of a mechanism that could have mediated between x and y makes it more likely that x caused y).

Preview

I have argued that neither covariation alone nor theory alone constitute algorithms that guarantee the right answer in scientific reasoning. Theory and data are both crucial, and theory and data are interdependent. Sound scientific reasoning involves bootstrapping: considerations of theory or mechanism constrain data, and data in turn constrain, refine, and elaborate theory. Therefore, to demonstrate whether subjects are reasoning scientifically, it is not sufficient to demonstrate only that subjects rely on causal theories when they evaluate covariation information or that they sometimes use theoretical considerations to override the conclusions suggested by covariation information. This has already been amply demonstrated. Rather, to demonstrate that subjects are reasoning in a methodologically legitimate way, one must demonstrate that subjects are relying on considerations of theory or mechanism in ways that are judicious rather than mechanical. The experiments that follow represent a preliminary attempt to do this.

Part II
Experimental Evidence

A Note about Subjects

With the exception of experiment 14, reported in chapter 11 (which was based on ninth-graders and college students), all experiments in this book were based on subjects from three age groups: sixth-graders, ninth-graders, and college students. The college students were drawn from courses at area colleges and universities that attract students from a variety of majors. Ninth-grade and sixth-grade subjects were attending local public schools. To make the age groups as comparable as possible, we interviewed ninth-graders who were enrolled in "honors" courses in either English or mathematics and who, given past patterns, would almost invariably enroll in college preparatory programs in high school. Because "honors" courses were sometimes not available in the sixth-grade, in choosing sixth-graders, we relied on teachers' judgments. Furthermore, since some of our college students had transferred from community colleges, we emphasized to teachers that we hoped their selection would include students who might attend a community college before transferring to a four-year program.

Chapter 4

When Non-Humean Indices Replace or Override Covariation

In this chapter I summarize two experiments. Although the experiments were preliminary ones, the results demonstrated two things. First, they made it clear that there was a phenomenon to be pursued. In showing that considerations of theory or mechanism do play a role in evaluating explanations, the results of the two experiments legitimized the subsequent research. Second, in raising more specific questions about the role of theory in evaluating explanations, the experiments motivated several additional studies.

Experiment 1
Barbara Koslowski and Lynn Okagaki

The aim of the first study (Koslowski and Okagaki 1986) was a simple one, namely to document that in deciding whether a factor is likely to be causal, college students and college-bound adolescents take into account more than just information about covariation. College students and college-bound ninth- and sixth-graders were each presented with a set of eight story problems in which a problem solver was trying to decide whether a target factor was likely to have been the cause of an event. In one problem, for example, a potter was trying to decide whether baking pottery in a low-heat kiln is likely to cause it to crumble easily.

In all the problems, there was an "initial report" in which the subject was told that the target factor was associated with the event. (To avoid suggesting at this point that the target factor covaried with the effect, it was made explicit that "nothing is now known" about the situation in which the effect did *not* occur.) In the initial report, the subject was also told that there had not yet been time to check and rule out the usual causes.

Each subject was then presented with a "more recent report" that included an additional piece of information about one of three causal indices: covariation, mechanism, or analogous effects. Specifically, in some stories the subject was told that the target factor either had or had not been found to covary with the effect. In some stories the subject learned that there either was or was not a possible mechanism that could explain how the factor could have brought about the effect. And in some stories the subject was told that the factor either had or had not been associated with analogous effects (such as, for example, the tendency of baked-on enamel to peel off). Finally, in two control conditions, subjects were told simply that there had not been time to gather any additional information (about covariation, mechanisms, or analogous effects). Also, in one of the two control conditions, subjects were told that the usual causes of the event had been checked and ruled out; in the other control condition, subjects simply learned that there had "still not been time" to check and rule out the usual causes. Therefore, by comparing the two control conditions, we were able to determine whether being told only that the usual causes had been ruled out was sufficient to induce subjects to rate the target factor as having been causally relevant.

The results were straightforward. Relative to the control condition, causal ratings were significantly higher when target factor and effect covaried and significantly lower when they did not. This was hardly surprising. The Humean index of covariation certainly often indicates causation. But for my purposes, the more relevant results occurred for those stories in which covariation information was not available. For such stories, causal ratings were higher, relative to the control condition, when a possible mechanism was present and when the factor had been associated with analogous effects in the past; in contrast, causal ratings were lower when possible mechanisms and analogous effects were absent. In addition, when the usual causes had been checked and ruled out, ratings were higher than when there had "not been time" to check on the alternatives.

In short, the results of this study supported our general hypothesis that when making causal judgments, subjects rely on information in addition to Humean information about covariation. The results therefore legitimized subsequent studies that sought to specify more precisely how various non-Humean indices are used.

Finally, because they will become relevant in some of the studies that follow, two features of the experiment are worth mentioning: One is that in this study the target factor was not one of the "usual" causes. In consequence, it was fairly nonstandard. This raises the question of whether non-Humean information would have a comparable effect on standard causes. And as we will see in experiments 9 and 10, chapter 8, information about mechanism has different effects, depending on whether the target possible cause is standard or nonstandard (and depending, of course, on other information as well). However, as we will see in experiment 8, chapter 7, even when the target cause is a standard one, there is a sense in which subjects treat it as they did the nonstandard causes in experiment 1, namely as becoming increasingly credible when alternatives are ruled out.

Furthermore, I also draw attention to the fact that there were no age differences (this despite sufficient power to detect age effects of reasonable size). The discussion of when age differences do and do not occur will be deferred until the results of additional studies have been described. At this point I simply note that for each problem, subjects were evaluating only two pieces of causal information: whether or not the usual causes had been ruled out and whether covariation, mechanism, or analogous effects were present or absent. That is, the information-processing demands were fairly low.

Experiment 2
*Barbara Koslowski, Lynn Okagaki, Cheryl Lorenz, and
David Umbach*

The preceding study demonstrated that when covariation information is not available, then various sorts of non-Humean information play a role in causal judgments. In experiment 2 (Koslowski, Okagaki, Lorenz, Umbach 1989) we asked about situations in which covariation information is available but is accompanied by, and in some cases in conflict with, other sorts of information. As I argued earlier, clearly there are situations in scientific inquiry in which the presence and absence of covariation do not indicate the respective presence and absence of causation. We were interested in whether, when making causal judgments in nonscientific situations, college students and college-bound adolescents would also sometimes override judgments suggested by covariation alone.

To do this, we included conditions that pitted covariation information against information about other sorts of causal indices. As in the previous study, we presented subjects with a series of story problems in which a problem solver was trying to find out whether a target factor was likely to be causally related to a particular effect (for example, whether using gasoline with a special additive results in worse mileage than does using ordinary gasoline.)

To answer this question, the problem solver designed an experiment. For each problem, the subject was presented with the following four pieces of information about the experiment:

• *Experimental design* When the experimental design consisted of controlled, direct experimental intervention, then, for example, cars were matched in terms of model and age. When the design relied on confounded, naturally occurring or correlational data, cars were chosen that had already been using different types of gasoline with no attempt to control for model and age of cars.

• *Sample size*   Either the sample was large (for example, a total of eight cars with four cars in each of the gasoline groups) or small (with only one car using the additive gasoline and one car using ordinary gas).

• *Mechanism status*   Either the problem solver learned that a mechanism existed that could explain how the factor caused the effect (the additive contains impurities that interfere with combustion) or else she learned that several possible mechanisms had been ruled out.

• *Covariation status*   Either the target factor and the effect did covary, or else they did not.

Thus we were able to ask, for example, whether the presence of covariation was less likely to be judged causal if it resulted from a confounded design rather than controlled design or if it was based on a small rather than a large sample. On the other hand, we were also able to ask whether, in spite of the absence of covariation, subjects would be more likely to assume that causation was nevertheless present if an explanatory mechanism was present than if likely mechanisms had been ruled out.

Possible Beliefs about Covariation and Undiscovered Mechanisms

In terms of age differences, the results were more complex than those of the preceding study. When covariation was absent, age differences were negligible. Like college students, even the sixth-graders had learned that when covariation is absent to begin with, an unlikely causal relation becomes even more unlikely when mechanisms are absent and sample size is large.[1]

However, when covariation was present, age differences were substantial. With covariation present, older subjects lowered their causal ratings when mechanisms were absent rather than present and when sample size was small rather than large. In contrast, sixth-graders maintained their relatively high causal ratings when mechanisms were absent and sample size was small.

Note that the age differences when covariation was present cannot be attributed to the younger subjects' inability to coordinate information about several variables. When covariation was absent, the number of variables about which the subject was given information was the same as when covariation was present. Nevertheless, when covariation was absent, the younger subjects did take into account information about mechanisms and sample size but, when covariation was present, they did not. What, then, might explain the age differences when covariaton was present?

The subjects' qualitative justifications suggested two possible answers. One was that young adolescents hold a tacit theory of evidence in which the presence of covariation is accorded a kind of primacy, so that so long as covariation is present, adolescents judge causation to be present, even when mechanisms are absent and sample size is small. (One justification noted, for example, "Results are results. There *was* a difference.")

However, another reason is that covariation is taken seriously (though not necessarily accorded primacy) precisely because it is buttressed by other beliefs that might enable adolescents to render other evidence arguing against causation less convincing than adults find it. For example, the youngest subjects' justifications suggest that when told covariation is present, they might dismiss information that mechanisms are absent precisely because they assume that other mechanisms exist that will eventually be discovered. (This was suggested by justifications that noted, for example, "There still could be some way it could have happened.") Comments of this sort suggested to us that perhaps adolescents believe in an inflated range of possible mechanisms that can be operating in a situation, so they are more likely than college students to believe that unknown mechanisms exist to be discovered, and so mechanisms that a college student would treat as dubious adolescents treat as reasonable. Subjects' beliefs about mechanisms, undiscovered as well as already known, were examined in experiments 3, 4, and 5, chapter 5.

However, yet another possibility is that the age differences simply reflected the fact that subjects were not individually interviewed. We structured the ruled-out mechanisms to be as general and as exhaustive as we could make them. However, as the results of experiment 8, chapter 7, later suggested, when covariation is present to begin with, it is sometimes difficult, in a noninterview context, for adolescents to grasp the point that ruling out a generic phenomenon means ruling out the specific instances of that phenomenon. Therefore, in experiment 3 we also asked subjects to make causal judgments when mechanisms were ruled out, but we interviewed subjects individually so that we could make it clear, if questions arose, that when a generic mechanism was ruled out, this meant that its specific instances had been ruled out as well.

Possible Beliefs about Internal and External Validity

Finally, I draw attention to an additional result that was true across ages, namely that experimental design had no effect. Subjects were just as likely to infer causation when the experimental design was confounded as when it was controlled. Although this finding was certainly congruent with one of D. Kuhn et al.'s (1988) conclusions, we questioned its soundness for two reasons. One is that, as noted in chapters 2 and 3, we questioned the soundness of Kuhn et al.'s conclusions. The other is that, with the advantage of hindsight, we realized that the confounding in the stories had not been apparent; one had to infer confounding from the fact that specific controls were not explicitly mentioned. Therefore, we could not distinguish between two alternatives: One was that subjects failed to distinguish the confounded and controlled conditions because they did not infer that the confounded condition had in fact been confounded. The other was that subjects did infer confounding but did not regard it as problematic. These questions were pursued in experiment 6, chapter 6.

With respect to confounding, some of the adolescents' justifications suggested an additional point as well. When the design was based on a large sample, we did not specify whether the sample was characterized by external validity. However, many subjects assumed that it was—that, for example, the cars in the gasoline problem were of more than one type. As a result, when the design was confounded but the sample was large, some adolescents gave justifications of the following sort: "Well, it was probably the gas [that accounted for the mileage differences]. It could be that all the cars that were using the old gasoline were Toyotas and all the cars that were using the new gas were big Buicks, but with all those different cars you wouldn't have all the cars that used the old gas all being Toyotas."[2] That is, some subjects seemed to think, mistakenly, that at least one kind of systematic confounding (type of car with type of gas) would be attentuated by having a heterogeneous sample; they seemed to believe that the liklihood of systematic confounding (which would threaten internal validity) could be minimized by a sample that was characterized by external validity. We examined this possibility in more detail in experiment 6 by making explicit and systematically varying information about external validity.

General Summary

Both studies documented that even sixth-graders base their causal judgments on information other than information about covariation. Furthermore, both studies raised several issues that (along with others) were pursued in some of the studies described below. The first issue (examined in experiments 3, 5, and 6; chapters 5 and 6) asked whether young adolescents believe in the primacy of covariation to the extent that covariation is seen as indicating causation even when information is present that calls causation into question. The second issue (pursued in experiments 3, 4, and 5; chapter 5) asked whether adolescents believe that the presence of covariation indicates that some causal mechanism can be discovered to explain the covariation even if such a mechanism is not now known.

Two additional issues (both explored in experiment 6, chapter 6) involved subjects' awareness of the problems that result from confounded data and adolescents' beliefs about the relation between internal and external validity.

The three experiments in the next chapter pursued the question of adolescents' belief in the primacy of covariation and examined in more detail their beliefs about causal mechanisms.

Chapter 5

Beliefs about Covariation and Causal Mechanisms—Implausible as well as Plausible

Experiment 3
Elizabeth Bjick, Barbara Koslowski, and Elizabeth Allen

In this experiment we pursued two related questions that had been raised by subjects' spontaneous comments in experiment 2, chapter 4: One concerned whether adolescents hold a belief in the primacy of covariation to the extent that they treat the presence of covariation as indicating causation even when several plausible mechanisms have been ruled out. The other, related question concerned adolescents' beliefs about causal mechanisms—those ruled out as well as undiscovered. The beliefs are related because, as I suggested earlier, if adolescents do accord a primacy to covariation, one reason might be that they have an inflated notion of the range of possible mechanisms that can be operating in a situation. This would mean that even when several plausible mechanisms have been ruled out, adolescents might assume that other undiscovered mechanisms might be lurking in the bushes to render the covariation causal.

Our first aim was to see whether we could replicate the particular finding from experiment 2, chapter 4, that suggested a belief in the primacy of covariation. Recall that in experiment 2, when covariation was present, sixth-graders (in contrast to college students) did not lower their causal ratings when mechanisms were absent. Justifications such as "Results are results" suggested that for sixth-graders, the presence of covariation was so important that it could outweigh information that mechanisms were absent.

However, in experiment 2, subjects had not been individually interviewed. Therefore, it was possible that when they read that a general mechanism had been ruled out, they did not grasp that this meant that specific instances of the mechanism had also been ruled out. Accordingly, in this study we interviewed subjects individually to make it clear, if questions arose, that when a general mechanism was ruled out, that meant that its specific instances were ruled out as well.

In the interviews, we presented subjects with situations in which x and y covaried and asked them to rate how likely it was that x had caused y. Subjects then learned about several possible mechanisms that had been checked and ruled out and were asked to rate again how likely it was that x had caused y.

If the sixth-graders' ratings did take account of ruled-out mechanisms, this would suggest that a belief in the primacy of covariation had limits. However, it would not rule out such a belief entirely. Therefore, we also examined other situations in which a belief in the primacy of covariation might play a role. Specifically, we asked whether subjects' causal ratings would be lower if covariation were only partial rather than perfect. If adolescents do believe in the primacy of covariation, then one might expect that even when covariation is only partial, adolescents will be more likely than college students to infer causation. To address this question, we asked subjects to provide causal judgements in one of two conditions: In the perfect covariation condition, for each of six instances, when x was present, y was present, and when x was absent, y was absent. In the partial covariation condition, this was true for only four of the six instances.

In the same vein, we also reasoned that if adolescents had a belief in the primacy of covariation, then when covariation was only partial, ruling out possible mechanisms would decrease causal ratings less for adolescents than for college students.

Finally, we also wanted to explore the second issue raised in experiment 2 regarding subjects' beliefs about possible mechanisms. To this end, after mechanisms had been ruled out and subjects had given their second causal rating, we asked them whether they agreed with a statement that since x and y covary, there must be some way that x helps produce y, even if no one has yet discovered the way. We reasoned that if adolescents do have an inflated notion of the range of possible mechanisms that can be operating in a situation, then even if some mechanisms have been ruled out, adolescents might believe that other mechanisms exist that have yet to be discovered and that can render the covariation causal.

Method

Materials
Four story problems were constructed about the same content areas used in experiment 2. The content areas included the following: selling books, doing laundry, reducing shoplifting, and improving gasoline mileage. An example of one of the story problems in each of the two conditions can be found in the appendix to this experiment. The story format was the same across conditions. Each story consisted of two parts. Subjects com-

pleted the first part for all four stories before they were presented with the second part.

The first part of each story began by describing a problem situation in which an individual was trying to find out whether a target factor (for example, type of gas) was likely to be causally related to an effect (for example, mileage). Following this, an "Evidence" section described, with the aid of a chart, the procedure followed by the problem solver to answer the question. In all stories, the problem solver examined six pairs of instances, with each pair having one member in which the target factor was present and one in which it was absent. In both conditions, the "Evidence" section also made it clear that several plausible alternative causes had been controlled for.

In the "Results" section, in the perfect-covariation condition, in all six cases when the target factor was absent, the "usual" state of affairs obtained, but when the target factor was present, the results deviated from what was usual. In the partial covariation condition, this occurred in only four of the six pairs. In the two remaining pairs, the target factor did not produce any deviation from what was usual, and therefore the two pair members did not differ in terms of effect.

This information was followed by a nine-point rating scale in which the subject was asked to judge how likely it was that the target factor had caused the effect (question 1). Note that at this point the only difference among stories was whether the covariation was perfect or partial; information about mechanisms was not presented until after the initial rating had taken place.

The second part of the story problem followed the initial rating. In the mechanisms-ruled-out condition, we described several possible mechanisms that had been checked and ruled out. In the control condition, we noted that we had "no other information" and that we simply wanted to "double check" the subject's earlier rating. This information was followed by two additional questions. The first (question 2) asked subjects to rate once again how likely it was that the target factor had caused the effect. The second (question 3) asked whether or not the subject agreed with a statement that since the two groups did differ in outcome ("more often than not" in the case of partial covariation), "there must be some way that x helps produce y even if no one has yet discovered it."

Procedure

All subjects (including college students) were interviewed individually. Both interviewer and subject looked at the story problem while the interviewer read it aloud and the subject read it silently. When subjects gave truncated answers (for example, "It seems reasonable"), their answers were followed up with nondirective probes (for example, "Could you say a bit more?").

As in experiment 6, chapter 6, in reading the story problems, we relied on repetition, amplification and pointing to the chart. For example, while reading the "Evidence" section, when six car dealers were mentioned, the interviewer would point to the first column in the table and repeat, "See, here are the six dealers." While reading the "Results" section of the problem, the interviewer would also be pointing to the appropriate lines in the table of evidence that illustrated the results.

Subjects were first presented with and questioned about the first part of all of their story problems. After the initial rating had been completed in the first part for all of the stories, the interviewer returned to each of the four problems, reviewed each of them in turn (including the subject's rating), and, after each had been reviewed, presented subjects with the second part of the story problem (which included the information about ruled-out mechanisms and the question about mechanisms not yet discovered).

When they learned in the second part that several alternatives had been ruled out, some of the younger subjects speculated that perhaps alternative x might have been operating, when x was nothing more than a specific instance of one of the general alternatives that had already been ruled out. That is, some of the younger subjects seemed not to have inferred that ruling out a general alternative meant ruling out the specific instances of that alternative (including the specific's instance that they themselves had proposed). When this happened, the interviewer made it clear that the general alternative had included alternative x.

Design

The between-subjects variables were age, sex, and mechanism status (mechanisms ruled out versus control). The within-subject variables were covariation type (perfect versus partial) and story. At each age there were 48 subjects (24 females and 24 males).

Results and Discussion

Ratings of covariation as an index of causation

Perfect versus partial covariation   For the question 1 ratings, subjects judged how likely it was that x had caused y in both the perfect-covariation and partial-covariation conditions but before subjects had been presented with information about mechanisms. Question 2 ratings involved the same judgment but after subjects had been presented with information about mechanisms. An age × sex × covariation type × mechanism status × story analysis of variance for repeated measures was used

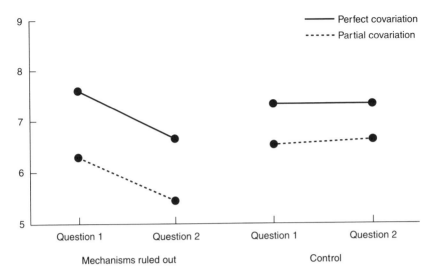

Figure 5.1
Question 1 and question 2 ratings as a function of mechanism status (ruled out versus control) and covariation type (perfect versus partial).

to analyze the ratings for question 1, the ratings for question 2, and the difference between the question 1 and question 2 ratings.[1] As can be seen from the question 1 and question 2 ratings in figure 5.1, both question 1 ratings and question 2 ratings were higher when covariation was perfect than when it was only partial, $F(1, 360) = 75$, $p = .0001$; $F(1, 359) = 62.2$, $p = .0001$; for questions 1 and 2, respectively. That is, across age, partial covariation was judged as less likely than perfect covariation to indicate causation both before and after information about mechanisms was presented.

Mechanism status   Recall that subjects were presented with information about mechanisms after the question 1 ratings were completed. Therefore, it is not surprising that for question 1 ratings there was no main effect for mechanism status, $F(1, 360) = .01$, $p = .93$. However, there was an effect of mechanism status on question 2 ratings, $F(1, 359) = 53.8$, $p = .0001$, and there was also an effect of mechanism status on the difference between question 1 and question 2 ratings, $F(1, 359) = 87.4$, $p = .0001$. As can be seen in figure 5.1, when mechanisms were ruled out, question 2 ratings were lower than question 1 ratings while, in the control condition, the change from question 1 to Question 2 ratings was virtually nil. Furthermore, the decrease in ratings caused by learning that mechanisms had been ruled out was comparable in both the perfect-covariation and partial-covariation conditions, $F(1, 359) = .03$, $p = .85$.

In a word, when plausible mechanisms that could explain how x might have caused y were ruled out, then across age groups, subjects found the covariation of x and y less likely to have been causal, and this occurred to the same extent when covariation was perfect as when it was partial.

Thus in terms of one of the questions that motivated the present study, there was no support for the suggestion, from experiment 2, chapter 4, that subjects in general and adolescents in particular hold a belief in the primacy of covariation: across age groups, partial covariation was seen as less compelling than perfect covariation. And the presence of covariation did not compensate for evidence that called causation into question: across age groups, ratings decreased when subjects learned that plausible explanatory mechanisms had been checked and ruled out even when covariation was perfect.[2]

The absence of a difference among the age groups in the present experiment was in striking contrast to the difference between the sixth-graders and the older age groups that had occurred in experiment 2. I attribute the difference between the two experiments to the fact that in the present study, subjects were individually interviewed, while in experiment 2, subjects merely read the story problems by themselves. I suggest that individual interviews made salient the point (in a way in which merely reading about absent mechanisms did not) that several likely mechanisms had indeed been ruled out. (I will report an analogous finding regarding the effect of interviews in experiment 8, chapter 7.)

Age and sex differences   There was an interaction of age × sex × covariation type for both question 1, $F(2, 360) = 3.9$, $p = .02$, and question 2, $F(2, 359) = 3.98$, $p = .02$. These are illustrated in figure 5.2. Recall that question 1 measured initial causal ratings and question 2 measured causal ratings after information about mechanisms had been presented. As can be seen in figure 5.2, for both questions, with increasing age, females become more convinced than males that a causal relation exists when covariation is perfect and less convinced that a causal relation exists when covariation is partial. (However, note that for both questions, the sex differences were small—always less than one point.) Thus, for both questions, with increasing age, females were more likely than males to behave in accord with what one would expect, given the principles of scientific inquiry, namely that the more consistent the covariation, the more likely it is to indicate causation.

Ratings of the likelihood of undiscovered mechanisms
Recall that question 3 asked subjects how likely it was that an undiscovered mechanism existed that could explain how x could have caused y even if no one had yet discovered the mechanism. In asking this question,

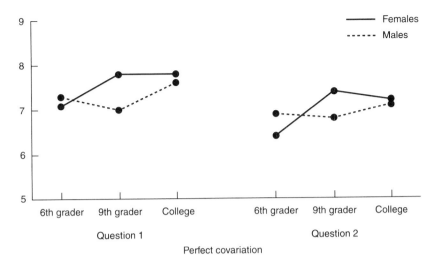

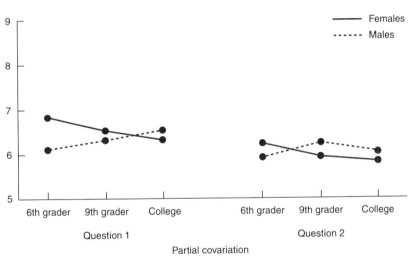

Figure 5.2
Question 1 and question 2 ratings as a function of grade, sex, and covariation type (perfect versus partial).

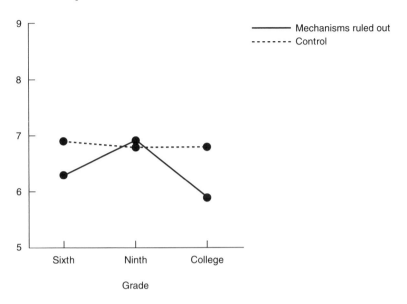

Figure 5.3
Question 3 ratings of the likelihood of undiscovered mechanisms, as a function of grade and of mechanism status.

we had reasoned that if adolescents hold a belief in the primacy of covariation, it might be because they believe that when covariation occurs, a mechanism will eventually be discovered to explain it.

Effects of covariation type   In terms of our initial question, there was a main effect for covariation type, $F(1, 478) = 20.3$, $p = .0001$, with subjects at all ages more likely to believe in the possibility of undiscovered mechanisms when covariation was perfect rather than partial—again a finding that supports neither a belief in the primacy of covariation nor a belief in an inflated range of possible mechanisms.

Effects of mechanism status and age   There was also a main effect of mechanism status, $F(1, 478) = 9.93$, $p = .002$, and a main effect of Age, $F(2, 478) = 4.6$, $p = .01$, as well as an interaction of the two, $F(2, 478) = 3.72$, $p = .02$. However, the interaction was due largely to the ninth-graders' deviation. As figure 5.3 illustrates, ratings in the mechanisms-ruled-out versus control conditions for sixth-graders were comparable to those of college students, $F(1, 478) = .79$, $p = .37$, while ratings of the ninth-graders were different from the ratings of the other two age groups averaged together, $F(1, 478) = 6.53$, $p = .01$. Specifically, ratings in the control condition were comparable across ages. However, when mechanisms were ruled out, ninth-graders were more likely than the other two age groups to believe in the possibility of undiscovered mechanisms. We note that several ninth-graders made comments like "Well people didn't know a lot of stuff in the Middle Ages, and we know them now, so maybe other people later on will discover even more things." I suggest that this in turn reflects the fact that the ninth grade is a time when students are being formally taught about science as a vehicle for unearthing new discoveries and that the ninth-graders in our sample have learned this lesson.

Sex differences   Finally, there was a main effect of sex, $F(1, 478) = 7.58$, $p = .006$. Across conditions, females rated it as more likely than males did that unknown mechanisms would eventually be discovered. However, the difference was a small one: less than 0.5 between the ratings of females and of males. Like the behavior of the ninth-graders, a sex difference was not anticipated but occurred in other experiments as well and will be discussed after the results of all the experiments have been reported.

General Discussion

Experiment 3 addressed two related questions raised in experiment 2, chapter 4: First, do adolescents hold a belief in the primacy of covariation and is the belief strong enough that covariation is seen as indicating causation even when ruled-out mechanisms make causation less likely? Second, do adolescents believe that if covariation is present, then some causal mechanism exists to explain the covariation, even if such a mechanism is not now known?

The answer to the first question was strikingly negative. Even sixth-graders were less likely to treat covariation as indicating causation when the covariation was only partial rather than perfect. Furthermore, even when covariation was perfect, subjects in all age groups decreased their ratings of causation when they learned that plausible mechanisms to explain the covariation had been checked and ruled out. That is, the presence of covariation did not compensate for evidence (regarding ruled-out mechanisms) that called causation into question. And when covariation was only partial, ruling out explanatory mechanisms decreased causal ratings as much for the adolescents as for the college students. In a word, there was no evidence in experiment 3 for an adolescent belief in the primacy of covariation.

The findings regarding ruled-out mechanisms contrast with the results of experiment 2. In that experiment, adolescents did not decrease their ratings of causation when mechanisms were absent. We suggest that the difference is due to the fact that in this experiment, subjects were individually

interviewed. The individual interviews seemed to make it especially salient to the subjects that possible mechanisms had been ruled out, and
when this information was salient, adolescents responded to it no differently from the way college students did. (I will note an analogous finding
regarding the effects of individual interviews in experiment 8, chapter 7.)

Finally, even adolescents were less likely to believe in the possibility of
an undiscovered mechanism when covariation was partial rather than perfect. In addition, sixth-graders were comparable to college students in
believing that undiscovered mechanisms were less likely to exist when
several plausible mechanisms had already been ruled out than in the control condition. That is, there was no evidence in this experiment that
sixth-graders had an inflated notion of the range of possible mechanisms
that could be operating in a situation; they were no more likely than the
college students to believe in an unknown mechanism that was yet to be
discovered.

As in other studies, the behavior of the ninth-graders differed from that
of the other two age groups: when mechanisms had been ruled out, ninth-
graders were more likely than the other two age groups to believe in the
possibility of undiscovered mechanisms. And as in other studies, there
were also sex differences: females were more likely than males to believe
in the possibility of undiscovered mechanisms, and with increasing age,
females became more convinced than males that a causal relation existed
when covariation was perfect and less convinced that a causal relation
existed when covariation was partial. As noted above, I will report other
experiments in which the behavior of the ninth-graders is anomalous and
in which there are sex differences. We had not anticipated either sort
of difference, and I stress that the suggested explanations for them are
working hypotheses that were generated after the fact.

Finally, by way of leading the next two experiments, I point out that
the results in experiment 3 formed a consistent pattern: At all ages, subjects treated covariation as less likely to be causal when it was partial
rather than perfect and when mechanisms that might account for it had
been ruled out. And congruent with this, subjects at all ages were less
likely to expect undiscovered mechanisms when covariation was partial
rather than perfect. That is, this experiment provided no evidence that
sixth-graders have an inflated notion of the range of possible mechanisms
that can be operating in a situation.

However, despite the results from experiment 3, it remained possible
that sixth-graders do believe in an inflated range of possible mechanisms
that can be operating but that the situations in the present experiment
were not ones in which such a belief plays a role. Therefore, in experiments 4 and 5 we examined other situations in which such a belief might
be functioning.

Appendix to Experiment 3

Perfect covariation, mechanisms ruled out

Problem   Larry wants to know, Does using gasoline with a new additive help make cars get better mileage?

Evidence   Larry visits 6 car dealers. At each dealership, he chooses one car to use gas with the new additive and one to use normal gas.

Dealer	Additive gasoline	Normal gasoline
1	Buick	Buick
2	Toyota	Toyota
3	Chrysler	Chrysler
4	Chevrolet	Chevrolet
5	Honda	Honda
6	Ford	Ford

At each dealership, the cars that get the additive gas are *similar* to the cars that get the normal gas in terms of

- year and model,
- size,
- driving conditions when tested.

That is, the only difference between the groups is the type of gasoline.

Results   For all 6 dealers, the cars with the *normal* gasoline got the same mileage as usual, but the cars that used the *additive* gasoline got better mileage than usual.

Questions   Think about the 6 dealerships. Given what Larry found, do you think that type of gasoline has something to do with making cars get better mileage?

1	2	3	4	5	6	7	8	9
Type of gas definitely did *not* help		Type of gas probably did *not* help		Type of gas may or may not have helped		Type of gas probably helped		Type of gas definitely helped

Why?

[New page]

Larry checks on possible ways that the additive gas could improve mileage. For example, he checks on whether the additive gas burns more completely, and therefore more efficiently, and on whether the additive gas has fewer impurities, and is thus less likely to clog the engine. But Larry can find no evidence for any of the possible ways that he checks out. Now that you have learned this, do you now think that the additive gas makes cars get better mileage?

1	2	3	4	5	6	7	8	9
Additive gas definitely did *not* help		Additive gas did *not* help		Additive gas may or may not have helped		Additive gas probably helped		Additive gas definitely helped

Why?

Larry decides, The cars with the additive gas did get better mileage, so there must be some way that the additive gas improves mileage—even if no one has yet discovered the way. Do you agree or disagree?

1	2	3	4	5	6	7	8	9
Strongly disagree		Disagree		No opinion		Agree		Strongly agree

Partial covariation, control condition

Problem   Larry wants to know, Does using gasoline with a new additive help make cars get better mileage?

Evidence   Larry visits 6 car dealers. At each dealership, he chooses one car to use gas with the new additive and one to use normal gas.

Dealer	Additive gasoline	Normal gasoline
1	Buick	Buick
2	Toyota	Toyota
3	Chrysler	Chrysler
4	Chevrolet	Chevrolet
5	Honda	Honda
6	Ford	Ford

At each dealership, the cars that get the additive gas are *similar* to the cars that get the normal gas in terms of

- year and model,
- size,
- driving conditions when tested.

That is, the only difference between the groups is the type of gasoline.

Results   For 4 of the 6 dealers, the cars with the *normal* gasoline got the same mileage as usual, but the cars that used the *additive* gasoline got better mileage than usual. However, for the other 2 dealers, the cars that used *normal* gasoline and the cars that used the *additive* gasoline all got the same mileage as usual.

Questions   Think about the 6 dealerships. Given what Larry found, do you think that type of gasoline has something to do with making cars get better mileage?

1	2	3	4	5	6	7	8	9
Type of gas definitely did *not* help		Type of gas probably did *not* help		Type of gas may or may not have helped		Type of gas probably helped		Type of gas definitely helped

Why?

[New page]

We have no other information to give you. We would just like to remind you of the earlier information and double check to see whether you want to change your rating or keep your judgment the same.

1	2	3	4	5	6	7	8	9
Additive gas definitely did *not* help		Additive gas did *not* help		Additive gas may or may not have helped		Additive gas probably helped		Additive gas definitely helped

Why?

Larry decides, The cars with the additive gas did get better mileage more often than not (4 out of 6 times), so there must be some way that the additive gas improves mileage—even if no one has yet discovered the way. Do you agree or disagree?

1	2	3	4	5	6	7	8	9
Strongly agree		Agree		No opinion		Disagree		Strongly disagree

Experiment 4
Barbara Koslowski, Kirsten Condry, Kimberley Sprague, and Michelle Hutt

Experiment 2, chapter 4, raised two main questions about age differences in causal reasoning. One had to do with whether, and if so, to what extent, sixth-graders hold a belief in the primacy of covariation. The other concerned the related issue of subjects' beliefs about causal mechanisms, ruled-out as well as undiscovered. Both questions were pursued in experiment 3.

In experiment 3 we found no evidence that young adolescents have an inflated notion of the range of possible mechanisms that can be operating in a situation: recall that sixth-graders and college students were comparable in believing that undiscovered mechanisms were less likely to exist when covariation was partial rather than perfect and less likely when some plausible mechanisms had already been ruled out than in the control condition.

In experiment 4 we wanted to examine subjects' beliefs about causal mechanisms in more detail. Although there was no evidence in experiment 3 that sixth-graders believe in an inflated range of possible mechanisms, it was nevertheless conceivable that they did hold such a belief but that the situations in that experiment were not ones in which that belief plays a role. Therefore, in experiment 4 (as well as in experiment 5), we examined other situations in which such a belief might be functioning.

We had three questions: Question 1 was, Are there age differences in how subjects rate possible mechanisms that are implausible (from an adult perspective)? Question 2 was, Are there age differences in the types of mechanisms that subjects generate on their own to explain covariations and in the extent to which they rate their generated mechanisms as being credible? We reasoned that if adolescents do, in fact, have an exaggerated notion of the range of possible mechanisms that might be operating in a situation, then they might also judge implausible mechanisms to be likely and might generate, on their own, mechanisms that would appear to a college student to be implausible. Question 3 was, Are there age differences in subjects' beliefs about the likelihood of mechanisms that have not yet been discovered? A version of this question was also asked in experiment 3 (where it resulted in no age differences). In this experiment, subjects were asked to rate the liklihood of undiscovered mechanisms after they had been asked to generate mechanisms on their own. We reasoned that if adolescents do hold a (possibly tacit) belief that unknown mechanisms exist, then generating their own mechanisms might activate this belief.

We presented subjects with shortened versions of the same story problems used in experiment 2. Because we were interested in tapping subjects' belief about mechanisms, we did not want subjects to conclude that no mechanisms were likely because a flawed design had made causation itself unlikely. Therefore, all stories were presented in the controlled (direct-intervention) condition rather than in the confounded (natural-occurrence) condition. Furthermore, in this experiment the sample size of the story problems was not a concern. Therefore, exact sample size was not specified in the story problems in the present study, although the wording certainly suggested more than two instances. Finally, since we were interested in age differences in reasoning when covariation was present, all of the stories were presented as ones in which factor and effect perfectly covaried.

Methods and Procedures

Materials
The six story problems used were identical to the ones used in experiment 2. An example can be found in the appendix to this experiment. The

story problems were presented only in the controlled (direct-intervention), covariation-present condition with a wording that did not specify sample size but that suggested more than two instances. Information about mechanism, present in the previous study, was omitted from this study because that was what we were interested in tapping.

Each story problem consisted of four parts. The first described the problem, evidence about the (direct-intervention) sampling method, and evidence that the target factor and the effect were found to covary. The second part asked subjects to rate the likelihood that the target factor and the effect were causally related. The third part asked subjects to generate possible ways in which the target factor could have brought about the effect and to rate each of the generated ways in terms of credibility. The ratings of generated mechanisms controlled for the possibility that subjects were generating mechanisms merely to comply with our demands rather than because they actually believed the mechanisms to be reasonable ones. The fourth part consisted of various questions. One asked subjects how likely it was that an undiscovered mechanism existed that could explain how the target factor might have brought about the effect. Another question asked subjects to rate the plausibility of two possible mechanisms (one that was plausible, and one that was implausible, to college students) and to explain their ratings.

Procedure

All subjects (including college students) were interviewed individually. During the interview, the interviewer and the subject both read a copy of the story problem, the interviewer out loud, the subject silently. The subject's answers and ratings were written down by the interviewer, and in answering the questions, subjects were allowed to refer back to the story problem.

In the third section of the interview, whenever a subject generated a possible mechanism to explain how the target factor could have brought about the effect, the interviewer always followed up the response with the general question "Are there any other ways that you can think of?" This section of the interview was terminated either when the subject said that she could think of no other ways or else when five seconds went by without a response. After the subject finished generating possible mechanisms, she was reminded of what she had generated and was asked to rate the likelihood of each mechanism. (The question and the interviewer made it clear that low as well as high ratings were acceptable.)

The last question (about two possible mechanisms) was on a separate sheet of paper. This meant that the two specific mechanisms (one likely, one unlikely) that subjects were presented with and asked to rate did not affect their answers to the earlier question about undiscovered mechanisms.

Design
The between-subjects variables were age (sixth-graders versus ninth-graders versus college students) and sex. The within-subject variable was story.

Ten females and ten males were interviewed at each of the three age levels. Although we wanted to use all six of the stories used in the previous study, pilot testing made it clear that subjects could best deal with being interviewed about only three stories. Therefore, we used a balanced incomplete block design in which each story was presented with each other story an equal number of times for each age × sex group but in which each subject was interviewed about only three stories. At each age level, each combination of stories was given to one female and one male.

Results and Discussion

Initial causal ratings
Recall that in the first part of each story problem, subjects were asked to rate how likely it was that x had caused y, given the result that x and y covaried. These initial ratings were analyzed with an age × sex × story analysis of variance. There were no significant main effects or interactions.

Undiscovered mechanisms
In the second part of each story problem, subjects were asked to rate how likely it was that there was "another way" (mechanism) that had not yet been discovered but that could explain how x might have caused y. Ratings were analyzed with an age × sex × story analysis of variance.

Age differences did not reach significance at even the .60 level: young subjects were just as likely as older subjects to believe in the existence of as yet undiscovered mechanisms. That is, these results converge with the results of experiment 3. Recall that in one of the conditions in that study, covariation was perfect, as it was in the present study. And in this condition (as well, of course, as when covariation was partial) there were also no age differences in subjects' beliefs in the likelihood of undiscovered mechanisms.

However, this question was subtly different from the analogous question in experiment 3, and subjects' comments suggested that it was often interpreted in two different ways. One way asked whether an undiscovered mechanism existed that no one (not even, for example, experts in the field) had yet thought of. (Witness comments like "Even experts discover more things, so there could be another way even if no one's thought of it yet.") That is, the question could have been treated as comparable to the question about undiscovered mechanisms in experiment 3. However, the other way asked about an undiscovered mechanism that the subject herself did not know about. (Consider comments like "Well, *I* probably haven't thought of it, but someone else probably has.") Therefore, in the following experiment this question was disambiguated into two separate questions: One about experts in the relevant field and another about the subject herself.

Mechanisms generated by subjects

Recall that in the third part of each story problem, subjects were asked to generate possible mechanisms that could explain how *x* might have caused *y* and to rate the likelihood of each mechanism that they generated. (Recall also that the ratings controlled for the possibility that subjects were generating mechanisms merely to comply with our requests rather than because they actually believed the mechanisms to be reasonable.)

At each age, there was a total of 60 stories for which subjects could generate possible mechanisms. We considered only those mechanisms that had been generated as a first response to this question. Sixth-graders, ninth-graders, and college students generated at least one mechanism as a first response for 54, 54, and 55 stories, respectively. (In the remaining 6, 6, and 5 cases, the first response to this question consisted of a simple paraphrase of the story problem or the subject's claim that she simply could not think of any possible ways.)

Types of mechanisms generated

The mechanisms generated in experiment 4 and experiment 5 were coded at the same time and were coded in terms of typicality (dubious, reasonable, ambiguous) and specificity (specific, general, ambiguous).

If adolescents had an inflated notion of the range of possible mechanisms that might be operating in a situation, then we might expect that they would generate possible mechanisms that an adult would find unlikely. Therefore, one dimension along which we coded generated mechanisms was typicality.

When we did the interviews, it also seemed to us that adolescents were more inclined than college students to generate mechanisms that were specific rather than general. This put us in mind of the finding of Bruner and his colleagues (Bruner, Goodnow, and Austin 1956; Mackworth and Bruner 1966) that children, in contrast to adults, sometimes focus on details at the expense of synthesis. Therefore, we also coded generated mechanisms in terms of specificity.

Coding categories   *Reasonable* mechanisms were mechanisms that were plausible. For example, "If people have longer visiting hours, they have friends and relatives around more often. And a positive attitude helps

Table 5.1
Number of mechanisms generated as a first response, and their mean ratings, grouped by specificity and by typicality, for each age group

	Sixth grade		Ninth grade		College	
	Number	Mean rating	Number	Mean rating	Number	Mean rating
Specificity						
Specific	25 (15)[a]	6.2	26 (16)	5.7	25 (17)	6.3
General	22 (13)	6.4	23 (17)	6.8	23 (15)	7.0
Ambiguous	7 (7)	6.8	5 (4)	7.8	7 (7)	7.6
Typicality						
Dubious	5 (5)	6.2	4 (4)	6.5	10 (8)	6.3
Reasonable	36 (19)	6.1	37 (20)	6.5	35 (18)	6.8
Ambiguous	13 (10)	6.9	13 (9)	6.4	10 (10)	7.3

a. Numbers in parentheses indicate the total number of subjects who gave the response type at least once.

healing." Or, "With longer visiting hours, there's more likely to be someone around who can call a doctor if there are problems."

Dubious mechanisms were relatively less plausible. For example, "With longer visiting, they'd keep awake more and keep their blood flowing; they wouldn't get too much sleep."

Coding a generated mechanism as dubious was conservative: whenever the two raters disagreed about whether a mechanism was dubious or reasonable, the mechanism was coded as *ambiguous*.

Note also that "plausible" does not mean "possible." One can tell a story according to which increasing blood flow, for example, does improve recovery rate. Thus this mechanism is possible. Given our current knowledge, it is simply not very plausible. Intercoder reliability was .9 or above.

General mechanisms included, for example, "Longer visiting hours will make them feel better and that helps healing."

Specific mechanisms were relatively more focused. For example, "Longer visiting hours will make them feel more worthwhile, less isolated and depressed." Or, "It might make them feel better because it'll be like they're at home and nothing is really wrong."

Coding a generated mechanism as specific was also conservative: whenever the two raters disagreed about whether a mechanism was general or specific, it was coded as *ambiguous*.

Table 5.1 presents the total number of mechanisms that were generated as a first response, grouped by specificity and by typicality, for each of the three age groups.

Specificity   There were no age differences in terms of specificity, $\chi^2(4) =$ .46, $p = .97$. As can be seen in table 5.1, the distribution of specific, general, and ambiguous responses was comparable across ages.

Typicality   As can be seen in table 5.1, there were also no age differences in terms of typicality, $\chi^2(4) = 3.78$, $p = .44$. The distribution of dubious, reasonable, and ambiguous responses was comparable across ages.

Subjects' ratings of generated mechanisms

Although there were no age differences in types of mechanisms generated, it was possible that there were age differences in subjects' judgments of the generated mechanisms. In particular, it was possible that when adolescents generated mechanisms that were dubious, they judged them to be likely whereas when college students generated dubious mechanisms, they did not. To test this, we analyzed subjects' ratings of generated mechanisms with an age × sex × type of generated mechanism (dubious versus reasonable and ambiguous) × story analysis of variance. There was a remarkable lack of significant differences. In particular, there were no significant differences for age, $F(2, 121) = .86$, $p = .42$, or for type of mechanism generated, $F(1, 121) = .39$, $p = .53$, or for the interaction age and type of mechanism generated, $F(2, 121) = 1.14$, $p = .32$. In summary, when subjects generated a possible mechanism as a first response, all age groups rated the dubious mechanisms as being comparable in likelihood to the nondubious mechanisms. (This result will be discussed in experiment 5.)

In summary, there was a remarkable lack of age differences in the kinds of mechanisms generated by the subjects and in subjects' ratings of how likely their generated mechanisms were.

Plausible versus implausible mechanisms

In the last section of each story problem, subjects were presented with one plausible and one implausible mechanism that could explain how x might have caused y and were asked to rate each of the two mechanisms in terms of the likelihood that it was operating.

Ratings of these other-generated plausible and implausible mechanisms were each analyzed with an age × sex × story analysis of variance. As figure 5.4 illustrates, when other-generated mechanisms were plausible, age differences did not reach even the .60 level of significance. In contrast, when other-generated mechanisms were *im*plausible, age differences were striking, $F(2, 144) = 26.69$, $p = .0001$. A mechanism that, to an older subject, sounds quite implausible sounds, to a younger subject, to be quite plausible indeed. This finding was congruent with the suggestion that

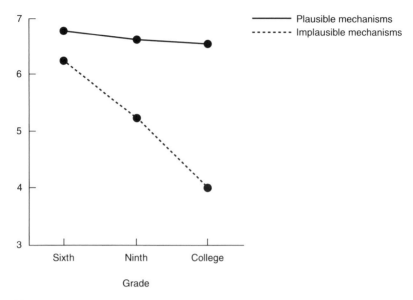

Figure 5.4
Ratings of plausible and of implausible mechanisms as a function of grade.

young adolescents have an inflated notion of the range of possible mechanisms that might be operating in a situation and that consequently they rate as plausible mechanisms that are in fact quite dubious.

Discussion

Our aim in this experiment was to examine in more detail the hypothesis that adolescents do have an inflated belief in the range of possible mechanisms that might be operating in a situation even though the belief was not tapped in experiment 3. The adolescents' ratings of other-generated implausible mechanisms were certainly congruent with this hypothesis: with decreasing age, subjects found implausible mechanisms increasingly likely, to the point where, for sixth-graders, there was very little difference between other-generated implausible mechanisms and other-generated plausible mechanisms.

But if adolescents hold an inflated belief in the range of possible mechanisms, then it is puzzling that they were no more likely than adults to generate implausible mechanisms on their own. A possible clue to this puzzle is that in this experiment subjects were generating mechanisms to explain plausible covariations. Perhaps asking adolescents to explain implausible covariations would be especially likely to tap a belief that dubious mechanisms are reasonable because dubious mechanisms might be the only way of explaining implausible covariations. Therefore, in the following experiment, we asked subjects to generate mechanisms to explain implausible as well as plausible covariations.

We also pursued an additional question in the next experiment. Recall that in explaining their judgments about the likelihood of undiscovered mechanisms, some of the subjects in this experiment gave responses that indicated that our question was ambiguous between asking about mechanisms unknown to them personally and mechanisms unknown to experts in the relevant field. In experiment 5 we disambiguated this question into two separate questions.

Appendix to Experiment 4

Controlled, covariation-present condition

Problem   The head administrator of a hospital wants to find out whether having longer visiting hours might have something to do with bringing about higher recovery rates in the patients.

Way of finding out   The way the administrator decides to find out is by having his hospital arrange for odd-number rooms to have longer visiting hours than even-numbered rooms and then to compare the recovery rates.

Results   When the administrator compares the recovery rates from his hospital, he finds that there was a difference between the two sorts of visiting hours. The patients who had longer visiting hours did have higher recovery rates that the patients who had shorter visiting hours.

Questions   Think about the evidence. Patients with longer visiting hours had higher recovery rates. Do you think this was chance or coincidence? Or did the longer visiting hours actually make or cause the higher recovery rates?

1	2	3	4	5	6	7	8	9
Definitely a coincidence		Probably a coincidence		Maybe a coincidence		Probably coincidence		Definitely a coincidence

Now the administrator is trying to understand why it is that patients with longer visiting hours have higher recovery rates. Can you think of how longer visiting hours might lead to higher recovery rates?

[New page]

You've thought of some ways in which having longer visiting hours might lead to higher recovery rates. When people propose reasons, they often propose reasons that are not likely as well as reasons that are likely. Could you think of each of these ways and tell me whether you think it's a likely way or a not likely way?

1	2	3	4	5	6	7	8	9
Definitely not likely				As likely as not				Definitely likely

[New page]

Here are two possible way in which longer visiting hours might have led to higher recovery rates. Tell us how likely or believable you find each one.

Longer visiting hours could make it more likely that someone would report any problems that the patient was having.

1	2	3	4	5	6	7	8	9
Definitely not likely		Probably not likely		As likely as not		Probably likely		Definitely likely

Why did you choose this rating?
    Longer visiting hours make patients more excited. It could be that their blood flows more rapidly when they're excited. This might bring more white blood cells to the diseased area and therefore cause faster healing.

1	2	3	4	5	6	7	8	9
Definitely not likely		Probably not likely		As likely as not		Probably likely		Definitely likely

Why did you choose this rating?

[New page]

How likely do you think it is that there's another way that nobody has yet discovered and that you have not thought of—another way that longer visiting hours might lead to higher recovery rates?

1	2	3	4	5	6	7	8	9
Definitely *no* other ways		Probably no other way		Might or might not be another way		Probably another way		Definitely another way

Experiment 5
Barbara Koslowski, Kimberley Sprague, Kirsten Condry, and Michelle Hutt

In this experiment we wanted to pursue the suggestion, made in experiment 4, that the adolescents' tendency to treat dubious mechanisms as reasonable might be especially likely to play a role when the covariations to be explained are implausible rather than plausible. To this end we included two types of events to be explained: Plausible events were ones in which the covariation described was congruent with reasonable adult expectations, such as that the type of gasoline used was related to mileage. Implausible events were ones in which the covariation described was unexpected by ordinary adult standards, such as that the color of a car (whether it was red or blue) would be related to mileage.

We asked subjects to generate, on their own, and to rate the likelihood of, possible mechanisms to explain the implausible as well as the plausible covariations. We reasoned that if subjects were asked to explain a plausible covariation, then all age groups would be able to rely on plausible explanatory mechanisms to do the job. However, if asked to explain an implausible covariation, then the college students' ability to generate (and speculate about undiscovered) explanatory mechanisms would be restricted somewhat by their beliefs about what sorts of mechanisms are reasonable. Adolescents' beliefs, in contrast, might be restricted to a lesser extent because mechanisms that a college student would find dubious would appear to an adolescent to be quite sound.

In asking subjects about undiscovered mechanisms, we disambiguated the question from experiment 4 regarding the likelihood of undiscovered mechanisms into two distinct questions: one concerning undiscovered mechanisms that the subject herself did not know about and another concerning undiscovered mechanisms currently unknown even to experts in the relevant field. And we asked subjects to rate the likelihood of undiscovered mechanisms when covariations were implausible as well as plausible.

Methods and Procedures

Materials and procedures

The format of the story problems and the interview procedure was analogous to the format and procedure used in the previous study. An example of one of the story problems in the plausible and the implausible conditions can be found in the appendix to this experiment. For purposes of comparison, the sample story is about the same event as the sample story in the previous study.

The six story problems that involved plausible covariates were the same as the ones in experiment 4 (which, recall, were the same as the ones used in experiment 2).

The six story problems about implausible covariates involved the same content as the implausible covariates used in experiment 9, chapter 8. Therefore, we had independent evidence from experiment 9 that our judgments of implausibility were shared at least by college students. Three of the implausible stories were parallel to three of the plausible ones except that the target possible cause varied. (For example, in the plausible version, the type of gas was related to mileage, while in the implausible version, the color of the car was related to mileage.) The remaining three implausible stories were different from the first three implausible stories both in terms of possible cause and in terms of observed effect.

In each story problem (as in experiment 4), subjects were first asked to rate the likelihood that the target factor and the effect were causally related. Subjects were then asked to generate possible ways in which the target factor could have brought about the effect and to rate the generated possibilities in terms of credibility.

The next questions[3] asked subjects to rate the likelihood that an undiscovered mechanism existed that could explain how the target factor could have brought about the effect. However, in contrast to the analogous question in experiment 4, the questions in this experiment asked about two types of undiscovered mechanisms: those unknown to the subject herself and those unknown to experts in the relevant field.

(After subjects had answered all of these questions for each of their three story problems, subjects were asked to consider again each of the story problems in turn. Subjects were then asked, for each story problem, to generate and to rate the likelihood of possible alternative causal factors that could have brought about the observed effect. In spite of pilot testing, this question was ambiguous; subjects often interpreted it as a request for more possible causal mechanisms, in addition to the one they had already generated, rather than as a request for alternative causal factors. Because of the ambiguity in the question, we did not have confidence in the resulting data, and so did not analyze them.)

Design

The between-subjects variables were age (sixth-graders versus ninth-graders versus college students) and sex. The within-subject variables were plausibility type (plausible versus implausible covariates) and story.

There were two constraints on the design. As in the previous study, each interview had to be limited to three story problems. In addition, plausibility type had to be a within-subject variable to avoid having some subjects receive only implausible stories. Therefore, within each age × sex group, half the subjects were given two stories about plausible covariates and one about an implausible covariate, while the other half were given two stories about implausible covariates and one about a covariate that was plausible. Each pair of stories was given to 8 subjects: 4 females and 4 males. At each age there were 40 subjects: 20 females and 20 males.

Results and Discussion

There was a significant effect for plausibility, $F(1, 288) = 38$, $p = .0001$, with plausible covariations receiving higher causal ratings than implausible covariations.[3] And the interaction of age and plausibility was not significant, $F(2, 288) = 1.61$, $p = .20$. That is, when subjects were merely rating covariations, rather than trying to explain them, there were no age differences; at all ages, plausible covariations were judged as more likely to be causal than were implausible covariations. (As we will see, analogous results obtained in experiments 9 and 10, chapter 8.)

Undiscovered mechanisms

Mechanisms unknown to the subject   Recall that the "undiscovered mechanisms" question from the previous study was disambiguated into two separate questions. The first question yielded ratings of how likely it was that there was another mechanism that the subject personally did not know about that could have explained how x caused y. These ratings were analyzed with an age × sex × plausibility status (plausible versus implausible covariation) × story analysis of variance for repeated measures.[4]

There was a main effect for plausibility of covariation, $F(1, 288) = 21.8$, $p = .0001$. However, the interaction of age and plausibility of covariation was not significant, $F(2, 288) = 1.52$, $p = .22$. That is, across age groups, subjects were more likely to assume that there was a mechanism that they personally did not know about when covariations were plausible rather than implausible.

Mechanisms unknown to experts   The second question yielded ratings of how likely it was that there was another mechanism, one that was unknown to experts but that scientists might eventually discover, that could explain how x caused y. These ratings were also analyzed with an age × sex × plausibility type (plausible versus implausible covariation) × story analysis of variance for repeated measures. In contrast to the preceding question, this question did yield age differences. There was a main effect for plausibility, $F(1, 288) = 9.08$, $p = .0028$, and for age, $F(2, 288) = 3.12$, $p = .045$, as well as an interaction of plausibility and age, $F(2, 288) = 3.00$, $p = .05$.

As can be seen in figure 5.5, when the covariations were plausible, there were essentially no age differences. However, the difference between ratings when covariations were plausible versus when they were implausible was smaller for sixth-graders than for college students, $F(1, 288) = 1.67$, $p = .09$ (one-tailed). (The plausible versus implausible difference for the ninth-graders is larger than that of the other two groups averaged together, $F(1, 288) = 4.71$, $p = .03$.) In short, when the covariations were implausible, there was a trend for sixth-graders to be more likely than the other two age groups to believe that a mechanism currently unknown to experts will eventually be discovered to explain the implausible covariations.[5]

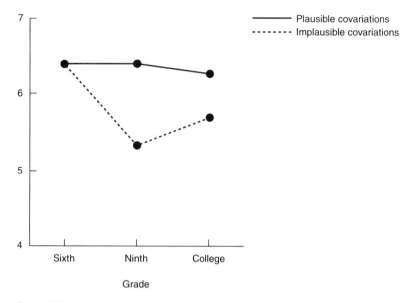

Figure 5.5
Likelihood of mechanisms unknown to experts as a function of grade and plausibility of covariation.

I suggest that this is because, for sixth-graders, the range of possible mechanisms that could have been operating was larger than for college students.

As for the ninth-graders, their ratings, when the covariations were implausible, were closer than the ratings of the other two age groups to the indeterminate rating of 5—there "might or might not be another way" that experts might discover that could explain how x caused y. That is, they were more likely than the other two age groups to be uncertain. This result, along with other, related results, will be discussed in the last chapter in terms of Keating's (1990) notion of the generalization of uncertainty.

Mechanisms generated by subjects
Recall that in the third section of each story problem, subjects were asked, as they were in experiment 4, to generate possible mechanisms that could explain how x might have caused y and to rate the plausibility of each mechanism they generated.

As in experiment 4, we considered only those mechanisms that had been generated as a first response to the question. Recall that the first-response mechanisms generated in experiments 4 and 5 were coded at the same time and were coded in terms of specificity (specific, general, ambiguous) and typicality (dubious, reasonable, ambiguous). And as in experiment 4, the coding of generated mechanisms as dubious was very conservative: whenever the two raters disagreed about whether a mechanism was dubious, the mechanism was coded as ambiguous.

At each age, there were 120 stories for which subjects could generate possible mechanisms as their first response. Sixth-graders, ninth-graders, and college students generated at least one mechanism for 93, 80, and 71 stories, respectively.

Types of mechanisms generated

Table 5.2 presents the total number of mechanisms that were generated as a first response, grouped by specificity and typicality, for each of the three age groups in response to both the plausible and the implausible covariations.

Specificity   There were no age differences in terms of specificity when mechanisms were grouped into three categories (specific, general, ambiguous) for either the plausible covariations, $\chi^2(4) = 2.4$, $p = .66$, which echoed the results of experiment 4, or for the implausible covariations, $\chi^2(4) = 4.09$, $p = .39$. Nor were there age differences in specificity when mechanisms were grouped into only two categories (specific versus general and ambiguous) for either the plausible covariations, $\chi^2(2) = 2.37$, $p = .31$, or for the implausible covariations, $\chi^2(2) = 3.34$, $p = .19$.

Typicality   As we had expected, there were also no age differences in terms of typicality when mechanisms were grouped into three categories (dubious, reasonable, ambiguous) for the plausible covariations, $\chi^2(4) = 3.62$, $p = .46$, but there were for the implausible covariations, $\chi^2(4) = 6.98$, $p = .06$ (one-tailed).

Similarly, when mechanisms were grouped into only two categories (dubious versus reasonable and ambiguous), there were also no age differences for the plausible covariations, $\chi^2(2) = 2.22$, $p = .33$, but age differences were even more significant for the implausible covariations, $\chi^2(2) = 5.39$, $p = .03$, (one-tailed).

In a word, when covariations were implausible to begin with, sixth-graders were more likely than the other two age groups to generate mechanisms that were, by adult standards, dubious. Indeed, when covariations were implausible, more than half of the sixth-graders (10 females and 13 males), but only one fourth of the subjects in each of the other two age groups, generated a dubious mechanism at least once. (And recall that for half of the subjects, there was only one implausible covariation that was included in the interview.)

Table 5.2
Number of mechanisms generated as a first response and their mean ratings, grouped by specificity and by typicality, for each age group to plausible and implausible stories

	Plausible story						Implausible story					
	Sixth grade		Ninth grade		College		Sixth grade		Ninth grade		College	
	Number	Mean rating	Number	Mean rating	Number	Mean rating	Number	Mean rating	Number	Mean rating	Number	Mean rating
Specificity												
Specific	17 (16)[a]	6.4	18 (17)	6.5	11 (11)	7.7	38 (33)	6.3	25 (20)	9.8	24 (19)	6.8
General	12 (12)	7.6	10 (10)	5.5	12 (12)	4.9	6 (5)	6.0	8 (8)	5.9	3 (3)	7.0
Ambiguous	17 (15)	6.7	13 (13)	4.7	17 (16)	6.8	3 (3)	7.3	6 (6)	6.0	4 (4)	7.8
Typicality												
Dubious	6 (5)	6.5	6 (6)	3.3	2 (2)	9.0	24 (23)	6.3	11 (11)	7.1	10 (10)	6.9
Reasonable	32 (29)	7.0	29 (22)	6.1	34 (27)	6.1	18 (18)	6.1	25 (22)	6.3	19 (18)	7.1
Ambiguous	8 (8)	6.3	6 (6)	6.2	4 (4)	8.7	5 (5)	6.8	3 (3)	6.0	2 (2)	4.5

a. Numbers in parentheses indicate the total number of subjects who gave the response type at least once.

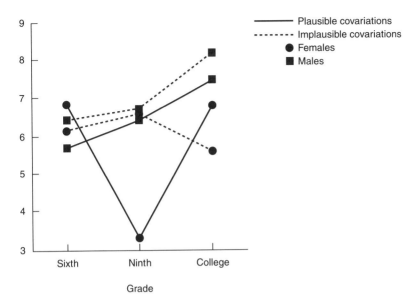

Figure 5.6
Ratings of initial mechanisms generated by subjects as a function of grade, sex, and plausibility of covariation.

Subjects' ratings of generated mechanisms

Our next question was whether, when sixth-graders generated dubious mechanisms, they in fact judged them to be dubious. To answer this question, we analyzed subjects' ratings of generated mechanisms with an age × sex × plausibility of covariation × type of generated mechanism (dubious versus reasonable and ambiguous) × story analysis of variance, with story nested in plausibility.[6]

In terms of our initial question, there was a striking absence of various effects. Specifically, there were no main effects for age, $F(2, 162) = 1.52$, $p = .22$, or for type of mechanism generated, $F(1, 162) = .14$, $p = .71$, or for the interaction of age and type of mechanism generated, $F(2, 162) = .77$, $p = .47$. In short, as in experiment 4, when adolescents generated mechanisms, they rated their dubious mechanisms as being comparable in likelihood to their nondubious mechanisms, but in doing so, they were not different from college students.

There was an interaction of age × sex × plausibility of covariation, $F(2, 162) = 3.41$, $p = .04$. As can be seen in figure 5.6, when covariations were plausible, ninth-grade females provided lower ratings than did the other age × sex groups. Perhaps ninth-grade females are especially susceptible to what Keating (1990) has called the "overgeneralization of uncertainty," characteristic of certain aspects of adolescent thinking.

To summarize, what we have is a situation in which over half the sixth-graders (in contrast to only one-fourth of each of the other two age groups) were generating dubious mechanisms (where dubiousness was conservatively coded) but in which all the age groups were rating their dubious mechanisms to be as likely as their nondubious mechanisms.

General Discussion

One of the questions examined in experiments 4, 5, and 6 was whether adolescents hold an inflated belief in the range of possible mechanisms that can be operating in a situation. To the extent that they do, the belief seems to affect explanations of covariations rather than assessments of covariations. Assessments of covariations are comparable across ages. In this experiment, subjects in all age groups treated implausible covariations as less likely to be causal than plausible covariations, and in experiment 3 they treated partial covariations as less likely to be causal than perfect covariations.

Furthermore, even when subjects move from assessing covariations to explaining them, age groups are still comparable so long as the covariations being explained are plausible rather than implausible. In the present experiment, when subjects were asked to explain plausible covariations, adolescents and college students were comparable in generating reasonable mechanisms and in rating them as reasonable.

However, when subjects are asked to explain covariations that are implausible, age differences become apparent. Implausible covariations call up implausible explanatory mechanisms. For college students, this restricts the sorts of mechanisms proposed because college students are reluctant to propose dubious mechanisms. In contrast, sixth-graders' explanations are not restricted to the same extent. Because they treat dubious mechanisms as reasonable, sixth-graders are more likely than older subjects to propose dubious mechanisms to explain implausible covariations. That is, when reasonable mechanisms do not come to mind, sixth-graders rely on a default apoach and generate dubious mechanisms. (And when covariations are implausible, there is a trend for adolescents to be more likely than college students to expect that experts will eventually discover currently unknown mechanisms to explain the covariations.)

Furthermore, even when adolescents are not generating their own dubious mechanisms, their exaggerated notion of the range of possible mechanisms can nevertheless be activated. In experiment 4, when subjects were asked to generate explanations for plausible covariations, they generated reasonable mechanisms. However, when they were asked to evaluate a dubious mechanism proposed by someone else to explain a plausible covariation, they rated the dubious mechanism as reasonable (even though they did not generate implausible mechanisms to account for plausible covariations on their own).

Finally, there is a sense in which sixth-graders have not completely integrated covariations and mechanisms. On the one hand, sixth-graders are more likely than college students to generate dubious mechanisms to explain implausible covariations and to judge dubious mechanisms generated by others to be as likely as plausible mechanisms. On the other hand, like college students, sixth-graders judge implausible covariations as less likely to be causal than plausible covariations and partial covariation as less likely to be causal than perfect covariation. Hence the nonintegration. If implausible mechanisms are viable, why do sixth-graders treat implausible and imperfect covariation as less convincing than plausible and perfect covariation? Why do they not merely assume that there must be mechanisms (including mechanisms that adults find unconvincing) that can render the deficient covariations causal?

Had we known in advance what the data were going to consist of, we would have asked subjects to rate the plausibility of the initial covariations *after*, as well as before, they had generated possible mechanisms to explain them. We would have wanted to know whether, after generating mechanisms (even dubious mechanisms) to explain the implausible covariations, subjects find the implausible covariations to be more likely than before the mechanisms were generated. (What we do know from experiments 9 and 10, chapter 8, is that when subjects are *presented* with mechanisms to account for implausible covariations, they find the covariations increasingly likely. The mechanisms presented in experiments 9 and 10 were neither generated by subjects on their own nor as unreasonable as the dubious mechanisms that subjects generated in this study. However, they do demonstrate that at least in some situations, judgments about the plausibility of covariations depend on the presence of explanatory mechanisms.)

With regard to the sixth-graders' inflated belief in the range of possible mechanisms, I suggest that what might look, at first glance, like an instance of qualitatively different thinking can instead be attributed to a particular sort of knowledge-base deficit: sixth-graders do not know enough about various aspects of the world to realize that some possible mechanisms are simply not very likely to be operating. And because of this, when a causal judgment requires them to consider explanation as well as covariation and the covariation to be explained is implausible, adolescents often treat as reasonable mechanisms that are, in fact, dubious.

These results also raise another question about the relation between covariation and mechanism. The first concerns the behavior of the college students. When subjects generated their own mechanisms in experiments 4 and 5, all age groups (even college students) rated their dubious mechanisms to be as likely as their nondubious mechanisms. However, in experiment 4, when we presented subjects with other-generated mechanisms to evaluate, college students gave much lower ratings to the dubious mechanisms than they did to the reasonable mechanisms. One possibility is that dubious mechanisms generated by the subject herself are seen as more reasonable than dubious mechanisms generated by someone else simply because of personal involvement.

Another possibility turns on the fact that in experiment 4, when the covariations were plausible, there was a reasonable as well as a dubious mechanism offered to explain each covariation. Therefore, there was no reason to treat the dubious mechanism as likely; the covariation could be accounted for quite adequately by relying on the reasonable mechanism. However, in this experiment, some of the covariations were implausible, and implausible covariations tend to call up dubious mechanisms. Therefore, subjects may have judged their dubious mechanisms to be reasonable not merely because of personal involvement but also because they treated the presence of a covariation (even though it was an implausible one) as indicating that there was something to be explained. And given that the covariations were implausible, a dubious mechanism (called up by the implausible covariation) seemed to be the explanation that was likely.

Appendix to Experiment 5

Plausible event

Problem   A medical researcher notices that some patients have visitors who stay longer than others. He wants to find out whether having longer visiting hours might have something to do with bringing about higher recovery rates in the patients.

Way of finding out   The way he decides to find out is by having his hospital arrange for half the rooms to have longer visiting hours and the other half to have regular visiting hours and then to compare the recovery rates.

Results   When the medical researcher compares the recovery rate from his hospital, he finds that there *was* a difference. The patients who had longer visiting hours *did* have higher recovery rates than the patients who had shorter visiting hours.

Think about the evidence. Patients with longer visiting hours had higher recovery rates. Do you think this was chance or coincidence? Or did the longer visiting hours actually make or cause the higher recovery rates?

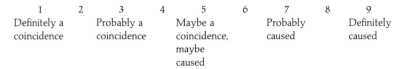

1	2	3	4	5	6	7	8	9
Definitely a coincidence		Probably a coincidence		Maybe a coincidence, maybe caused		Probably caused		Definitely caused

Why did you choose this rating?

Think of *how* longer visiting hours might make people recover better. Can you think of *how* that might happen? *How* could it be that having longer visiting hours might make patients recover better?

[New page]

You've thought of some ways in which patients with longer visiting hours might have higher recovery rates. When people propose reasons, they often propose reasons that are not likely as well as reasons that are likely. Could you think of each of these ways and tell me whether you think it's a likely way or a not likely way?

1	2	3	4	5	6	7	8	9
Definitely				As likely				Definitely
not likely				as not				likely

[New page]

How likely do you think it is that there's another way that you, personally, don't know about—another way that having longer visiting hours might make patients have higher recovery rates?

1	2	3	4	5	6	7	8	9
Definitely		Probably no		Might or		Probably		Definitely
no other		other way		might not		is another		another
ways				be another		way		way
				way				

Why?

How likely do you think it is that there's another way that no one else has yet discovered but that the medical researcher or somebody else will eventually discover if they look hard enough—another way that having longer visiting hours might make patients have higher recovery rates?

1	2	3	4	5	6	7	8	9
Definitely		Probably no		Might or		Probably		Definitely
no other		other way		might not		is another		another
ways				be another		way		way
				way				

Why?

Implausible event

Problem   A medical researcher notices that some patients have heavy drapes on their windows and others have curtains. He wants to find out if having heavy drapes on the windows has something to do with making patients recover faster.

Way of finding out   The way the researcher decides to find out is by having one group of patients have heavy drapes on their windows and another group have only curtains.

Results When the researcher compares the two groups of patients, he finds that there *was* a difference. The patients who had heavy drapes on their windows *did* recover faster than the patients who had curtains on their windows.

Think about the evidence. The patients who had heavy drapes on their windows did recover faster. Do you think this was just chance or coincidence? Or did having heavy drapes on the windows actually make or cause the patients to recover faster?

1	2	3	4	5	6	7	8	9
Definitely a coincidence		Probably a coincidence		Maybe a coincidence, maybe caused		Probably caused		Definitely caused

Why did you choose this rating?

Think of *how* having heavy drapes on the windows might make the patients recover faster. Can you think of *how* that might happen? *How* could it be that having drapes on the windows might make patients recover faster?

[New page]

You've thought of some ways in which having drapes on the windows might make patients recover faster. When people propose reasons, they often propose reasons that are not likely as well as reasons that are likely. Could you think of each of these ways and tell me whether you think it's a likely way or a not likely way?

1	2	3	4	5	6	7	8	9
Definitely not likely				As likely as not				Definitely likely

[New page]

How likely do you think it is that there's another way that you, personally, don't know about—another way that having heavy drapes on the windows might cause patients to recover faster?

1	2	3	4	5	6	7	8	9
Definitely *no* other ways		Probably no other way		Might or might not be another way		Probably is another way		Definitely another way

Why?

How likely do you think it is that there's another way that no one else has yet discovered but that the medical researcher or somebody else will eventually discover if they look hard enough—another way that having drapes on the windows might make patients recover faster?

1	2	3	4	5	6	7	8	9
Definitely *no* other ways		Probably no other way		Might or might not be another way		Probably is another way		Definitely another way

Why?

General Summary

This chapter reported three experiments that asked subjects to evaluate various sorts of covariations (plausible covariations rather than implausible covariations and plausible covariations that were perfect rather than partial), to judge the causal likelihood of plausible covariations after mechanisms to explain them had been ruled out to generate and rate the likelihood of mechanisms to explain plausible as well as implausible covariations, and to rate the likelihood of plausible and of implausible mechanisms generated by others to explain the plausible covariations.

Assessments of covariations were comparable across ages. Adolescents as well as college students treated implausible covariations as less likely to be causal than plausible covariations and partial covariations as less likely to be causal than perfect covariations. Furthermore, even when subjects moved from assessing covariations to explaining them, the age groups were still comparably likely to generate plausible mechanisms so long as the covariations being explained were plausible.

However, when subjects were asked to explain implausible covariations, the sixth-graders were more likely than the older subjects to do so by generating dubious mechanisms. And when subjects were asked to evaluate mechanisms proposed by others to explain plausible covariations, sixth-graders, in contrast to college students, judged dubious mechanisms to be as likely as reasonable mechanisms.

I suggest that the age difference occurred because adolescents hold an inflated belief in the range of possible mechanisms that can be operating in a situation, so they treat as reasonable mechanisms that older subjects find dubious.

Chapter 6

Assessing Internal and External Validity

Experiment 6
Barbara Koslowski, Lynn Okagaki, Kimberly Sprague, Kay Forest

Like experiments 3, 4, and 5, experiment 6 was motivated by some of the results in experiment 2.[1] The first result dealt with internal validity. Recall that in experiment 2, subjects in one of the conditions were presented with story problems in which x covaried with y and were asked to rate the likelihood that x had caused y. In experiment 2 the covariation had resulted either from direct experimental intervention (which had controlled for several factors) or else from natural occurrence (in which no factors were mentioned as having been controlled for). We found no difference in causal ratings between the direct-intervention condition and the natural-occurrence condition. That is, subjects judged data that resulted from a controlled experiment to be no more conclusive than data that resulted from a confounded experiment.

This finding was certainly congruent with one of D. Kuhn et al.'s (1988) conclusions. They had suggested that subjects in general and adolescents in particular mistakenly treat confounded data as being conclusive. Recall that in one of their studies, subjects who were shown that, for example, type of texture covaried with degree of bounce in sports balls concluded that texture was a causal factor even though type of texture itself covaried perfectly (that is, was perfectly confounded) with, for example, color.[1]

Nevertheless, in spite of the congruence of our findings and Kuhn et al.'s, we were not confident of our results, for two reasons. One is that, as I argued in chapters 2 and 3, we were not confident of D. Kuhn et al.'s (1988) results. Their results may have occurred because, outside of the laboratory, even adolescents have learned that color (unless it is an index of some deeper causal property) is, indeed, irrelevant to how well a ball will bounce; there is no plausible causal mechanism that can explain how color could affect bounce. I suggested that their subjects' behavior did not reflect an insensitivity to confounding. Rather, it reflected the kind of assessment of plausibility that is reasonable scientific practice. Therefore, we did not treat as bolstering our results the fact that our results were congruent with those of Kuhn et al.

The other reason we questioned the validity of our finding that subjects did not distinguish controlled from confounded data had to do with a flaw in our own experimental design. Consider the information that specified (and which we had expected to distinguish) the controlled from the confounded conditions: As I noted in chapter 4, with the clarity of hindsight, we realized that in the confounded condition of experiment 2, chapter 4, it was in fact not very clear that confounded factors had been operating; one had to infer this from the fact that specific controls were not explicitly mentioned.

Thus in experiment 2 we could not distinguish between two alternatives: One was that subjects failed to distinguish the confounded and controlled conditions because they did not infer that the confounded condition had, in fact, been confounded. The other was that subjects did infer confounding but did not regard it as being causally problematic. Therefore, one aim of this study was to see whether, when confounding was made explicit, subjects would judge data that resulted from a confounded design to be less conclusive than data that resulted from a controlled design. That is, one motive for the present study was to examine subjects' awareness of internal validity.

The second motive for this experiment was to examine subjects' beliefs about external validity. In this regard, we had two specific questions. One was the straightforward question of whether subjects would realize that the presence of external validity would make it more likely that the results of a study could be generalized to a new sample. (A corollary question was whether subjects would also treat a controlled design as making it more likely than a confounded design that the results would generalize to a new sample.)

The other question was whether subjects conflated external and internal validity and therefore mistakenly believed that external validity (by minimizing confounding) would increase the likelihood of attaining internal validity. This question was suggested by some of the adolescents' justifications in experiment 2. For the story problems in experiment 2, we did not specify whether the large samples were externally valid. However, subjects frequently assumed that they were; that is, they assumed that, for example, the cars in the gasoline problem were of more than one type. As a result, in the large-sample condition, some adolescents gave justifications of the following sort, "Well it was probably the gas [that accounted for the difference in mileage]. It could be that all the cars that got good mileage [and that used the old gasoline] were Toyotas or something like that and all the cars that got bad mileage [and that used the new gas] were big Buicks, but with all those different cars, you wouldn't have all the cars that used the old gas all being Toyotas." This subject was clearly aware of an alternative factor that could have been systematically confounded with the target factor and that could have explained the low mileage: it could have been type of car rather than type of gasoline. However, the subject seemed also to think that the variety of cars sampled would insure that the confounding would be taken care of, that is, not be systematic: "You wouldn't have all the cars that used the old gas all being Toyotas."[2] (But, of course, in the natural-occurrence condition, even if type of car had been ruled out as an alternative, the possibility would still remain of other systematic confounding. The drivers who chose one type of gas could have had different driving patterns, kept their cars differentially maintained, etc.)

In short, some subjects gave justifications that suggested that the notions of external and internal validity were not clearly distinguished. Subjects seemed to be aware that they should be concerned about alternative causes (which is a question of internal validity), but they seemed mistakenly to think that having variety in the sample (external validity) would take care of that problem. We wanted to examine more directly the relation, for adolescents, between internal and external validity.

To address the two aims of the present study, we asked subjects to evaluate covariations that resulted from various sorts of experiments. In some of the experiments, the designs were controlled, while in others they were confounded. In some of the experiments, the samples were homogenous, and therefore had little external validity, while in others the samples were varied.

We wanted to avoid Kuhn et al.'s (1988) difficulties caused by having the confounded factor be implausible. Therefore, for each story, we arranged to have both the target factor and the confounding factor be plausible possible causes.

Subjects were presented with story problems in which a target factor (for example, type of gasoline: regular versus additive) covaried with a particular effect (for example, mileage). In all the story problems the sample size was analogous to the large-sample condition in experiment 2: there were four pairs of instances (in this example, four pairs of cars), with one member of each pair being in the treatment group (additive gasoline) and one member in the control group (regular gasoline). In the controlled condition, it was made explicit that the pairs were matched on relevant factors, so the two members of a pair were extremely similar with the only relevant difference being whether the member received the experimental treatment. In the confounded condition, it was made equally explicit that the treatment and control groups differed in terms of two

factors: the target factor and an additional factor systematically confounded with the target factor. Within each of these two conditions
(controlled versus confounded), subjects were also presented with information about external validity. When external validity was present, the
pairs of instances varied (for example, one pair of small Hondas, one pair
of large Chevys, etc.). When external validity was absent, the four pairs of
instances were all the same (e.g., four pairs of small Hondas).

Questions about whether x causes y are ambiguous between "Did x
cause y this time?" and "Does x cause y in general, in a lot of circumstances?" Therefore, when we questioned our subjects, we asked two separate questions: one was about whether x caused y for the four pairs of
instances that were actually studied; the other asked about whether the
results from the four pairs could be generalized to a new instance. In
short, we explicitly distinguished our question about internal validity
from our question about external validity.

Because we were making the confounding very explicit in the natural-
occurrence condition and because the confounding factor was a plausible
cause, we expected that, in contrast to experiment 2, subjects at each age
(even sixth-graders) would indeed judge the confounded data to be less
conclusive than the controlled data. However, we wanted to anticipate
the possibility—though we thought it remote—that even with the confounding made explicit, subjects would still fail to see the confounded
design as flawed. Therefore, after subjects had been interviewed on all of
the story problems, we returned to each of the story problems to ask two
additional questions. Both questions were couched in terms of what the
problem solver in the story believed (to make it more likely that we were
measuring subjects' cognitive evaluation of the evidence rather than their
emotional commitment to the conclusions that they themselves had earlier
reached). The first additional question described the problem solver's conclusions about the internal validity of the study. (Depending on the condition, the problem solver concluded either that the target factor was the
only difference between the two groups and was therefore probably the
causal factor, or that the target factor was confounded with another factor
and therefore one could not tell whether it was causal). The second additional question summarized the problem solver's views about the external
validity of the study. (Depending on the condition, the problem solver
either could not generalize the results because the study was confounded
and/or the sample was very restricted or could generalize the results
because the study was controlled and the sample was extremely varied.)
After each of the additional questions, we asked the subject whether she
thought the problem solver's conclusions were right or wrong.

Given that the confounded factors in the present study were both plausible possible causes, we expected that even the adolescents would judge

confounded data to be less conclusive than controlled data. We also expected that subjects would judge the results of the initial study to be more likely to generalize to a new situation when the sample was varied rather than homogeneous, that is, when external validity was present rather than absent. Finally, we expected that adolescents would treat external validity and internal validity as being related, although we did not have clear expectations about what the nature of the relation would be. The sorts of comments subjects had made in experiment 2, chapter 4, suggested that adolescents might treat external validity as actually compensating for a lack of internal validity, that is, as being a reason for increasing causal ratings in the confounded condition. However, if, as we expected, even adolescents had a robust understanding that controlled data are more convincing than confounded data, then one might expect that for adolescents, even external validity would not salvage a confounded study. Instead, one might expect that external validity would increase causal ratings only if internal validity were already present, that is, that it would increase causal ratings only when the design was controlled to begin with.

Method

Materials
The six story problems used in experiment 2 were modified for use in this study. The appendix to this experiment presents one of the story problems as it appeared in two of the conditions (controlled, external validity present and confounded, external validity absent). The stories all followed the same format in each of the conditions.

As can be seen in the appendix, each story began with a description of a problem situation in which an individual was trying to find out whether a target factor (e.g., a new kind of gasoline) was likely to be causally related to a particular effect (improved mileage). This part of the experiment was the same in all conditions. Following this, a method section described the strategy that the problem solver had used to gain information. In all stories, the problem solver examined four pairs of instances, each pair having one treatment and one control member (e.g., for each pair of cars, one used regular gasoline and one used the gasoline with an additive).

The rest of the information in the method section varied across the four conditions: (controlled versus confounded) × (external validity present versus external validity absent). In the controlled condition, subjects were told that several alternative causes had been controlled for. In the confounded condition, variation in the target factor (type of gas) was confounded with variation in another factor (type of car). When external validity was present, the method section made it clear that different types of pairs had been examined. When external validity was absent, subjects were told the problem solver had restricted himself to only one pair type.

After the prose description of the method, the same information was presented in tabular form. For three of the stories, the treatment group was in the right column; for the other three, the treatment group was in the left column.

For three of the stories, the treatment group had a lower score on the dependent measure than the control group (e.g., the cars that received the additive gasoline got worse mileage), and for three stories, the treatment group had higher scores. The results section was constant across conditions and noted that the treatment instances differed from the control instances.

After the results information, subjects were asked a series of four questions, each accompanied by a rating scale. The first asked, for the four pairs of instances studied, how likely it was that the treatment-control difference (in mileage) had occurred because of the target factor (type of gasoline) or because of some other reason. The second question reminded subjects of the method and results and asked how likely it was that the target factor would bring about the same difference in a sample that had not been represented in the study.

The third and fourth questions described what the problem-solver in the story believed about questions 1 and 2 and asked the extent to which the subject agreed or disagreed with the problem solver. (Recall that the third and fourth questions were not asked until after subjects had answered questions 1 and 2 for all three story problems.)

Procedure

All subjects (including college students) were interviewed individually. Both interviewer and subject looked at the story problem while the interviewer read it aloud and the subject read it silently. When subjects gave truncated answers (e.g., "It seems reasonable"), their answers were followed up with nondirective probes ("Could you say a bit more?").

I draw attention to two other points about the procedure. One is that the subject was not given questions 3 and 4 until she had completed all three story problems. We wanted to make certain that the subject was not exposed to the problem solver's answers to questions 1 and 2 until after the subject had given her own answers to these questions for each of the story problems.

The second point is that we conducted individual interviews in a way that minimized potential information-processing problems (see experiment 8). We did this by relying heavily on repetition, amplification, and pointing. For example, when an interviewer was reading the method section, she would accompany each line with appropriate pointing to the table. Thus when four car dealers were mentioned, the interviewer would point to column 1 in the table and repeat, "Here are the four dealers, dealer 1, dealer 2, etc." Similar pointing and repetition accompanied the rest of the story. For example, when the interviewer read that some cars were given regular gasoline and some the additive, she would first point to column 2 in the table and say, "These cars were given the regular gasoline," and would then point to column 3 and say, "These cars were given the additive gasoline."

In the confounded condition, we wanted to measure not whether subjects were picking up on the confounding but rather whether they were judging the confounding to be a problem. Therefore, after the interviewer had read the description of the method, she would summarize, while pointing to the relevant sections in the table, in the following, very explicit way: "So this group of cars was given the regular gasoline, and these cars were also small; and this group over here was given the additive gasoline, and these cars were also large. And the ones that were large and that got the additive gasoline also got worse mileage," and the interviewer would then write "worse" under the second group of cars.

Analogous repetition, amplification, and pointing also occurred when reading the questions and the summaries that preceded them. With questions 2 and 4, we took special care to emphasize: "Now John is asking about a *different* kind of car. He's no longer asking about these eight cars over *here* (pointing); he's asking about these cars over *here* (pointing). Will type of gasoline make a difference for *these* two cars?"

Design

There were three between-subjects variables: age, sex, and design type (controlled versus confounded). The within-subject variables were external-validity status (external validity present versus external validity absent) and story.

Because of the length of time required to complete an interview about a single story problem, each subject was interviewed about only three stories. Therefore, within each age × sex × design type group, half the subjects received one story in the external-validity-present condition and two stories in the external-validity-absent condition, while for the other subjects, one story was in the external-validity-absent condition and two were in the external-validity-present condition. To construct the story combinations within each age × sex × design type group, we used a balanced incomplete-block design in which each story (in each external-validity condition) was presented with each other story (in each external-validity condition) an equal number of times but in which each subject was presented with only three stories. There were 12 subjects within each of the twelve age × sex × design type groups, yielding a total of 48 subjects (24 males and 24 females) at each age.

Results and Discussion

For each of the four questions separately, responses were analyzed with an age × sex × design type × external validity status × story analysis of variance.

Question 1: assessments of causation

Controlled versus confounded designs   Recall that the first question asked subjects how likely it was that the target factor had caused the effect in the sample actually studied.[3] And as figure 6.1 illustrates, subjects were much more likely to infer causation when the design was controlled rather than confounded, $F(1, 216) = 209$, $p = .0001$. When the design was confounded, causal ratings were closer to the indeterminate rating of 5 (x may or may not have caused y).

Furthermore, from the lack of a significant interaction of design type and age, we can infer that even the sixth-graders found a controlled design more indicative of causation than a confounded design. In light of D. Kuhn et al.'s (1988) data, the ability to distinguish controlled from confounded designs was most unexpected for the sixth-graders. Therefore, we also tested this difference for sixth-graders directly and found that it too was highly significant, $F(1, 216) = 44$, $p = .0001$. In short, even for the youngest subjects, confounded designs were seen as problematic with respect to inferring causation.

Internal and external validity   There was also a three-way interaction of grade × design type × external validity, $F(2, 216) = 4.4$, $p = .01$. As can be seen in figure 6.1, when the design was controlled to begin with, sixth-graders (in contrast to college students) judged causation to be more likely when external validity was present rather than absent, $F(1, 216) = 6.64$, $p = .01$. That is, in spite of some subjects' justifications in experiment 2, sixth-graders did not treat external validity as compensating for the absence of internal validity. However, they did treat external validity as enhancing the likelihood of causation when internal validity was present to begin with.

Thus, the question to be explained is why external validity enhanced internal validity for adolescents but not for college students. In light of the subjects' justifications, I suggest the following working hypothesis: The college students were answering the question we actually asked them, namely, "Did the target factor play a causal role *in the particular*

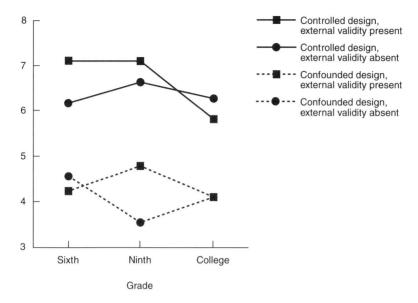

Figure 6.1
Question 1 ratings as a function of grade, design type, and external-validity status.

sample studied?" And for this question, external validity is irrelevant. What was relevant was internal validity, the fact that the target factor was the only difference between the two groups.

The younger subjects, in contrast, were concerning themselves with this question but also with another question, which we did not ask, about the general causal picture. Specifically, the younger subjects were concerned with whether, beyond the confines of the target experiment, the target factor is an important cause or merely a minor one. And it is this that makes external validity relevant. When a younger subject learns that gas with an additive produced worse mileage in four different sorts of cars, she treats this as evidence that the target cause is important enough to operate across many situations. However, when she learns that external validity is absent, she wonders whether the target factor is merely a minor cause that operates only in cars of a certain sort. Witness comments like "Maybe it works but only for BMWs" or "Maybe with other kinds of cars it wouldn't work as well."

The three-way interaction also reflects the fact that when the design was confounded, the difference in ratings when external validity was present versus when it was absent was greater for the ninth-graders than for the other two age groups. An admittedly ad hoc hypothesis is that, just as sixth-graders concerned themselves with the general causal picture when the design was controlled, ninth-graders concerned themselves with the general causal picture when the design was confounded. For ninth-graders, the absence of external validity made the target factor less likely to be a major cause and therefore less likely to be causal in the general scheme of things. In contrast, the presence of external validity made the target factor more likely to be a major cause and therefore made it harder to choose between the target factor and the confounded factor, which resulted in a score closer to the indeterminate 5. (A somewhat similar finding occurred in response to question 4, below.)

Question 3: agreement with statements about control versus confounding

Recall that in the third question, we asked whether subjects would agree with the problem solver's conclusions about controlled versus confounded designs.[4] (When the design was controlled, the problem solver argued that the target factor was the only difference between the two groups and was therefore probably the causal factor. When the design was confounded, the problem solver argued that one could not tell whether the target factor or the confounding factor was the cause.)

As figure 6.2 illustrates, subjects' agreement with the problem solver's statements depended on whether the design was controlled or confounded, $F(1, 216) = 12.2$, $p = .0006$, but the effect varied with age, $F(2, 216) = 37.5$, $p = .0001$.

I draw attention to two features of the results. First, consider the condition in which the design is controlled and external validity is absent. As figure 6.2 illustrates, in this condition, the age groups were roughly comparable in the extent to which they agreed with the problem solvers' conclusions that the target factor was probably causal because it was the only difference between the two groups. In the controlled conditions, the one age difference was that sixth-graders, in contrast to college students, were even more likely to agree that the relation was causal when external validity was present rather than absent, $F(1, 216) = 4.14$, $p = .04$. That is, as with the parallel ratings for question 1, for sixth-graders, external validity enhanced causation so long as internal validity was already present.

I argue that this age difference reflects the adolescents' greater tendency to be concerned with the general causal picture. External validity enhances adolescents' assessments of causation because it indicates that the target cause is important enough to operate across many situations, that it is important not only in the target experiment but also relative to other causal factors in general.

The second point I draw attention to is the age difference in the extent to which subjects agreed with the problem solvers' statements that a confounded design was inconclusive. The college students agreed with this

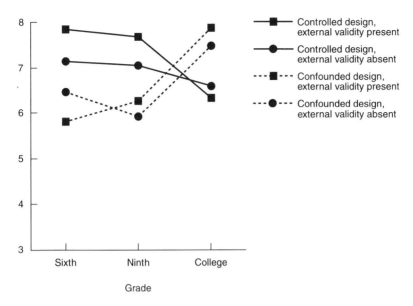

Figure 6.2
Question 3 ratings as a function of grade, design type, and external-validity status.

statement, rating it roughly between 7 and 8. The ratings of the adolescents, in contrast, hovered around 6, that is, were close to the midpoint, which indicated that the problem solver might be right or might be wrong in concluding that causation was indeterminate. This result is surprising, given the fact that in question 1 all age groups judged controlled designs to permit causal conclusions and confounded designs to yield indeterminate conclusions. Therefore, there must have been some feature of the wording in the two questions in the confounded condition that accounts for the difference.

Question 1 asks about the subject's causal conclusion and stresses with gestures and words that the subject's conclusion should be restricted to what she learned about the particular instances in the target experiment. And when the conclusion is thus restricted, the adolescents (like the college students) conclude that in the confounded condition, causation is indeterminate. Question 3, in contrast, asks about the problem solver's mental state and does so in what was, in retrospect, a misleading way. The problem solver's conclusion in question 3 was the same as the subjects' conclusions in question 1: the problem solver feels that causation is indeterminate. But the subject is asked to rate whether the problem solver (not the problem solver's conclusion) was right or wrong. And because of the wording, the problem solver could be construed as concluding that he cannot *ever* identify the cause. This shifts the focus of the question away from what could be learned from the particular instances in the target experiment to what the problem solver could learn *in principle* by not restricting himself to the target experiment alone. And in principle, the problem solver certainly could learn what the cause was; he would simply have to gather a different kind of data. Witness comments like, "He could probably find out what did it. He'd just need to look at different cars." Therefore, adolescents, misled by unclear working, found less compelling than the college students did the problem solver's conclusion that in the confounded condition, he "cannot tell" what the cause was. Maybe he could tell if he just worked at it a bit.

In short, the age groups are roughly comparable in agreeing with the statement that controlled designs make causation more likely. However, sixth-graders find this conclusion especially compelling when external validity is present (and this echoes the question 1 ratings). When internal validity is already present, external validity indicates that the cause is important enough to operate across many situations.

Question 2: assessments of generalizability

Question 2 asked subjects to rate how likely it was that the results of a study could be generalized to a new sample.[5] The results of the target experiment were seen as more likely to be generalizable when external validity was present rather than absent, $F(1, 216) = 5.7, p = .017$. And the effects of external validity were not significantly different for the three age groups, $F(2, 216) = .6, p = .5$.

Furthermore, the results were more likely to be seen as generalizable if the initial design had been controlled rather than confounded, $F(1, 215) = 22, p = .0001$, and there was no significant interaction of design type with age, $F(2, 216) = .3, p = .7$. That is, not only did all age groups find that confounding was problematic for inferring causation about the original sample (as was evident from the question 1 ratings), but they also judged confounding in the original sample to be problematic for generalizing to a new sample.

In short, subjects' understanding of confounding is robust: It includes an awareness not only that confounding limits internal validity (question 1) but also that it limits generalizability. And conversely, subjects also understand that external validity increases generalizability.

Question 4: agreement with statements about external validity

In the fourth question, we asked whether subjects would agree with the problem solver's statements about generalizability to a new sample.[6] (Recall that, when the design was controlled, the problem solver argued that generalizability was more likely when the sample was heterogeneous

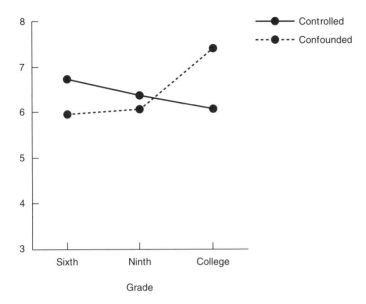

Figure 6.3
Question 4 ratings as a function of grade and design type.

rather than homogenous. When the design was confounded, the argument was that it was simply not clear whether x would cause y in a new sample because it was not clear that x had caused y in the initial sample.)

Ratings depended on the interaction of design type and age, $F(2, 216) = 15.17$, $p = .0001$. As figure 6.3 indicates, when the initial design was controlled, the three age groups were comparably likely to agree with the statement that the results would generalize to a new sample. However, when the initial design was confounded, younger subjects were less likely than college students to agree with the statement that because causation was indeterminate in the initial sample, it was not clear that the target factor would be causal in a new sample.

What was striking and, to us, counterintuitive was that for sixth-graders and for college students, external validity had no significant effect on judgments about generalizability. That is, considerations of generalizability to a new sample were based on internal rather than external validity.

Thus the results from question 4 were parallel to the results from question 3. When the design was a controlled one, the age groups were roughly comparable in agreeing that the results would generalize to a new sample. However, when the initial design was confounded, adolescents found less compelling than college students did the problem solver's

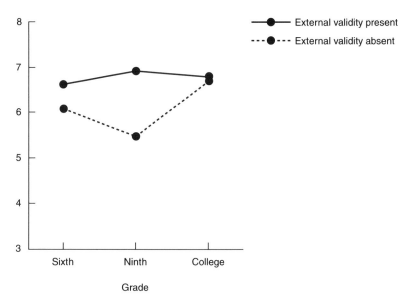

Figure 6.4
Question 4 ratings as a function of grade and external-validity status.

statement that he "cannot tell" whether the results would generalize. Like the ratings for question 3, the question 4 ratings make sense if one recognizes that the wording was ambiguous, with the result that the college students were focusing on the target experiment and the younger subjects were concerning themselves with what the problem solver could do in principle. Because of their qualitative responses, I suggest that, in the confounded condition, the younger subjects reasoned that if many pieces of information were considered, not just the results of the target experiment, the problem solver probably could determine whether the results would generalize.

Ratings for question 4 were also affected by external-validity status, $F(1, 216) = 9.87$, $p = .0019$, but the effects varied with age, $F(2, 216) = 4.17$, $p = .016$, and as one can see in figure 6.4, this interaction was due largely to the ninth-graders' ratings when external validity was absent, and in this regard, it was similar to the ratings for question 1. The ratings of the sixth-graders were not significantly different from those of the college students, $F(1, 216) = 1.27$, $p = .26$. However, as with the question 1 ratings, although we had not anticipated this, the ratings of the ninth-graders differed significantly from the ratings of the other two age groups averaged together, $F(1, 216) = 7.07$, $p = .0084$. I suggest, as I did earlier, that the absence of external validity triggered the ninth-graders' concern with the general causal picture. However, this suggestion is definitely ad hoc.

General Discussion

I draw attention to several points.

Internal validity
Perhaps the most salient point is that at all ages, even among six-graders, confounded data are treated as being more problematic than controlled data with respect to drawing causal conclusions about experimental results (question 1). These results are in striking contrast to D. Kuhn et al.'s (1988) findings that people in general and adolescents in particular have trouble realizing that confounded data are causally inconclusive. As noted earlier, I attribute the difference to plausibility. In Kuhn et al.'s study, one of the confounded factors was one that subjects had antecedently identified as being an implausible cause. In the present study, both of the confounded factors were plausible possible causes. I argue that not taking account of implausible confounded factors is congruent with sound scientific practice; it is what allows one appropriately to dismiss some correlations as noise or random error.

Am I arguing that implausible correlations ought never to be taken seriously? Certainly not. To begin with, one's judgments about what is plausible and what is not could be wrong. Furthermore, in some situations, correlations serve to correct mistaken estimates of plausibility by causing us to take a second look at correlations that we initially thought to be implausible. (Indeed, in experiments 9 and 10, chapter 8, we see that subjects do, in fact, sometimes take seriously implausible correlations. However, as we will see in experiments 9 and 10, they do so judiciously rather than mechanically or at random.) Rather, what I am arguing is that it would be mistaken to assume an insensitivity to confounded data simply on the basis of situations in which one of the confounded factors is (or is antecedently thought to be) an implausible cause at the outset.

The present results dovetail with the findings from Bullock's (1991) "lantern" study, described in chapter 2. Recall that in that study, subjects were asked to test whether having a roof makes lanterns less likely to go out in the wind. In that study, when presented with a set of instances that could be used to answer the question, even most fourth-graders chose instances in which everything was held constant except the presence of a roof. In the present study, when presented with a confounded design, even sixth-graders understood that the design was problematic. In addition, even the sixth-graders realized that the absence of internal validity, which resulted from a confounded design, could not be compensated for by the presence of external validity—a finding to which we now turn.

The relation of internal and external validity

At all ages, whether or not subjects generalized from the initial sample to a new sample was certainly affected by whether or not the initial sample was a heterogeneous one (question 2). But it was also affected by whether or not the initial sample was confounded (question 2). That is, at all ages, subjects were aware that, even when external validity was present, results that were suspect to begin with (because the design was confounded) could not easily be generalized. In short, at all ages, the absence of internal validity, which resulted from a confounded design, could not be compensated for by the presence of external validity. This shows a very robust appreciation of the advantages of control over confounding.

However, in spite of their appreciation of controlled designs, adolescents nevertheless did not treat internal validity as being totally independent of external validity. When the design was a controlled one to begin with, adolescents (but not college students) were more likely to infer causation when the sample was heterogenous rather than homogeneous (question 1). That is, although adolescents did not treat external validity as compensating for the absence of internal validity, they did treat external validity as enhancing the likelihood of causation when internal validity was present to begin with.

I suggested the working hypothesis that the older subjects are restricting themselves to the question that we actually asked: whether the target factor was playing a causal role in the particular sample studied. And for this question, it was internal validity that was relevant and not external validity. The sixth-graders, in contrast, were concerning themselves with this question but also with an additional question that we did not ask, one about the general causal picture in which the target factor may have been operating. In this framework, external validity was relevant because it demonstrated that in the general scheme of things, the target factor was important enough that it operated across many situations.

It would be easy to use this argument as an excuse for dismissing this age difference on the grounds that the sixth-graders had simply not understood our question and were therefore "not playing our game." However, the sixth-graders certainly understood at least some of the presentation to be able to conclude, as the college students did, that controlled designs are more convincing than confounded designs (question 1). Therefore, from my perspective, their answers suggest not simply a misunderstanding of our question but rather a possible limitation on the way sixth-graders assess the data from particular experiments. Their answers suggest that when sixth-graders treat experimental data as a single piece of a larger puzzle, attention to the other pieces of the puzzle might make it difficult for them to assess the results of a particular experiment in isolation.

The coordination of theory and evidence
Finally, consider again our finding (from questions 1 and 2) that when two factors are confounded, even sixth-graders recognize that causation is indeterminate, provided that the confounded factors are both plausible causes. Is this finding compatible with D. Kuhn's et al.'s (1988) argument that people have trouble coordinating theory (about what is plausible) and evidence (about what is confounded)? We think not.

Kuhn et al.'s basic finding is that people ignore a confounded factor if they have theoretical reasons to believe that the factor is causally irrelevant. However, Kuhn et al. treat this as the *absence* of an ability to coordinate theory and evidence, because theoretical considerations lead people to dismiss a certain type of evidence (namely, evidence of a confounding factor) as insignificant. I recognize this finding but also add an additional one, namely that people do take account of confounding if they have theoretical reasons to believe that both confounded factors are potentially causally relevant. I treat these findings, taken together, as indicating the *presence* of an ability to coordinate theory and evidence because they indicate that subjects are relying on theoretical considerations to decide that some possible causes are plausible and ought to be taken seriously while others are implausible and ought properly to be dismissed as noise (unless there are, as we will see in experiments 9 and 10, compelling reasons for taking them seriously). That is, on my view, neither theory nor evidence are evaluated in isolation; rather, they are coordinated in that consideration of one informs decisions of how to evaluate the other.

In short, on D. Kuhn et al.'s view, ignoring an implausible cause because of theoretical considerations reflects the absence of an ability to coordinate theory and evidence, and the absence is problematic. On my view, ignoring an implausible possible cause because of theoretical considerations but taking seriously a plausible possible cause, also because of theoretical considerations, reflects the presence of an ability to coordinate theory and evidence (because it involves relying on theory to decide which evidence to take seriously). And on my view, far from being problematic, this is in fact scientifically legitimate.

Relevance to confirmation bias
The fact that confounded data were treated as more problematic than controlled data suggests the absence of a confirmation bias. Had subjects been

relying on a confirmation bias when evaluating the target account, one would not have expected them to lower their ratings when confounding factors were present. However, they did. Nevertheless, one could argue that subjects' behavior was not relevant to the question of confirmation bias, because the target accounts had not been proposed by the subjects themselves. We will return to this issue in experiments 13, 14, and 15, chapters 10 and 11.

Science as bootstrapping

Finally, the results of this experiment illustrate a more general claim about scientific practice, namely that following the principles of scientific inquiry does not guarantee success. In the present experiment, subjects took the confounding factors seriously precisely because they had theories according to which the confounding factors were plausible causes. However, if the subjects' theories had been mistaken (or if the subjects had held no beliefs one way or another about the confounding factors), then they might well have judged the confounding to be irrelevant, and their judgment would have been mistaken. (See Schauble 1990 for a compatible view.)

In a word, since the world is rife with correlations, it is impossible to take them all seriously. Therefore, one rule of thumb congruent with the principles of scientific inquiry is to take seriously those that are plausible. However, this rule of thumb yields success only to the extent that beliefs about what is plausible are approximately correct. That is, relying on the principles of scientific inquiry makes us more likely to get the right answer to the extent that the background beliefs that we use in conjunction with the principles are approximately true. This point will be taken up again in the last chapter.

In the following chapter, I address the other side of bootstrapping, namely how it is that following the principles of scientific inquiry can help us discover beliefs that are approximately correct.

Appendix to Experiment 6

Condition: controlled, heterogeneous sample

Problem   Larry wants to know, Does gasoline with a special additive make cars get worse mileage?

Method   Larry talks to four used car dealers. Larry asks each dealer to choose two cars. The cars are similar and are similar types. One car gets regular gasoline; the other gets the gasoline with the additive.

Dealer	Regular gasoline	Gasoline with additive
1	Small Honda	Small Honda
2	Small Volkswagen	Small Volkswagen
3	Large Chevy	Large Chevy
4	Large BMW	Large BMW

Results   For each dealer, the car that got the *additive* gasoline got *worse* mileage.

Question 1   Think about these eight cars. Do you think one group got worse mileage because of the gasoline or for some other reason?

1	2	3	4	5	6	7	8	9
Definitely for some other reason		Probably for some other reason		May or may *not* be because of gasoline		Probably because of gasoline		Definitely because of gasoline

Why?

Question 2   Think again about the evidence:

1. The dealers sold four different types of cars.
2. For each dealer, the cars were as similar as possible.
3. For each type of car, the car that got the additive gasoline got worse mileage.

Larry now plans to drive a different car—a Ford. None of the cars already studied was a Ford. Given what the four dealers found, do you think a Ford would also get worse mileage if it used the additive gasoline?

1	2	3	4	5	6	7	8	9
Definitely for some other reason		Probably for some other reason		May or may *not* be because of gasoline		Probably because of gasoline		Definitely because of gasoline

Why?

[New page]

Question 3   Think again about the evidence: Larry decides that it *was* the additive gasoline that made some cars get better mileage than the others. He remembers that the cars in the two groups were similar and were similar types. Since the *only* difference between the groups was that one had the additive gasoline and one did not, Larry decides that it must have been the additive gasoline that made one group get worse mileage. Do you think he's right or wrong? Why?

1	2	3	4	5	6	7	8	9
Definitely wrong		Probably wrong		May be right; may be wrong		Probably right		Definitely right

Question 4   Larry also decides that the additive gasoline would probably also make a Ford get worse mileage. He decides that because so many different kinds of cars got worse mile-

age with the additive gasoline, Fords would also probably get worse mileage with the additive gasoline. Do you think he's right or wrong? Why?

1	2	3	4	5	6	7	8	9
Definitely wrong		Probably wrong		May be right; may be wrong		Probably right		Definitely right

Condition: confounded, homogeneous sample

Problem   Larry wants to know, Does gasoline with a special additive make cars get worse mileage?

Method   Larry talks to four used car dealers. Larry asks each dealer to choose two cars. Some cars are small; others are large. Some cars use regular gasoline; others use the gasoline with the additive.

Dealer	Regular gasoline	Gasoline with additive
1	Small BMW	Large BMW
2	Small BMW	Large BMW
3	Small BMW	Large BMW
4	Small BMW	Large BMW

Results   The cars that used the *additive* gasoline got *worse* mileage.

Question 1   Think about these eight cars. Do you think one group got worse mileage because of the gasoline or for some other reason?

1	2	3	4	5	6	7	8	9
Definitely for some other reason		Probably for some other reason		May or may *not* be because of gasoline		Probably because of gasoline		Definitely because of gasoline

Why?

Question 2   Think about the evidence:

1. The cars were the same type.
2. The cars that got the additive gasoline were larger.
3. The cars that got the additive gasoline got worse mileage.

Larry now plans to drive a different car—a Ford. None of the cars already studied was a Ford. Given what the four dealers found, do you think a Ford would also get worse mileage if it used the additive gasoline?

1	2	3	4	5	6	7	8	9
Definitely would *not* get worse		Probably would *not* get worse		May or may *not* get worse mileage		Probably would get worse mileage		Definitely would get worse mileage

Why?

[New page]

Question 3   Think again about the evidence: Larry decides that he can*not* tell whether the additive gasoline made some cars get worse mileage than the others. He remembers that the cars that used the additive gasoline also were larger than the others. Therefore, he decides that he cannot tell whether they got worse mileage because they used the additive gasoline or because they were larger. Do you think he's right or wrong? Why?

1	2	3	4	5	6	7	8	9
Definitely wrong		Probably wrong		May be right; may be wrong		Probably right		Definitely right

Question 4   Larry also decides that he can*not* tell whether the additive gasoline would make a Ford get worse mileage. The cars that got the additive gasoline also were larger than the others. Therefore, he cannot tell whether these cars got worse mileage because they used the additive gasoline or because they were larger. Since he cannot tell whether it was the additive gasoline thaat made the *other* cars get worse mileage, he also decides he cannot tell whether the additive gasoline would make Fords get worse mileage. Do you think he's right or wrong? Why?

1	2	3	4	5	6	7	8	9
Definitely wrong		Probably wrong		May be right; may be wrong		Probably right		Definitely right

General Summary

Our main aim in carrying out this study was to test our hypothesis that in drawing causal conclusions, even sixth-graders would treat confounded data as more problematic and inconclusive than controlled data. And they did. I suggest that the difference between our findings and those of D. Kuhn et al. (1988) is that in our study the confounding factor was itself a plausible cause, whereas in Kuhn et al.'s study, the confounding factor was (or was judged to be) implausible. I argue that not taking account of implausible confounded factors is congruent with sound scientific practice; it is what allows one appropriately to dismiss some correlations as noise. (In experiments 9 and 10, chapter 8, I address the question of when implausible correlations should be taken seriously.)

Furthermore, even sixth-graders' appreciation of control is robust. When the design is confounded to begin with, then even with a heterogeneous sample, the results are treated as being less generalizable than the results of a controlled experiment. That is, even for sixth-graders, external validity cannot salvage a design that lacks internal validity.

Nevertheless, there is a sense in which the sixth-graders' approach to issues of control and confounding is different from that of the college students. One is that, when the design is a controlled one to begin with, sixth-graders, but not college students, are more likely to infer causation when the sample is heterogeneous rather than homogeneous. That is, although external validity cannot salvage a design that lacks internal validity, external validity can, for sixth-graders, enhance the likelihood of causation if internal validity is already present. I suggest that sixth-graders are not restricting themselves to the question of whether the target factor was operating in a particular experiment. Rather, they are also concerned with whether the target factor plays an important role in the general causal picture. And for this concern, external validity is relevant because it indicates that the target factor is important enough that it operates across many situations.

In trying to explain the difference between our results and those of D. Kuhn et al. (1988), I have argued that dismissing implausible correlates (even when they covaried perfectly with the target cause) was a reasonable way of keeping noise at bay. However, I also acknowledged that sometimes noise should not be ignored, because it reflects causal relations that have yet to be discovered. The question of when to ignore the noise of implausible covariation and when to take it seriously (that is, the question of what makes implausible covariation plausible) is a question that will be addressed in the next two chapters.

Chapter 7
Evaluating Explanations in Light of Alternative Accounts

In this chapter I return to the general issue, also addressed in experiments 1 and 6, chapters 4 and 6, regarding the effect of ruling out competing alternative accounts.

Recall the general point that in scientific inquiry, possible causes are evaluated not in isolation but rather in the context of rival alternative accounts: Possible causes are judged as more likely to be actual causes to the extent that competing causes are ruled out. Conversely, they are more likely to be judged as indeterminate if alternative causes remain in the running.

In experiment 6 we examined this point in the context of confounding: we found that if an alternative cause is confounded with the target cause so that both are viable possible causes, then the target is seen as more likely to be indeterminate than if the alternative is ruled out or controlled for. Similarly, in experiment 1 the target cause was more likely to be judged to be causal when several alternative causes had been ruled out than when the alternatives remained as competitors.

Experiment 7
Barbara Koslowski, Patricia Bence, Nancy Herse

In experiment 7 we had two aims. One was to examine the effects of control versus confounding in another context. In experiment 6 the problem solver began with a possible causal factor and tried to discover whether it produced a particular effect. In the present experiment the problem solver began with an effect and tried to work backward to identify the likely cause. In experiment 6 the subject was presented with information about several instances of a contrast. In the present experiment each story problem reported a single instance. It was conceivable that a single instance would be treated as such weak initial evidence of causality that ruling out alternatives would have little additional effect. Alternatively, it was possible that even a single instance would be treated as requiring explanation and therefore that ruling out alternatives would make the target account seem more likely to be causal. To examine the effects of control versus confounding, the target possible cause in some of the story problems was confounded with an alternative, while in other story problems the alternatives were controlled for. In addition, in contrast to the unusual target causes in experiment 1 but like the target causes in experiment 6, the target causes in this experiment were fairly usual possible causes.

The second question asked whether the effects of ruling out alternative hypotheses interacts with information about causal mechanisms. To examine this question, for half the subjects in the controlled and in the confounded conditions, a possible mechanism was present that could explain how the target factor had produced the effect, while for the other half of the subjects, there was no mention made of a mechanism that might have been operating. In line with the arguments set out in the first three chapters and in line with the results of experiments 1 and 2, chapter 4, we expected that the presence of a mechanism would make the target accounts more likely to appear causal.

We also expected that the presence of a mechanism would have a greater effect when alternatives were still present rather than ruled out. We speculated that for target factors that are "usual causes" (as they were in the present experiment), if competing causes have already been ruled out, this in itself might increase ratings of the remaining target factor to such an extent that the additional presence of a possible mechanism might have only a negligible additional effect. In contrast, when competing factors are still viable alternatives, then the presence of a possible mechanism might give the target factor a causal edge over its competitors.

Methods and Procedures

Materials
Six story problems were constructed, one about differences within each of the following areas: gas mileage, hospital recovery rates, growth rates of plants, effectiveness of pain killers, efficiency of mail delivery, sales of books. The stories all followed the same format in each of the conditions.

Each problem consisted of three parts. The first described a difference between two events (for example, that one of two cars had gotten better gas mileage that the other).

The second part provided information about alternative accounts and about causal mechanisms. In the alternatives-ruled-out condition, it was made clear that several standard possible causes had already been ruled out (for example, "The two cars were the same year and model and were driven at the same times of day with the same type of gasoline"). Only one factor remained that distinguished instances in which the effect obtained from those in which it did not. However, in the condition in which alternatives were still present, the target factor was only one of many differences between the two events.

The second part also included explicit information about mechanism. In the mechanism-present condition, a mechanism was explicitly identified that could have enabled the target factor to bring about the effect. (For example, when the target factor was the newness of the factory in which the target car had been built, it was pointed out that a newer factory would have better equipment, and the cars would be assembled better and would therefore get better mileage.) In the control condition, there was no mention made of a specific mechanism that might have been operating.

The appendix to this experiment includes one story in each of two of the four conditions: when mechanisms were present and alternatives were ruled out and when mechanisms were present and alternatives were not ruled out.

Design

The between-subjects variables were age, sex, and mechanism status (mechanism present versus absent). The within-subject variable was alternatives status (ruled out versus not ruled out).

At each age, 12 subjects (6 males and 6 females) were randomly assigned to each of the mechanism-status conditions. Within each of the two groups, half the subjects received stories 1, 2, and 3 in the mechanisms-present condition and stories 4, 5, and 6 in the mechanisms-absent condition. For the other subjects, stories 1, 2, and 3 were used in the mechanism-absent condition, and stories 4, 5, and 6 were used in the mechanisms-present condition.

Results

Results were analyzed with an age $\times$ sex $\times$ mechanism status $\times$ alternatives status analysis of variance.[1] There was a main effect for alternatives status, $F(1, 408) = 53.4$, $p = .0001$. Causal ratings of the target factors were higher when alternatives had been ruled out than when they were still viable (which is congruent with the results of experiments 1, 6, and 8, chapters 4, 6, and 7).

The interaction that we had expected (that mechanism status would have a greater effect when alternatives were viable rather than ruled-out) was not significant, $F(1, 408) = 1.6$, $p = .2$. The presence of a possible mechanism increased causal ratings no more when alternatives were viable than when alternatives had been ruled out.

Discussion

In contrast to what we had expected, the target factors in the present study were no more likely to be treated as causal when mechanisms were present than when they were not mentioned, and this was true irrespective of whether alternatives were present or had been ruled out.

In this experiment the target factors we used were all fairly plausible possible causes. With the benefit of hindsight, I suggest that one of the things it means for a target factor to be a plausible cause is that a mechanism is known to exist that can mediate between the factor and the effect. Therefore, when a factor seems like a plausible cause to begin with, being told that a mediating mechanism exists may constitute receiving redundant information.

If this suggestion is correct, we should expect that the presence of a mechanism will have an effect when the target possible cause is a fairly nonstandard one. We examine this possibility in experiments 9 and 10, chapter 8.

In contrast to the effects of mechanism, learning that alternatives had been ruled out did make the (plausible) target accounts in the present experiment more likely to be seen as causal for all the age groups and did so even though the story problems presented only a single instance of a treatment/control contrast. We suggest that for most ordinary events, even if they are only single instances, there is a set of plausible or likely causes that could have brought about the event. The set includes the target cause, but it also includes other, equally plausible alternative causes that compete with the target cause. To the extent that the competing alternatives in the set are ruled out, subjects (even adolescents) treat the factor that remains as increasingly likely to be the actual cause. And this strategy makes sense. It constitutes, for example, the rationale for the use of control groups in scientific inquiry.

However, this strategy also has limits and the limits illustrate the point about bootstrapping made in earlier chapters. Treating the target cause as increasingly likely when alternatives have been ruled out breaks down when the actual cause, because it has not yet been discovered, is not one of the alternatives that is controlled for. In such cases, ruling out the known competing alternatives still leaves the unknown cause confounded with the known target account. And this is why science involves bootstrapping. On the one hand, the strategy of ruling out alternatives increases the liklihood that the target account is the actual cause. On the other hand, the effectiveness of this strategy depends on whether one's background knowledge is extensive enough to have correctly identified all of the likely alternative causes.

Appendix to Experiment 7

Mechanism present, alternatives ruled out

Event   A professional driver noticed that one of his cars had gotten much better gas mileage than the other.

Information   The two cars were the same year and model and were driven at the same times of day with the same type of gasoline. The only difference that the driver could find was that the one that had gotten better mileage was built in a new factory, and the other in an older factory. The driver is also reminded that new factories have more modern equipment, which makes it easier to assemble the cars properly.

Do you think the better mileage was caused by being built in a new factory or by something else?

1	2	3	4	5	6	7	8	9
Definitely due to something else		Probably due to something else		May or may not be due to a new factory		Probably due to a new factory		Definitely due to a new factory

Why did you choose the rating that you did?

Mechanism present, alternatives not ruled out

Event   A professional driver noticed that one of his cars had gotten much better gas mileage than the other.

Information   The cars were made in different years, were different models, were driven at different times of day, and were used with different brands of gasoline. In addition, the car that had gotten better mileage was built in a new factory, and the other in an older factory. The driver is also reminded that new factories have more modern equipment, which makes it easier to assemble the cars properly.

Do you think the better mileage was caused by being built in a new factory or by something else?

1	2	3	4	5	6	7	8	9
Definitely due to something else		Probably due to something else		May or may not be due to a new factory		Probably due to a new factory		Definitely due to a new factory

Why did you choose the rating that you did?

Experiment 8
Barbara Koslowski, Patricia Bence, Jonathan Tudge, Eileen Gravani

In experiment 8 we continued to examine the effects of ruling out competing alternative accounts. Experiment 6 and experiment 7 examined the effect of ruling out alternatives in the context of control and confounding and found that confounding an alternative cause with the target cause made the target seem less likely to be causal than when the alternative was controlled for or ruled out.

In both experiments 6 and 7 the treatment/control contrast was explicit. For example, one car (or set of cars) was driven with a new type of gas, while the other car (or set of cars) was driven with ordinary gas. However, outside of the laboratory, this kind of format does not always obtain. Often when an event is to be explained, it consists of a single instance that requires explaining because it is a deviation from a usual state of affairs. (For example, John does better than usual on an exam.) Thus there is a sense in which the event to be explained is analogous to a treatment condition, with the usual state of affairs being the control condition, but the contrast is implicit; it does not occur in a traditional experimental format. In the present experiment, the story problems described events that consisted of a single instance in which the treatment/control contrast was only implicit.

To assess the effects of ruling out alternative causal factors, some story problems were ones in which a set of explicitly enumerated but quite general alternatives had been ruled out, while other story problems were in a control condition in which there was no information about alternatives.

We also had an additional question: In some of the pilot interviews for this experiment (as well as in some of the interviews for experiment 3), we had noticed that subjects' grasp of the information about ruled-out alternatives was sometimes initially incomplete. Specifically, when they initially learned that several alternatives had been ruled out, a few of the younger subjects speculated that perhaps alternative x might have been operating when x was nothing more than a specific instance of one of the general alternatives that had already been ruled out. That is, some of the younger subjects seemed not to have inferred that ruling out a general alternative meant ruling out the specific instances of that alternative (including the specific instance that they themselves had proposed). In experiment 3, of course, this was taken care of in the interview situation: if a subject speculated about an alternative x that might have been operating, the interviewer made it clear that the generic alternative includes alternative x. (In experiment 7, this problem did not arise, because, I suggest, the story problems contained much less information in general than did the story problems in experiment 3 or in this experiment.)

In the present experiment, we wanted to examine whether this kind of incomplete understanding of information about alternatives was systematic. To do this, we interviewed two groups of subjects. One group was interviewed in a "read and comment" condition in which, if the subject did speculate about a particular instance of one of the general ruled-out alternatives, it was made explicit to her that her particular alternative had indeed been ruled out. In contrast, for the "read only" group, the problem stories were simply read aloud by the experimenter with no additional comments.

Method and Procedure

Materials

Six story problems were constructed, one about each of the following events: a car accident, performance on an exam, business plans, missing jewelry, laundry, and a personnel decision.

The appendix to this experiment includes an example of one of the story problems in the condition in which alternatives have been ruled out. The initial description was the same in all conditions and consisted of three parts. The first part described an event to be explained, for example, "John, a high school student, does much better than he usually does on a geography exam. The geography teacher is trying to figure out why."

The second part described some initial evidence along with the target explanation that the initial evidence suggested, for example, "The teacher remembers that during the exam, John sat near a top student, someone who gets very high grades in geography. Although John could have been sitting near a top student for some other reason, this could also suggest that John was planning to cheat on the exam."

In the third part, the subject was asked to rate, on a scale of 0 to 10, how likely it was that the event was caused by the target factor ("How likely do you think it is that John did well on the exam *because he cheated* from one of the top students?") and how likely it was that the event was caused by some alternative factor ("How likely do you think it is that John did well on the exam because of *some other reason?*"). Subjects were asked to explain whey they chose the ratings they did. After the initial description and the ratings, subjects were given a "later report" that contained additional information and were then asked to rate again the target and the alternative explanations. Unlike the initial description, the information in the later report varied across conditions. When alterative accounts had been ruled out, the subject was told about several general alternatives that were checked but for which no evidence had been found. The alternatives were very general and were chosen to comprise a fairly exhaustive list. In the control condition, subjects were told, for example, "And there also has not been time to find out whether there could be some other reason why John did well on the exam."[2]

Procedure

All subjects were individually interviewed. In the alternatives-ruled-out and read-and-comment condition, whenever a subject proposed an alternative that might have been operating, she was told that the particular alternative had been ruled out because it was merely a specific instance of one of the general alternatives that had been ruled out in the story. (Recall that we were able to do this because the ruled-out alternatives were very general and were designed to comprise a fairly exhaustive list.) In the other conditions, the interviewer simply read the story problems out loud without commenting while the subject followed along, reading silently from the same protocol.

Design

Between-subjects variables were age, sex, and interview type (read only versus read and comment). The within-subject variables were alternatives information (alternatives ruled out versus control) and story.

At each age, 24 subjects were tested, with 12 subjects (6 female and 6 male) in each of the two interview-type conditions. Each subject received 4 stories, 2 in the alternatives-ruled-out condition and 2 in the control condition. A randomized block design was used to rotate the 4 stories (out of the 6 available) across subjects.

Results

An age × sex × interview type × alternatives information × story analysis of variance was separately carried out on each of four dependent measures: initial target ratings, initial alternatives ratings, the change from initial to final target ratings, and the change from initial to final alternatives ratings.

Initial ratings

Each of the main effects of age, sex, and interview type on initial target ratings, as well as the interaction of age × sex, were nonsignificant, with p values equal to or greater than .20.[3] For initial alternatives ratings, all of the main effects and interaction effects had p values equal to or greater than .20.

Changes from initial to final ratings

The main results are graphically depicted in figures 7.1 (for target ratings) and 7.2 (for alternatives ratings) and can be summarized very simply. As we had expected, in the read-only condition (depicted by the broken lines) there was an age difference: learning that alternatives had been ruled out had a greater effect on the ratings of the college students than on the ratings of the younger subjects. (This information increased target

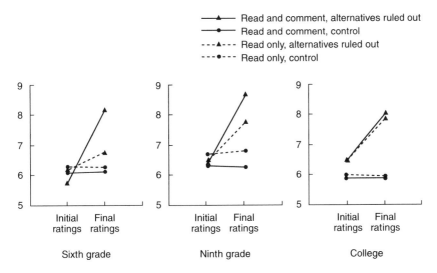

Figure 7.1
Initial and final target ratings as a function of age, interview type, and alternatives
information.

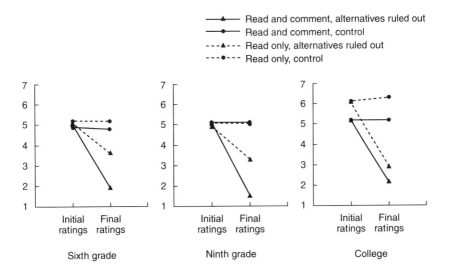

Figure 7.2
Initial and final alternatives ratings as a function of age, interview type, and alternatives
information.

ratings and decreased ratings of "some other" alternative more for college students than for adolescents.) However, ratings in the read-and-comment interview (depicted by the solid lines) brought the adolescents' ratings into alignment with those of the college students. That is, so long as it was made clear to the younger subjects (as it was in the read-and-comment condition) that the particular alternatives they were considering had in fact been ruled out as special cases of the general alternatives, then younger subjects increased their target ratings and decreased their alternatives ratings to roughly the same extent that the college students did. The statistical results that support this conclusion follow.

There were main effects of interview type on the change in target ratings, $F(1, 60) = 13.87$, $p = .0004$, as well as on the change in alternatives ratings, $F(1, 60) = 9.55$, $p = .003$. There were also main effects of alternatives information on both target change scores, $F(1, 144) = 162$, $p = .0001$, and alternatives change scores, $F(1, 144) = 224$, $p = .0001$. And the interaction of interview type × alternatives information also affected both target change scores, $F(1, 144) = 19.31$, $p = .0001$, and alternatives change scores, $F(1, 144) = 10.13$, $p = .0018$.

However, both main effects and the two-way interactions have to be qualified by the interaction of interview type × alternatives information × age for target change scores, $F(2, 144) = 4.07$, $p = .019$, as well as for alternatives change scores, $F(2, 144) = 3.20$, $p = .044$. Figures 7.1 and 7.2 illustrate this interaction. I draw attention to four points.

The first thing to note is the ratings in the read-only condition, depicted by the broken lines. In the read-only condition, for both target and alternatives ratings, the difference between alternatives-ruled-out ratings and control ratings was greatest for college students and decreased with decreasing age. That is, in the read-only condition, learning that alternatives had been ruled out increased target ratings and decreased the ratings of "some other" competitor more for college students than for younger subjects.

The second point is that in terms of the difference between alternatives-ruled-out versus control ratings, the type of interview had little effect on college students. The alternatives-ruled-out versus control difference in the read-only interview (broken lines) was comparable to the alternatives-ruled-out versus control difference in the read-and-comment interview (solid lines).

However, in terms of the difference between alternatives-ruled-out and control ratings, the type of interview did have an effect for the younger subjects (for both target and alternatives ratings). For younger subjects, the alternatives-ruled-out versus control difference in the read-and-comment interview (solid lines) was greater than the alternatives-ruled-out versus control difference in the read-only interview (broken lines).

That is, as can be seen in figures 7.1 and 7.2, in the control conditions, the type of interview had little effect on the change from initial to final ratings. However, in the alternatives-ruled-out conditions, read-and-comment interviews produced more extreme changes than did read-only interviews for the younger subjects but not for the older subjects.

In a word, the read-only interview produced age differences, whereas the read-and-comment interview brought the adolescents' ratings into alignment with those of the college students. That is, so long as it was made clear to younger subjects that the particular alternatives they were considering had, in fact, been ruled out, the younger subjects increased their target ratings and decreased their alternatives ratings to roughly the same extent that college students did.

General Discussion

Most generally, these results make the point that explanations are evaluated in the context of indirect evidence, namely evidence about competing explanations. Specifically, the present results extend the findings of experiments 1, 6, and 7. Experiment 1 demonstrated that at all ages, when target accounts were fairly nonstandard, then ruling out standard alternatives made the target accounts seem increasingly likely. The present findings (along with the results of the experiments 6 and 7) demonstrate that for all age groups, even when the target accounts are fairly standard, they nevertheless seem increasingly likely when alternative accounts have been ruled out. The present results also demonstrate that ruling out alternatives has comparable effects, regardless of whether the ruling out takes place in a traditional experimental format or in a less explicit context.

In line with the argument offered in experiment 7, I suggest that even when the possible cause is standard to begin with, ruling out alternatives means that there are fewer possibilities in the set of standard causes. (In contrast, when the possible cause is nonstandard, as it was in experiment 1, ruling out standard alternatives indicates to subjects that they may need to go beyond the set of standard causes and consider a possible cause that is somewhat unusual.)

Although these findings demonstrate that even adolescents treat as evidentially relevant information that alternative accounts have been ruled out, there is an age difference: the younger subjects had more difficulty than did the college students in inferring that ruling out a general alternative meant ruling out specific instances of that alternative. The read-and-comment condition in this study made this inference explicit by pointing out that the particular alternatives that subjects proposed were merely specific instances of general alternatives that had already been ruled out. And when this inference was made explicit, the adolescents were comparable to the college students in how they treated information about ruled-out alternatives.

I suggest that the age difference in this study is analogous to what other researchers have noticed, namely the increasing ability with age to engage in increasingly deeper levels of processing. For example, Markman (1977, 1979) has pointed out that because of the younger child's diminished ability to engage in "constructive processing," she is less likely than an older child to realize, for example, that obviously incomplete instructions are incomprehensible or that contradictory passages are inconsistent. That is, the younger the child, the less able she is to process material at a level deep enough to be able to draw the appropriate inferences.

To return to an earlier issue raised in chapter 3, the present findings are also relevant to the question of confirmation bias. Recall that in chapter 3, I argued that the real measure of whether someone is open to having her hypothesis disconfirmed is not whether she chooses a disconfirming test as opposed to a confirming test but rather whether she considers plausible alternative hypotheses. And in these experiments, there was certainly evidence that in all age groups, subjects took alternative hypotheses into account.

Finally, these findings also raise a question for further research and, in doing so, point up one of the limitations of the present experiments. Throughout this chapter (as well as in experiments 1 and 6), I have been discussing the effects of ruling out alternative accounts. However, in terms of how the issue was operationalized, it was in fact only plausible alternatives that were ruled out. And this is an important point. In principle, it is always possible to offer an alternative explanation to account for observed data. As a limiting case, one can always consider the possibility that little green women from Mars brought about the data in question. But as this example illustrates, not every alternative explanation is, or should be, taken seriously, because not every alternative is plausible. In this chapter I chose alternatives that were intuitively plausible. What was not addressed was the question of what it is that makes some alternatives more plausible than others.

And this, in turn, is related to the question of bootstrapping in science: the scientific principle "Rule out alternative hypotheses" is an important canon of scientific inquiry, but the success of this rule depends on the extent to which the alternative hypotheses have all been identified and are plausible. Trying to test a hypothesis about gasoline while ruling out a hypothesis about little green women but ignoring a hypothesis about car size would not be a good approach. That is, in terms of my earlier comments about science as bootstrapping, the principles of scientific inquiry are successful to the extent that the background beliefs (in this case, beliefs about which alternatives are plausible) that are used in conjunction with the principles are approximately correct.

Appendix to Experiment 8

Alternatives-ruled-out condition

Event   John, a high school student, does much better than he usually does on a geography exam. The geography teacher is trying to figure out why.

Early evidence   The teacher remembers that during the exam, John sat near one of the top students, someone who gets very high grades in geography. Although John could have been sitting near a top student for some other reason, this could also suggest that John was planning to cheat on the exam.

A possible explanation for the event   How likely do you think it is that John did well on the exam *because he cheated* from one of the top students?

0	1	2	3	4	5	6	7	8	9	10
Not at all possible		Very unlikely		A little unlikely	As likely as not	A little likely		Very likely		Abso-lutely certain

Why?

How likely do you think it is that John did well on the exam because of *some other reason?*

0	1	2	3	4	5	6	7	8	9	10
Not at all possible		Very unlikely		A little unlikely	As likely as not	A little likely		Very likely		Abso-lutely certain

Why?

[New page]

The teacher wants to see (a) whether there could be another reason why John was sitting near one of the top students, and (b) whether there could be another reason why John did well on the exam.

Later report   There has just not been time to find out whether there could be some other reason why John was sitting near one of the top students.

But the teacher also checks whether there could be some other reason why John could have done well on the exam. For example, she checks on whether John spent a lot of time studying for that exam, or whether the exam was an especially easy one, or whether the exam was about something that John had already learned on his own outside of the class, etc. But even though she checks very carefully, she can find no evidence of any other reason why John did well on the exam.

Think again about the Early Evidence and about both parts of the Later Report. *Now* how likely do you think it is that John did well on the exam *because he cheated* from one of the top students?

0	1	2	3	4	5	6	7	8	9	10
Not at all possible		Very unlikely		A little unlikely	As likely as not	A little likely		Very likely		Abso-lutely certain

Why?

And now how likely do you think it is that John did well on the exam because of *some other reason?*

0	1	2	3	4	5	6	7	8	9	10
Not at all possible		Very unlikely		A little unlikely	As likely as not	A little likely		Very likely		Abso-lutely certain

Why?

Think about each part of the Later Report. Was it relevant to your answers? If so, why? If not, why not?

General Summary

One of the important canons of scientific inquiry is that explanations become increasingly credible when alternative accounts have been ruled out. In experiment 1, we found that for fairly nonstandard target accounts, credibility of the target increases when alternatives have been ruled out. This study (along with experiments 6 and 7) extended these results: for fairly standard target accounts as well, credibility increases when alternatives have been ruled out. In a word, as I noted in chapter 2, neither standard nor nonstandard explanations are evaluated in isolation; rather, they are evaluated in the context of rival alternative accounts. Evidence for an explanation can be indirect as well as direct.

Furthermore, this effect is true across ages. That is, in terms of evaluating information about alternative accounts, adolescents and college students rely on comparable rules of evidence. So long as they are individually interviewed, younger subjects, like older subjects, treat information about ruled-out alternatives as making target accounts more credible and alternative accounts less credible. The age difference that does occur (whether because of differences in attentiveness, in ability to draw inferences, or in ability to extract information from wordy prose) has to do with the difficulty in conveying to the younger subjects that ruling out a general alternative means ruling out specific instances of that alternative.

To summarize the results in this chapter (along with those of experiments 1 and 6), for all age groups, explanations that are standard as well as nonstandard are evaluated in the context of rival alternative accounts, and this is true irrespective of whether the explanation is accounting for a single instance or for multiple instances. In experiment 11, chapter 9, we explore how explanations are evaluated in the context of anomalous information. In the next chapter we address the question of what makes an explanation plausible.

Chapter 8
Rendering Implausible Causes Plausible

One of the general themes of this book is that all covariations are not equally likely to be causal. That is, some factors that correlate with an effect are plausible causes, while others are implausible causes.

In the following two studies, we examine some of the factors that render implausible causes plausible.

Experiment 9
Barbara Koslowski, Patricia Bence, Nancy Herse

In experiment 6, chapter 6, and less conspicuously in experiments 7 and 8, chapter 7, we found that subjects do view covariation as more indicative of causation when it results from experiments that are controlled rather than confounded. Indeed, even sixth-graders treated confounded data as problematic. These results were in contrast to D. Kuhn et al.'s (1988) results. I argued that the difference obtained because in Kuhn et al.'s study the alternative cause confounded with the target cause was one that subjects had antecedently identified as being implausible. (Indeed, when the confounded cause was color, the experimenters had also identified it as implausible.) In contrast, in experiments 6, 7, and 8, each of the confounded factors was a plausible possible cause.

I argued that with respect to scientific practice, the strategy that Kuhn et al.'s subjects were using makes sense. In actual practice, confounded factors that are implausible causes have to be ignored so that one can avoid being overwhelmed by noise. If developmental progress covaried with both extra cuddling and blanket color, it would not be very pragmatic to take seriously the latter as a plausible cause of the progress.

Having argued that implausible confounding factors ought to be ignored, I now add the qualification "most of the time" because there are some situations in which scientific discovery actually hinges on taking implausible factors seriously. Cases of medical diagnosis provide some classic instances. For example, in identifying the cause of Kawasaki's syndrome, what eventually mattered was taking seriously the finding that what distinguished victims from nonvictims was that the victims lived in homes in which carpets had recently been cleaned—clean carpets being, indeed, a very implausible cause of illness.

There is a tension between, on the one hand, taking seriously all implausible possible causes (and, in consequence, traveling along many deadends) and, on the other hand, ignoring all implausible possible causes (and, in consequence, possibly overlooking some genuine and unexpected discoveries). The obvious compromise is to take seriously only some implausible possibilities. However, for such a strategy to be useful, there have to be guidelines that help one decide which implausible possibilities to take seriously and which to ignore. Choosing at random would be neither efficient nor informative.

In this study we focused on two such guidelines suggested by examples of medical problem solving (for example, Hempel 1966, Rouche 1988). In diagnosing medical problems, before implausible causes even become an issue, an initial strategy is to consider the catalogue of standard causes likely to be responsible for the observed symptoms. The problem is that when the symptoms are those of a previously undiagnosed disease, the catalogue of standard causes might not include the actual cause. For example, the standard possible causes of the symptoms of Kawasaki's syndrome did not distinguish children who had the syndrome from those who did not. When this happens, the next step is to consider factors that are not in the catalogue of standard causes but that are nevertheless associated with the effect. These may include possible causes that are relatively unlikely though nevertheless plausible as well as those that are straightforwardly implausible. And here is where guidelines come into play: in helping to decide which implausible factors are worth pursuing and which should probably be ignored.

One guideline involves considering whether the association of factor and effect is systematic or one time only. If the association occurs several times, then even if the factor is an apparently implausible cause, one might nevertheless want to give it a second look: a large number of associations might indicate that the factor is, in fact, causal but has not yet been identified as such. For example, on the face of it, the association of recently cleaned carpets with severe headaches, etc., would seem to be noncausal. But its appearance in several samples led epidemiologists to examine it more closely. And this relates to the second guideline.

The second guideline involves considering information about mechanism. When apparently implausible causal factors are given a second look, the look typically includes a search for a possible mechanism that might have mediated between the factor and the effect and that therefore might explain how the factor could have caused the effect. For example, the mechanism that was eventually discovered as mediating between recently cleaned carpets and Kawasaki's syndrome was the activation, by the cleaning fluid, of viruses that had been dormant. This mechanism rendered causal a factor that had initially appeared to be irrelevant noise.

However, the results of experiment 7 raised the possibility that being informed of the presence of a mechanism might make a factor appear more causally relevant only if the factor has not already been identified as a plausible possible cause. I suggested that part of what it means for a factor to be a plausible possible cause is that a mechanism is known that could have mediated between the factor and the effect. Therefore, when a factor seems like a plausible possible cause to begin with, being informed that there is a mechanism by which it could have operated might simply constitute redundant information. In contrast, a factor that seems to be an implausible possible cause can be rendered causal if a mechanism is discovered by which it could have brought about the effect.

That is, whether something is a causal factor is not a static phenomenon. A factor that seems to be an implausible possible cause should probably be given a second look if it is associated with the effect in a systematic, rather than one-time-only, fashion, and it will more likely be causal if a mechanism is discovered that can explain how it might have produced the effect.

In this experiment we presented college students and college-bound ninth- and sixth-graders with a set of story problems. In each problem some sort of effect had been noticed, and standard causes of the effect did not distinguish instances in which the effect occurred from those in which the effect was absent. Only one factor remained that did distinguish the two sorts of instances.

To test the effect of systematic versus one-time-only occurrence, in some conditions there were three instances in which the target factor was associated with the effect; in some conditions there was only one instance.

We also varied plausibility of the target factor. For example, one of the effects consisted of noticing that one car had gotten better mileage than another. In one condition, the car that got better mileage had been built in a new factory; the car that got worse mileage, in an old factory. Thus type of factory was a plausible cause but one that was relatively unlikely. In the other condition, the car with better mileage was red; the car with worse mileage, blue. And, obviously, car color was an implausible cause.

Finally, in some conditions there was a mechanism that could explain how the factor—even a seemingly implausible causal factor—could have brought about the effect; in some conditions, there was no mechanism present. Thus when color was the (implausible) target factor, subjects in the mechanism-present condition were told, "Red cars make drivers more alert; alert drivers are better drivers" and thus get better mileage.

For each story, subjects were asked to rate how likely it was that the target factor could have brought about the effect.

In line with the notion that the causal status of a factor is not a static phenomenon, we expected that the target factor would more likely be judged causal when there were more rather than fewer instances where factor and effect were associated, and when a possible causal mechanism was present rather than absent. In addition, we expected that the presence of a mechanism would have a greater effect when the target factor was implausible rather than plausible.

Method

Materials

The six story problems were similar in format to, and were about the same content areas as, the story problems in experiment 7, chapter 7. The stories all followed the same format in each of the conditions.

The appendix to this experiment presents one of the story problems in the condition in which the distinguishing factor was implausible, a possible mechanism was present, and the relevant differences had been observed in three instances.

Each problem consisted of three parts. The first described a difference between two instances (for example, that one of two cars had gotten better gas mileage than the other).

The second part provided several pieces of information. In all conditions, this section made it clear that several standard possible causes had already been ruled out (for example, "The two cars were the same year and model and were driven at the same times of day with the same type of gasoline"). Only one factor remained that distinguished instances in which the effect obtained from those in which it did not.

In the plausible condition, the factors were the same as the factors in experiment 7. That is, the plausible factors were certainly not standard causes, but it was relatively easy to generate the mechanisms by which they might have operated. (In this example, the plausible factor was that the car "that had gotten better mileage was built in a new factory, and the other in an older factory." It was easy to hypothesize—and our subjects did—that a newer factory would have better equipment, the cars would be assembled better, and they would therefore get better mileage.) In the implausible condition, the distinguishing factor was also not a standard cause. But in contrast to the plausible factor, the implausible factor was one for which it was difficult to generate the mechanism by which it might have operated. (In this example, the implausible factor was that the cars that had gotten better mileage were red rather than blue.)

When the distinguishing factor was an implausible one (for example, car color), the list of factors that had been ruled out also included the distinguishing factor from the plausible but unlikely condition (for example, type of factory).

The second part of the story problem also included explicit information about mechanism. In the mechanism-present condition, a mechanism was explicitly identified that could have enabled the factor to bring about the effect. (For example, when the factor was the implausible color, the mechanism was that the color red causes people to be alert and alert drivers are more likely to drive well, which conserves gas.) In the control condition, there was no mention made of a specific mechanism that might have been operating.

Finally, the second part also included information about the number of times the target factor had been associated with the effect. In the small sample, factor and effect were associated in one instance; in the large sample, in three instances.

The third section asked subjects to rate how likely it was that the distinguishing factor had something to do with causing the target difference. Subjects were also asked to justify their ratings.

Procedure

Subjects were tested in small groups. Subjects were requested to read the stories carefully and to respond to the rating scale below each story by considering the information given in each story problem. Subjects were given as much time as they needed to complete the six story problems, and all subjects finished the task in less than 45 minutes. Protocols were read by experimenters as they were completed, and subjects were asked to "say a bit more" about answers that were unclear. None of the subjects had any trouble understanding the task.

Design

The between-subjects variables were age, sex, mechanism status (mechanism present versus control) and number of instances (one versus three). The within-subject variable was plausibility status of the distinguishing factor (plausible versus implausible).

Thirty-two subjects were interviewed at each age. Within each age, four subjects were assigned to each of the eight groups formed by crossing the variables of sex, mechanism status, and number. Within each of the eight groups, two subjects were presented with a plausible factor for stories 1, 2, and 3 and an implausible one for stories 4, 5, and 6, while for the other two subjects the plausibility status of the stories was reversed.

Results

Results were analyzed with an age × sex × mechanism status × number of instances × plausibility status analysis of variance.

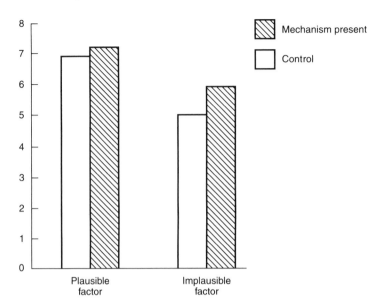

Figure 8.1
Causal ratings as a function of presence of mechanism and plausibility of target factor.

Plausibility × mechanism status

There were main effects of plausibility, $F(1, 336) = 109$, $p = .0001$, and mechanism status, $F(1, 72) = 6.7$, $p = .01$. Specifically, causal ratings were higher when factors were plausible rather than implausible and when mechanisms were present rather than not mentioned.

As we had expected, there was also an interaction of plausibility × mechanism status, $F(1, 336) = 3.4$, $p = .03$ (one-tailed). As figure 8.1 illustrates, when target factors were plausible causes to begin with, the additional presence of causal mechanisms did almost nothing to make the factors appear even more causally relevant. This result replicates the corresponding finding from experiment 7. (Furthermore, it is unlikely that this reflected a ceiling effect, as the ratings hovered around 7 on a 9-point scale.) In contrast, implausible possible causal factors did appear to be more causally relevant (that is, received higher ratings) when mechanisms were present rather than absent.

Number × sex

Although there were no main effects of either number, $F(1, 72) = .12$, $p = .73$, or sex, $F(1, 72) = .03$, $p = .86$, there was a significant and unexpected interaction of the two factors, $F(1, 72) = 6.1$, $p = .01$. As can be seen in figure 8.2, the interaction reflects the fact that females behaved

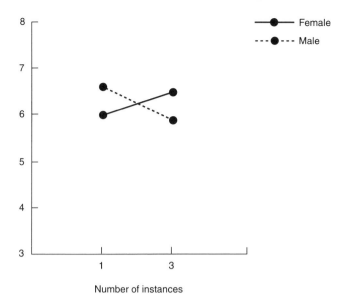

Figure 8.2
Causal ratings as a function of number of instances and sex.

as expected and gave the target factor higher causal ratings as sample size increased. In contrast, males provided lower ratings as sample size increased. (However, within each sex, the differences were borderline: males, $t(72) = 1.92$, $p = .06$; females, $t(72) = 1.57$, $p = .12$). Subjects' qualitative justifications suggested the following explanation: When males learned that additional instances had been found in which x and y covaried, they seemed to become skeptical, as though the findings were a bit too good to be true and this was cause for concern. The result was that they reduced their causal ratings.

Discussion

The role of mechanism
The results suggest that the apparent causal relevance of a factor is not a static phenomenon. Rather, it is in part a function of explanation. A factor that initially appears to be an implausible cause will come to be seen as causally relevant if subjects learn that there is a mechanism that can account for how the factor could have brought about the effect. Put differently, our subjects did take implausible possible causes seriously, but they did so judiciously, under only certain circumstances.

As we had expected, the presence of a mechanism had a greater effect on factors that were implausible rather than plausible possible causes. This was congruent with the suggestion in experiment 7 that for factors thought to be plausible possible causes at the outset, learning about a possible mediating mechanism may constitute receiving redundant information. In contrast, for target factors thought to be implausible possible causes, learning about a possible mediating mechanism renders the target factor a plausible possible cause.

The effect of number of instances
Finally, we were surprised both by the lack of a main effect for number of instances and by the interaction of number and sex. Earlier I suggested, on the basis of their qualitative justifications, that males reduced their ratings because they were skeptical that the results could have obtained that often.

The lack of an effect of number was pursued in experiment 10, which follows.

Appendix to Experiment 9

Distinguishing factor implausible, possible mechanism present, three instances

Event   A professional driver noticed that one of his cars had gotten much better gas mileage than the other.

Information   The two cars were the same year and model and were driven at the same times of day with the same type of gasoline. They were both built in the same factory. The only difference that the driver could find between the two was that the one that had gotten better mileage was red and the other one was blue. Later on, this driver meets three more professional drivers. All four drivers noticed the very same thing: for all four of these drivers, the car that got better mileage was red, and the other was blue. The driver also learns that the color red makes people more alert and thus more likely to drive well, which conserves gas.

Do you think that being a different color had something to do with making one of the cars get better mileage or was it just chance (or coincidence)?

1	2	3	4	5	6	7	8	9
Definitely was just chance		Probably was chance		May or may not have had something to do with it		Probably had something to do with it		Definitely had something to do with it

Why did you choose the rating that you did?

Experiment 10
Barbara Koslowski, Patricia Bence, Nancy Herse

In the previous study, the obvious explanation for why number of instances had no effect was that three instances was not large enough to be seen as being significantly different from one instance. Therefore, in this study, in the large sample condition the number of instances was changed from three to four. Using four instances to define a large sample was congruent with the design of other studies. For example, in experiment 2, subjects treated story-problem results based on four instances as significantly different, in the relevant conditions, from results based on only one instance.

Method

The procedure and design were identical to the procedure and design in the preceding study. The only difference between the two studies was in the story problems. In this study, when story-problem results were based on more than one instance, the number of instances was four rather than three. All other aspects of the story problems were the same as in experiment 9.

Results and Discussion

Plausibility × mechanism status
As in the previous study, there were main effects of plausibility, $F(1, 528) = 64.7$, $p = .0001$, and of mechanism status, $F(1, 528) = 12.2$, $p = .001$. There was also an interaction of the two, $F(1, 528) = 3.56$, $p = .06$. Figure 8.3 illustrates that, as in the previous study, the presence of a possible causal mechanism had a greater effect on causal ratings when target factors were implausible rather than plausible.

I draw attention to the striking similarity of the plausibility × mechanism interaction in the present and the previous studies. The actual average ratings plotted in figure 8.3 of experiment 9 are 6.9, 7.2, 5.0, 5.9, respectively. The corresponding ratings plotted in figure 8.3 of this study are 6.8, 7.07, 4.99, and 5.9. In a word, although the p value of the interaction in both studies was only .06, the present study strongly replicated the plausibility × mechanism interaction found in the previous study.

Number
In contrast to the previous study, there was also a significant main effect for number, $F(1, 528) = 16.7$, $p = .0001$, with causal ratings being higher

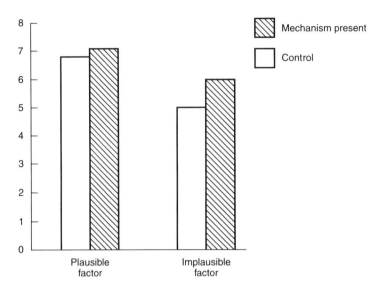

Figure 8.3
Causal ratings as a function of plausibility of target factor and presence of mechanism.

when the results were based on many instances rather than few. Furthermore, the effect of number was comparable for plausible, as well as for implausible target factors, $F(1, 528) = .07$, $p = .78$.

Sex

In contrast to the previous study, there was no significant interaction of number and sex, $F(1, 528) = .03$, $p = .84$. Recall that in the previous study, although the sex × number interaction was significant, for each sex the absolute differences between one versus three instances were quite small (approximately 0.5). Furthermore, subjects' qualitative justifications suggested that when males learned of additional instances, they seemed to become skeptical because the results sounded too pat and this caused them concern. In consequence, males actually reduced their causal ratings somewhat when the number of instances increased. In this study, the lack of a sex × number interaction (along with the main effect of number) suggests that when the number of instances is large enough, even skeptical males are convinced.

In this study, sex did interact with age, $F(2, 528) = 6.1$, $p = .002$. As can be seen in figure 8.4, for the younger subjects, females produced higher causal ratings than males. In contrast, for college students, the male-female difference was reversed, with males' ratings being higher than those of females.

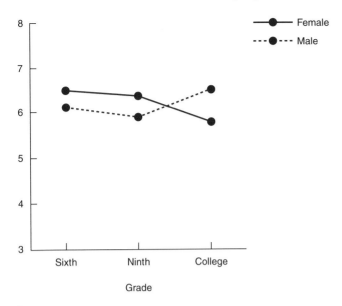

Figure 8.4
Average causal ratings as a function of age and sex.

In addition, sex also interacted with mechanism status, $F(1, 528) = 6.5$, $p = .01$. As figure 8.5 indicates, across conditions and age groups, the presence of a mechanism had a negligible effect for the males but did produce differences in the ratings of the females. However, I draw attention to the fact that there was no three-way interaction of sex and mechanism status with plausibility status, nor was there an interaction of grade with mechanism status and plausibility status. That is, the interaction of mechanism status and plausibility status, reported above, was not affected by sex or by grade.

Discussion

As in the previous study, when the target factor was plausible to begin with, the presence of a mechanism had almost no effect. However, when the target factor was implausible, the presence of a possible mechanism did make the factor seem more causal.

In addition, as we had anticipated, when the number of instances of covariation in the "large" condition was four (as it was in the present study) rather than three (as it was in the previous study), subjects at all ages rated the target factor as more likely to be causal when factor and effect covaried systematically, and not just once. Furthermore, the effect of the number of instances did not depend on whether the target factor

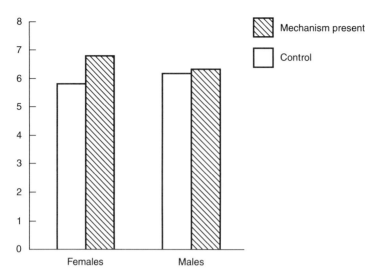

Figure 8.5
Causal ratings as a function of sex and mechanism status.

was plausible or implausible. Both types of factors were rated as more causal when the number of instances was large rather than small.

In short, the presence of a mechanism affected the ratings of only the implausible possible causes, whereas the number of instances affected the ratings of plausible as well as implausible possible causes.

At first glance, the results regarding number may seem counterintuitive, given that the effects of mechanism were restricted to only the implausible causes. I suggest, however, that the findings do make sense for the following reason: the presence of a mechanism indicates merely that the target factor could be a member of a set of plausible causes for this type of event; this is redundant information if the factor is already treated as one of the plausible causes but compelling information if the factor is treated as implausible. Therefore, with the clarity of hindsight, it is not surprising that mechanism affects the ratings of only the implausible causes.

However, even when the target factor is already a member of the set of plausible causes, a large number of covariations makes it seem even more likely to be causal because it gives that particular factor an edge over other, competing plausible causes. Furthermore, when the target factor is an implausible cause to begin with, a large number of instances might indicate that the factor should be moved into the set of plausible causes even though its causal relevance has not yet been discovered. A large number of instances indicates that the factor may be worth a second look (as is the case in many examples of medical diagnosis). That is, number of covariations affects the assessment of plausible, as well as implausible, causes.

In short, when target factors are implausible possible causes (such as car color as a cause of mileage differences), both mechanisms and number of covariations can put the factor in the running as a member of the set of plausible causes. However, when the target factor is already a member of the set of plausible causes (such as type of gasoline as a plausible cause of mileage differences), then learning that a mechanism is present simply constitutes redundant information, but a large number of covariations gives the target factor an edge over the other, competing plausible causes in the set.

(I will defer, for the time being, discussion of the two interactions involving sex. For now I note only that for the sex × mechanism interaction, mechanism status had a tangible effect only for females.)

In terms of current work in the field, several researchers (e.g., Schauble 1990) have noted that in solving causal problems, subjects preferentially test possible causes that they have deemed to be plausible. The results of this study identify two types of variables (presence of a mediating mechanism and number of occurrences) that affect judgments of plausibility.

Finally, in experiment 6, chapter 6, I argued that following the principles of scientific inquiry does not guarantee success. Successful science depends not only on following the principles of scientific inquiry but also on having approximately correct background information. The present results provide an example of how the two are related, because they illustrate how following the principles of scientific inquiry can aid in the discovery of additional background information. That is, these results provide an example of science as bootstrapping.

It makes sense to ignore irrelevant noise. The problem is that sometimes we are mistaken about what noise is. In some cases a factor initially dismissed as noise may actually be causally relevant. Hence the question, How are new relevant factors likely to be discovered if they are dismissed as noise and if dismissing noise is often a reasonable strategy? In experiments, 9 and 10, some of the factors initially dismissed as noise were found to be causal by relying on some of the principles of scientific inquiry having to do with frequency of occurrence and with causal mechanism.

Hence the notion of science as bootstrapping: On the one hand, having approximately correct background information increases the likelihood that when the principles of scientific inquiry are applied, they will add to our knowledge. (For example, applying the scientific principle "Rule out alternative hypotheses" is most likely to be effective when we have approximately correct background information about what the relevant alternatives are.) On the other hand, relying on the principles of scientific inquiry can add to our store of approximately correct background

information. (For example, as in the present experiment, relying on principles regarding mechanism and frequency of occurrence can add to our
store of background information about which factors are likely to be causally relevant.)

General Summary

We began experiments 9 and 10 with the question of how to compromise
between a strategy that would take seriously every implausible possible
cause (and run the risk of being overwhelmed by noise) and a strategy
that would ignore implausible possible causes (and run the risk of overlooking an actual cause that had not yet been identified). We examined
two guidelines that specify some situations in which nonstandard causes
ought to be given a second look. We found that when standard causes
have been ruled out, subjects (even sixth-graders) do sometimes take
implausible causes seriously, but they do so judiciously rather than either
mechanically or at random: at all ages, subjects are more likely to increase
the causal ratings of an implausible causal factor if a mechanism is discovered that can explain how the factor might have brought about the
effect. In contrast, when the factor is a plausible possible cause, the presence of a possible mechanism has no significant effect, and this is true
regardless of whether alternative causes have been ruled out or are still
viable. Furthermore, subjects are more likely to increase the causal ratings
of nonstandard causal factors (plausible as well as implausible) if the factors covary with the effect a sufficiently large number of times.

I suggest that for an implausible factor, either the presence of a mechanism or a large number of covariations can indicate that the factor could
be a member of the set of plausible causes. However, if the factor has
already been identified as a member of the set of plausible causes, then the
presence of a mechanism merely constitutes redundant information. However, a large number of covariations improves the ranking of a particular
factor relative to its competitors in the set. Therefore, the number of
covariations is relevant to a causal judgment even for plausible causes,
while presence of a mechanism primarily affects implausible causes.

In summary, plausibility is not a static phenomenon: it depends, at the
very least, on information about the number of instances of covariation as
well as on explanation or mechanism. And at least in the present study,
even sixth-graders were able to take account of this information. That is,
with regard to plausibility judgments, adolescents and adults are comparable in relying on the same rules of evidence.

Chapter 9

Deciding Whether Anomalies Refine a Theory or Call It into Question

Experiment 11
Barbara Koslowski, Margaret Adams, Nancy Herse, Eileen Gravani, David Umbach

As I argued in chapter 3, anomalous or disconfirming data do not always mean that an explanation ought to be treated as less credible or as something to be rejected. Sometimes anomalous data simply indicate that we now have more information and that the explanation ought to be modified or refined to take account of it. That is, in some cases, it is reasonable to modify an explanation in a way that accommodates or brings it into alignment with the anomalous data.

For example, imagine that penicillin were administered to patients infected with a new strain of bacteria, and imagine also that the treatment were found to be ineffective. The data from the new strain of bacteria would constitute problematic evidence for the explanation that penicillin kills germs. However, I submit that few of us would be tempted even to reduce, let alone to reject, our belief in the effectiveness of penicillin. I suggest that we would instead maintain the explanation that penicillin kills germs but modify it by restricting it to exclude the new strain of bacteria. That is, I suggest that in this instance it would be reasonable to modify the theory to accommodate the problematic data and unreasonable to reject outright our belief in the efficacy of penicillin.

In making this argument, I am taking a very different approach from the one taken by D. Kuhn et al. (1988). On their view, when theory and evidence are not in accord, the reasonable response is "to say in effect, 'This is what the theory says; this is what the evidence you have shown me indicates, and either the theory must be wrong or the evidence you have presented must be wrong, but it is not necessary that I decide which'" (D. Kuhn 1988, 221). That is, on their view, when theory and evidence are not in accord, one ought to conclude that the truth is indeterminate (one cannot decide whether theory or evidence is wrong), and one ought to expect that the eventual resolution will be all-or-none (either the theory will be wrong or the evidence will be wrong). In contrast, on my view, one can conclude that both theory and evidence are right; that is, one can conclude that the evidence has taught us that the theory is basically right but that it has to be modified so that it is seen as applying in only certain situations.

Nevertheless, my position also requires a caveat: In principle, theories can invariably be modified (and thus maintained) in the face of anomalous evidence. However, there are limits on the extent to which some modifications are seen as warranted. Therefore, in practice, some anomalous data do, in fact, call for rejecting the explanation. The tension between modifications seen as warranted and those seen as not warranted is reflected in the distinction between theory modification (which is treated as a methodologically legitimate response to anomalous data) and what is often pejoratively called "ad hoc theorizing" (which is seen as an unwarranted attempt to patch up a theory that, in fact, ought to be discarded). Therefore, the crucial question is, When do anomalous data call for rejecting an explanation, and when do they function instead as additional information that helps us refine or fine-tune our theory so that we can be more precise about when it is applicable?

Of course, part of the answer has to do with the nature and amount of evidence that supports the explanation. However, the answer also depends on the structure of the anomalies themselves, and it is this structure that is the focus of the present study.

We examined two situations in which modification rather than rejection is likely to be warranted. One situation occurs when the anomalies are characterized by a common feature, and thus form a pattern. For example, if drug x is effective in several populations but is ineffective in two populations both characterized by anemia, then one would be tempted to modify the theory by concluding that x is effective but only for nonanemic populations. Another situation occurs when there is a causal mechanism that can explain how the anomaly came to be. For example, if one of the anomalous populations was anemic and another characterized by high blood pressure, then one should modify the explanation if one learns, for example, that too little iron prevents the body from absorbing the drug and that the negative effects of high blood pressure override the beneficial effects of the drug. These are causal mechanisms that explain how anemia and high blood pressure could make the drug ineffective for these populations.

Philosophers of science argue that such characteristics as common features and explanatory mechanisms motivate modification rather than rejection of a theory because they enable the resulting modifications to be theoretically motivated. Such modifications fine-tune or amplify our understanding of the causal factor. The notion of theoretically motivated modifications acknowledges that theories, or explanations, aim to make sense of the world. To do this, theories identify patterns in the world (such as the pattern found when anomalies share a common feature), and they identify causal mechanisms to explain the patterns. Thus when anomalies involve common features or causal mechanisms, modifications that accommodate the anomalies will be seen as warranted in that they will add to our understanding of when and why the causal factor fails to operate. And by adding to our understanding of when the causal factor fails to operate, they also add to our understanding of when and why it does operate, as well.

In contrast, when the anomalies exhibit no pattern (that is, when they are characterized by idiosyncratic features) or if there is no causal mechanism that can account for how the anomalies could have come about, then the resulting modification would neither identify a pattern to the exceptions nor account for why the target factor failed to operate in the anomalous situations. But an insufficient understanding of why the target factor failed to operate in some situations would suggest an insufficient understanding of why the target factor did operate in the other situations. And a lack of understanding of how and when a factor operates raises the possibility that in any particular situation it was really chance (or something other than the target factor) that was responsible for the effect.

In this study we asked whether nonscientists would also find modification to be more warranted when anomalies were characterized by common rather than idiosyncratic features and when mechanisms to account for the anomalies were present rather than absent. However, we did not want the effects of different types of anomalous evidence to be masked by the subject's personal commitment to her own theory. Therefore, instead of asking subjects to generate theories, we presented subjects with theories to be evaluated. In addition, we wanted to assess subjects" reactions to anomalous data rather than their ability to seek it. Therefore, the anomalous instances that subjects were asked to take into account were also instances that were presented to them rather than instances that they had to identify on their own.

From previous research we knew that in at least some situations, even young children are attuned to whether anomalies form a pattern. In their classic study, Karmiloff-Smith and Inhelder (1974/1975) found that early in the problem solving process, preschool subjects did not seek anomalous evidence. Nevertheless, when they encountered it, they were most likely to treat it as suggesting an alternative explanation when the anomalies formed a pattern. We therefore expected subjects to be more likely to maintain an explanation when anomalies were characterized by common rather than separate features. We also expected subjects to be attuned to whether causal mechanisms were present. Several researchers (e.g., Bullock, Gelman, and Baillargeon 1982; Koslowski, Spilton, and Snipper 1981) have found that even preschoolers take account of causal mechanism when identifying causal factors. Therefore, we expected subjects to be more likely to maintain an explanation when mechanisms were present rather than absent.

Method

Materials

Six story problems were constructed, one about each of the following content areas: growing plants, delivering packages, winning legal cases, trying a new vaccine, treating emotional problems, and increasing book sales.

All stories followed the same format and consisted of five parts. Part 1 of the appendix to this experiment contains an example of one of the story problems in the common-feature and common-causal-mechanism condition.

As the example illustrates, the first, "Event," section of the story described the problem to be solved. The problem consisted of finding out whether a particular target factor could have produced a particular effect. The "Event" section also mentioned some of the other causes that sometimes produce the effect. The second section, "Relevant information," stated that when the target factor was present, the effect obtained in four out of six instances. That is, two anomalies challenged the rule that the target factor was associated with the effect. (We had the effect obtain in four out of six instances to avoid having the proportion of successes overwhelm the effects of the other variables.) For each story problem, the "Event" and the "Relevant information" sections were the same for all conditions.

The third section, "Additional information," was the only section that varied across conditions. This section provided additional information about the two anomalous instances. Part 2 of the appendix to this experiment presents, for the sample story problem, the information from this section in each condition. In the common-feature condition, both exceptions shared the same feature (in the book-sales example, both types of books that did not sell well were about biology); in the separate-features condition, each exception was characterized by a different feature (one type of book dealt with biology; the other with engineering). In the common-mechanism condition, one causal mechanism could explain how the feature(s) in question could have brought about the two exceptions. (In the example given, because biology books are expensive to print, even a new advertising program might not increase their sales.) In the separate-mechanisms condition, each feature brought about the exception by means of a distinct causal mechanism (for example, biology books are expensive, and engineering books go out of date quickly). In the control mechanism condition, no information was presented about causal mechanism; subjects were told merely, "There hasn't been time to get any more information."

The fourth, "Possible Explanations," section of each story described two possible ways of accounting for the initial association of target factor and effect in light of the anomalies. According to the "reject" explanation, the initial association (in four of the six instances) between target factor and effect did not reflect a causal relation; rather, the effect had probably been brought about by other causes. According to the "modify" explanation, the initial association between target factor and effect probably did reflect a causal relation, but the relation was of restricted scope. According to this explanation, the causal relation was restricted so that it did not obtain in instances characterized by the particular feature(s) that had distinguished the two anomalies. Subjects were asked to rate separately, on a scale of 0 through 10, both the reject and the modify explanations for each story.

Design

There were three between-subjects variables: age (sixth-grade versus ninth-grade versus college), feature type (common versus separate), and sex. There were two within-subject variables, causal-mechanism status (common versus separate versus control) and story. Thus at each age and sex level, there were two groups of subjects: separate features versus common feature. We tested 28 subjects (14 females and 14 males) in each age group: 12 subjects (6 females and 6 males) in the separate-features condition and 16 subjects (8 females and 8 males) in the common-feature condition. The design can be schematically represented as follows (numbers refer to the stories in one design sequence as described below):

Separate-features group
- control (1, 2)
- common mechanism (3, 4)
- separate mechanisms (5, 6)

Common-feature group
- control (1, 3, 5)
- common mechanism (2, 4, 6)
- (condition did not occur)

Separate-features group   At each age × sex level, six subjects in the separate features group received two story problems in each of the three mechanism conditions: common mechanism, separate mechanisms, control. To have each causal-mechanism condition appear an equal number of times with each story across subjects, three distinct story/mechanism design sequences were used. The first was, stories 1 and 2 in the common-mechanism condition, 3 and 4 in the separate-mechanisms condition, and 5 and 6 in the control condition. The other two design sequences were formed by systematically rotating pairs of stories across mechanism conditions. Design sequences did not correspond to the order in which subjects saw stories; order of story presentation was random.

One aim of the design was to avoid confounding story content with specific conditions. Associated with each story were two possible mechanisms and two possible features. Accordingly, for each story in the common-mechanism condition, the common mechanism was one of the mechanisms (M_1) for half the subjects and the other mechanism (M_2) for the other subjects. Similarly, in the separate-mechanisms condition, for half the subjects, the separate features F_1 and F_2 were associated with M_1 and M_2, respectively, while for the other subjects, F_1 and F_2 were associated with M_2 and M_1, respectively.

Common-features group   At each age × sex level, eight subjects in the common-feature group received three story problems in each of two mechanism conditions: common mechanism and control. Only two design sequences were required to balance stories with mechanism conditions. In the first sequence, stories 1, 3, and 5 were in the common-mechanism condition, and the other stories in the control condition. In the second sequence, the matching was reversed. Again, order of presentation of stories was random.

Within the common-feature group, subjects did not receive any stories in the separate-mechanism condition, because it did not make conceptual sense to have a common feature present in both anomalies but to have it operate via one (separate) causal mechanism in one case and via a different (separate) causal mechanism in the other. Although this is possible in principle, pilot investigations made it clear that practically, it was very difficult to construct story problems that subjects found plausible but in which one factor operated via two distinct causal mechanisms and in which each mechanism operated in only one and not both of the anomalous situations. Again, to avoid confounding story content with specific conditions, for each story in the absent-mechanism condition, the common feature was one of the features (F_1) for half the subjects and the other feature (F_2) for the other subjects. In the common-mechanism condition, the features and the mechanisms were associated in the following pairs with one fourth of the subjects receiving each pair: $F_1 + M_1$, $F_1 + M_2$, $F_2 + M_1$, $F_2 + M_2$.

Procedure
College students were tested in groups of three to fifteen, depending on how many subjects volunteered for a particular testing time. College students were not individually interviewed. Sixth- and ninth-graders were tested either individually or in groups, depending on the preferences of the particular schools.

Subjects were first presented with a practice story. While subjects read the practice story silently, the experimenter read it aloud. Subjects were requested to provide explicit reasons when they gave their qualitative responses, that is, to go beyond noting that, for example, "it seems reasonable" and to spell out why it seemed reasonable. After the practice story, subjects silently read each story to themselves and were allowed to refer back to the story while they rated the explanations. Subjects were given as much time as they needed to complete the story problems. All adolescent subjects finished the task in less than two 45-minute class sessions. College subjects completed the task during a single session. Protocols were read as subjects completed them, and subjects were asked whether they could "say a bit more" about answers that were sketchy. When testing occurred in groups, several experimenters were present to read the protocols and to ask individual subjects to elaborate their justifications.

Results

There were two dependent measures: subjects' ratings of the modify explanation and subjects' ratings of the reject explanation. Ratings for the two explanations were analyzed separately.

First, all of the data were used in order to construct pooled estimates of the between-subjects and within-subject error variances. However, recall that there was a missing cell (common feature and separate causal mechanism) in the design. Therefore, each of the two ratings was examined with two analyses, both of which used the pooled-variance estimates. For each rating, the main analysis considered only the control and the common-causal-mechanism conditions in both the common-feature and the separate-feature groups. That is, ratings for the reject and for the modify explanations were each analyzed separately with an age (sixth-grade, ninth-grade, college) × sex × type of feature (common versus separate) × type of causal mechanism (common mechanism versus control) × story analysis of variance for repeated measures.

In addition, a supplementary analysis dealt only with the separate-features group and tested the difference between the common-causal-mechanism and the separate-causal-mechanisms conditions and the interactions of this difference with age and sex.[1]

Supplementary analyses

Common versus separate causal mechanisms   This difference was analyzed separately for the modify and for the reject explanations. (Recall that this difference occurred only in the separate-features group.) For each

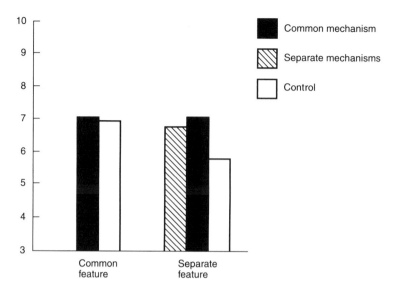

Figure 9.1
Ratings of the modify explanation as a function of feature type and mechanism status.

explanation, in the separate-features group, the common versus separate mechanisms difference and all interactions of this difference with age and/ or sex were nonsignificant. That is, in the separate-features group, there were no age or sex differences in subjects' tendency to treat the common-mechanism condition as being roughly comparable to the separate mechanisms condition.

Main analyses
Results of the main analysis are presented separately for the modify and for the reject explanations. (Recall that the main analysis omitted the data from the separate-features and separate-mechanisms condition. It considered data from both the common- and the separate-features groups but in only the common-mechanism and the control-mechanism conditions.)

Modify explanations   Although the main analysis omitted data from the separate-features and separate-mechanisms condition, they are, for the sake of completeness, included in figure 9.1.

Causal-mechanism status × feature type   The main finding regarding ratings of the modify explanation was the interaction of mechanism status and feature type, summarized in figure 9.1.
Main effects for feature type, $F(1, 72) = 5.16$, $p = .03$, and for causal-mechanism status, $F(1, 342) = 3.69$, $p = .0003$, were qualified by the inter-

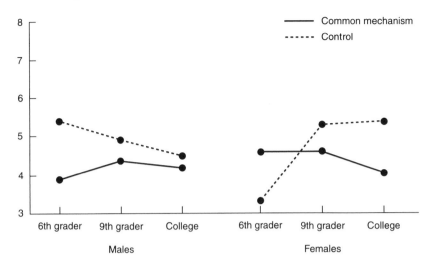

Figure 9.2
Ratings of the reject explanation as a function of grade, sex, and mechanism status.

action of the two, $F(1, 342) = 3.20$, $p = .002$. As can be seen in figure 9.1, across age, when features were common, mechanism information had no effect. That is, so long as features were common to both anomalies, modify ratings when mechanisms were absent were comparable to modify ratings when mechanisms were present. However, when anomalies were characterized by separate features, then ratings in the control condition were lower than when mechanisms were present.

One way of conceptualizing the modify ratings is to treat, as a baseline, the condition in which anomalies were expected to be most problematic, namely the separate-features and control-mechanisms condition (see figure 9.1). As expected, these anomalies were the most problematic: modify ratings in this condition were lower than in the other conditions. However, anomalies could become less problematic in two ways: if characterized by common rather than separate features or if accompanied by mechanisms to explain the anomalies. However, the presence of both types of information together (common features and explanatory mechanisms) made ratings no higher than the presence of either one alone.

Reject explanations   Results for the reject explanations are summarized in figure 9.2.

Feature type   There was a main effect for feature type, $F(1, 72) = 4.90$, $p = .03$. When ratings were pooled across subjects, then in both absent and common causal-mechanism conditions, reject explanations seemed more appropriate (that is, received higher ratings) when anomalies were characterized by separate rather than by common features.

Causal mechanism × age × sex   One way of summarizing the reject-explanation data is in terms of what we had expected, given the view of scientific inquiry that we were working with. On this view, we had expected that the reject explanation would be seen as more appropriate (and therefore receive higher ratings) in the control condition than when anomalies were explained by common explanatory mechanisms. Therefore, one way of interpreting the results is as showing that with increasing age, females become increasingly likely to follow the pattern congruent with this view of scientific inquiry, while males become decreasingly likely to do so. The statistics to support this interpretation follow.

For the reject ratings, there was a main effect of mechanism, $F(1, 342) = 2.84$, $p = .005$, with anomalies sharing a common mechanism receiving lower reject ratings than anomalies in the control condition. However, this effect must be qualified by the interaction of mechanism × age × sex, $F(2, 342) = 10.33$, $p = .0001$ (see figure 9.2).

As figure 9.2 illustrates, the pattern of responses in the sex × mechanism conditions was roughly comparable for ninth-graders and for college students, $t(342) = .97$, $p = .33$. Specifically, when averaged across sex, reject ratings of older subjects were higher in the control condition than when mechanisms were common, $t(342) = 2.26$, $p = .02$.

Furthermore, for older subjects, common-mechanism ratings were comparable for the two sexes, $F(3, 158) = 1.15$, $p = .33$. However, when mechanisms changed from common to control, females increased their reject ratings more than did males, $t(342) = 1.91$, $p = .05$. In addition, the pattern of reject ratings for the older subjects differed from that of the sixth-graders, $t(342) = 4.44$, $p = .0001$. For the sixth-graders, the difference between the two mechanism conditions was significant for males, $t(342) = 2.04$, $p = .04$, as well as for females, $t(342) = 2.44$, $p = .02$. However, for the sixth-graders, the differences were in the opposite directions for the two sexes.

Discussion

Modify explanations

Types of anomalies   With regard to ratings of the modify explanation, there are three findings worth noting:

The most salient is that some anomalies are more problematic for an explanation than others. So long as anomalies are characterized by a common feature, subjects are fairly content to modify and maintain the explanation, even if explanatory mechanisms are absent. Alternatively, when anomalies are characterized by separate features, subjects also choose to modify and maintain the explanation, provided that explanatory mechanisms are present. It is when neither common features nor explanatory mechanisms are present that anomalies are most problematic for an explanation. That is, different types of anomalous evidence have different causal consequences for the explanation being evaluated.

It is easy to see why causal mechanisms and common features make anomalies less problematic for an explanation. A complete understanding of why a target cause does operate usually also includes an understanding of when and why it fails to operate. Common features add to our understanding by identifying when it is that the factor does not operate (i.e., in situations sharing the common feature). Causal mechanisms provide us with an explanation of why it is that the target cause sometimes fails to operate. Thus anomalies characterized by common features and by causal mechanisms are less problematic for an explanation because they fine-tune our general understanding of the causal phenomenon by helping to delineate, in a systematic way, its boundaries.

Of course, another possibility is that when mechanisms are absent, anomalies sharing common features are less problematic for an explanation than are unrelated anomalies simply because the presence of a common feature effectively reduces two anomalies to just one. Although this possibility was not directly tested in this study, it would not be sufficient to explain the present findings, because the presence of a common feature was not the only way of making anomalies less damaging: the addition of causal mechanisms (when anomalies were characterized by separate features) served the same function. Furthermore, if a common feature does merely reduce two anomalies to just one, the reduction (that is, the change from separate features to a common feature) has no effect, provided that mechanisms are already present to make the anomalies less troublesome. And this relates to the second finding.

Specifically, although common features and explanatory mechanisms each increased ratings of the modify option, the presence of both together made subjects no more inclined to modify and maintain the explanation than did the presence of either one alone. I suggest the reason is that the two indices (common feature and causal mechanism) are treated as providing redundant information: the presence of a common feature, because it reflects a pattern in the anomalies, suggests an underlying causal mechanism that could have brought about the anomalies. Thus, learning that a causal mechanism is in fact present amounts to receiving redundant information.

In discussing the role of theory in deciding concept membership, Murphy and Medin (1985) have emphasized the extent to which theory or explanation determines which features are seen as being correlated. However, they also point out that correlations often reflect underlying causal structure. The present results speak to the latter point by suggesting that when adults and older adolescents try to account for anomalous data, one strategy is to notice which features are correlated with the anomalies and then to assume that the correlation probably reflects a mechanism (or explanation) that can account for it.

The third finding is that when anomalies are characterized by separate features, it does not matter whether a single causal mechanism accounts for both anomalies or a separate causal mechanism accounts for each one. Apparently, even unrelated anomalies are not very troublesome for an explanation, provided that explanatory mechanisms (even two separate explanatory mechanisms) exist that can account for each one.

In short, the behavior of the subjects was consistent with a theory of evidence in which explanation is crucial, so anomalies are least problematic when they are distinguished by mechanisms that explain how they might have come about or when they share common features that in turn suggest underlying explanatory mechanisms that might be discovered.

Relevance to Kuhn et al.'s work   The behavior of the subjects in this study is similar to the behavior of D. Kuhn et al.'s (1988) subjects who, in the face of imperfect covariation, maintained an explanation by bringing theory and evidence into alignment. In the present study, subjects in some conditions rated as reasonable, attempts to bring theory and evidence into alignment by modifying an explanation in order to take account of anomalies. For Kuhn et al., this sort of behavior reflects a general tendency to think *with*, rather than *about*, theories. That is, it reflects a flaw in the subject's basic cognitive ability.

We approach such behavior from a different perspective. First, we argue that modifying an explanation in the face of anomalous data is often reasonable: anomalous data can serve to refine an explanation, not merely to call it into question. However, not all evidence warrants modification. Therefore, if one is evaluating evidence thoughtfully, then some sorts of anomalies should be more problematic for an explanation and should therefore make modification less likely than others. And in fact this is exactly what happened. I conclude, therefore, that our subjects did not have a general problem distinguishing theory from evidence. Rather, in evaluating a theory, they found some types of evidence more problematic than others.

Modify versus reject explanations

Turn now to the other strategy for dealing with explanations in light of anomalous information, namely, rejecting the explanation. The striking finding is that the results for the modify and the reject explanations did not mirror each other. This is counterintuitive, since deciding in favor of one explanation would seem tantamount to deciding against the other. Nevertheless, the two explanations seem to have been rated independently: when the modify explanation was evaluated, it was the interaction of feature type and mechanism status that affected the ratings. When the reject explanation was evaluated, feature type affected subjects' ratings across age groups and conditions (while the effects of mechanism status depended on subjects' age and sex). One possibility is that reasoning with a negative (as subjects were required to do in rating the reject explanations that the target factor "did *not*" bring about the effect) is a cognitively demanding task that is made even more demanding by taking account of the way information about feature type and information about mechanism interact.

Another possibility turns on the fact that when rating the modify explanation, subjects considered one specific explanation, whereas when rating the reject explanation, they evaluated very nonspecific "other factors." It may be that when subjects consider a specific explanation, their judgments are subtle enough to include interaction effects, whereas when they consider the general class of unspecified alternatives, their judgments are less discriminating.

Limitations

Finally, one must also consider the limits on external validity of the present study. One is related to the finding that nonpatterned (separate-feature) anomalies are no more troubling than patterned (common-feature) anomalies so long as explanatory mechanisms are present. It is not clear whether this effect would continue to obtain if the number of separate-features anomalies were increased. The second limitation is that the story problems, features, and causal mechanisms all dealt with events that were neither emotion-laden nor of great consequence. It is not clear whether analogous results would obtain, for example, with the emotionally charged explanations offered during a jury trial. Finally, unlike the subjects in the studies discussed earlier, the subjects in this study were presented with the explanations they evaluated. It is an open question whether subjects would have behaved the same way had they generated the explanations on their own.

General Summary

For college students, anomalies are less problematic for an explanation when there are possible mechanisms to explain how they might have come about and when they are characterized by common rather than idiosyncratic features (thereby forming a pattern that might suggest an underlying mechanism). That is, college students are judicious in deciding when to modify an explanation in order to accommodate problematic data. Furthermore, it is reasonable for them to modify an explanation in the face of anomalies characterized by common features and for which there are explanatory mechanisms, because such modifications are theoretically motivated: by refining our understanding of when and why the causal factor fails to operate, the anomalies add to our understanding of where and why it does operate, as well. That is, college students do distinguish theory from evidence and realize that some types of evidence are more problematic than others.

For sixth-graders, in contrast, explanations do not become less likely when mechanisms are absent and characterizing features are distinct. One possibility is that the information-processing capacity of the sixth-graders was too limited to take into account all of the relevant information. The other is that because adolescents hold an inflated belief in the range of possible mechanisms that can be operating in a situation, they assume that undiscovered mechanisms exist that could account for the anomalies and could therefore make them less problematic for the explanation.

Appendix to Experiment 11

The story problem in the common-feature and common-causal-mechanism condition

Event The owner of a publishing house tries out a new advertising program designed to increase book sales. The owner of the publishing house knows that many factors can help to increase book sales (for example, times of the year such as Christmas or graduation, improvements in the economy so that people have money to spend on books, etc.). The owner wants to find out whether the *new advertising program* helped to increase sales.

Relevant information The owner looks at the records of six different types of books. He finds that four of these types of books *did* have higher sales while the new advertising program was operating. However, he also finds that two types of books did *not* have higher sales while the new program was operating.

Additional information Since two of the types of books did *not* have higher sales, the owner wonders whether the four types of books that *did* have higher sales had higher sales because of the advertising program or because of some other factors. He then learns that the two types of books that did *not* sell well have something in *common*. Both types are books on biology. The owner also learns that biology books usually cost a lot because they have to include a lot of drawings and diagrams that are expensive to print.

Possible explanations Thus the owner has to decide between two possible explanations: The *first possible explanation* is that the advertising program really does *not* help to increase book sales. That is, the increase in sales for the four types of books was probably caused by other factors besides advertising. The *second possible explanation* is that the advertising program *does* help to increase book sales but only for *some* types of books. Specifically, it does *not* help sales for books on biology because books on biology have to include so many drawings and diagrams that they are expensive to print.

[New page]

Consider the event and all of the information carefully. Given the event and the information, which of the two possible explanations is the more likely? (The more likely you find an explanation, the higher the number that you should circle.)

The *first* possible explanation is

0	1	2	3	4	5	6	7	8	9	10
not at all possible		very unlikely		a little unlikely	as likely as not	a little likely		very likely		abso- lutely certain

The *second* possible explanation is

0	1	2	3	4	5	6	7	8	9	10
not at all possible		very unlikely		a little unlikely	as likely as not	a little likely		very likely		abso- lutely certain

Why did you choose the rating that you did?

Additional information and possible explanations for the sample story problem in each of the feature type × mechanism status conditions

Additional information

Common feature, absent mechanism   Since two of the types of books did *not* have higher sales, the owner wonders whether the four types of books that *did* have higher sales had higher sales because of the advertising program or because of some other factors. He then learns that the two types of books that did *not* sell well have something in *common*. Both types are books on engineering. Because the owner just got the sales records, there hasn't been time to get any more information.

Common feature, common mechanism   Since two of the types of books did *not* have higher sales, the owner wonders whether the four types of books that *did* have higher sales had higher sales because of the advertising program or because of some other factors. He then learns that the two types of books that did *not* sell well have something in common. Both types are books on biology. The owner also learns that biology books usually cost a lot because they have to include a lot of drawings and diagrams that are expensive to print.

Separate features, absent mechanism   He then learns that the two types of books that did *not* sell well are quite *different*. The first type of books that did not sell well are books on engineering. The second type are books on biology. Because the owner just got the sales records, there hasn't been time to get any more information.

Separate features, common mechanism   He then learns that the two types of books that did *not* sell well are quite *different*. The first type of books that did not sell well are books on engineering. The second type are books on biology. The owner also learns that both of these types of books usually cost a lot because they have to include a lot of drawings and diagrams that are expensive to print.

Separate features, separate mechanisms   He then learns that the two types of books that did *not* sell well are quite *different*. The first type of books that did not sell well are books on engineering. The second type are books on biology. The owner also learns that engineering books usually cost a lot because they have to include a lot of drawings and diagrams that are expensive to print. In addition, the owner learns that biology books become outdated rapidly because they have to report the results of recent experiments.

Possible explanations

Common feature, absent mechanism   Thus the owner has to decide between two possible explanations: The *first possible explanation* is that the advertising program really does *not* help to increase book sales. That is, the increase in sales for the four types of books was probably caused by other factors besides advertising. The *second possible explanation* is that the advertising program *does* help to increase book sales but only for *some* types of books. Specifically, it does *not* help sales for books on engineering.

Common feature, common mechanism   Thus the owner has to decide between two possible explanations: The *first possible explanation* is that the advertising program really does *not* help to increase book sales. That is, the increase in sales for the four types of books was probably caused by other factors besides advertising. The *second possible explanation* is that the advertising program *does* help to increase book sales but only for *some* types of books. Specifically, it does *not* help sales for books on biology because books on biology have to include so many drawings and diagrams that they are expensive to print.

Separate features, absent mechanism   Thus the owner has to decide between two possible explanations: The *first possible explanation* is that the advertising program really does *not* help to increase book sales. That is, the increase in sales for the four types of books was probably caused by other factors besides advertising. The *second possible explanation* is that the advertising program *does* help to increase book sales but only for *some* types of books. Specifically, it does *not* help sales for books on engineering and it does not do so for books on biology, either.

Separate features, common mechanism   Thus the owner has to decide between two possible explanations: The *first possible explanation* is that the advertising program really does *not* help to increase book sales. That is, the increase in sales for the four types of books was probably caused by other factors besides advertising. The *second possible explanation* is that the advertising program *does* help to increase book sales but only for *some* types of books. Specifically, it does *not* help sales for books on engineering and books on biology because both of these types of books have to include so many drawings and diagrams that they are expensive to print.

Separate features, separate mechanisms   Thus the owner has to decide between two possible explanations: The *first possible explanation* is that the advertising program really does *not* help to increase book sales. That is, the increase in sales for the four types of books was probably caused by other factors besides advertising. The *second possible explanation* is that the advertising program *does* help to increase book sales but only for *some* types of books. Specifically, it does *not* help sales for books on engineering because these books have to include so many drawings and diagrams that they are expensive to print. And it also does not help sales for books on biology because, since these books have to report the results of recent experiments, they become outdated rapidly.

Experiment 12
Barbara Koslowski, Carol Katz, Kimberley Sprague, Michelle Hutt, Amy Susman

In the preceding experiment (experiment 11), we found that some anomalous evidence is less problematic than others. Specifically, we found that anomalies are less problematic for an explanation when they are theoretically informative, that is, when they are characterized by a common feature (which suggests a common causal pathway) and/or when there are (either common or distinct) explanatory mechanisms present that can account for how the anomalies came to be. This occurs, I argued, because anomalous evidence that is theoretically informative refines our understanding of when and why a causal factor operates and therefore puts a premium on modifying an explanation rather than on relinquishing it.

In the preceding experiment, the additional information (about features and mechanisms) that made some anomalies theoretically informative (and thus less problematic) was explicitly presented to the subjects to see whether they would take it into account. In this study we wanted to see what sort of assumptions people would make about anomalies if additional information were not explicitly provided. Our general question was, When people encounter anomalous information, how do they treat it? Specifically, is their initial assumption that the anomalies resulted from a common causal pathway? That is, do people assume that the anomalous evidence is the theoretically informative kind that enables us to refine our explanation?

Part of our motivation for asking this question was to shed additional light on the common conclusion that what is typically called "disconfirming" (but what I am calling "anomalous") evidence often does very little to reduce the credibility of an explanation. If people have a tendency to assume that anomalous evidence is the sort that is theoretically informative, then perhaps it does little to reduce the credibility of an explanation, in part because it is seen as simply refining the explanation rather than actually calling it into question.

We presented subjects with partial versions of the same story problems used in the preceding experiment. They were partial because they included no information about causal mechanisms. Depending on the condition, subjects were told that each anomaly was characterized by a separate feature or were told that both anomalies were characterized by a common feature or were given no information about distinguishing features. Therefore, in the "no information" (control) condition, we were able to ask whether subjects would assume that the anomalies had resulted from a common causal pathway when there was no additional information either about distinguishing features or about mechanisms. By contrasting the control condition with the common-feature condition, we could ask whether this tendency increased when a commonality was explicitly mentioned. And by contrasting the control condition with the separate features condition, we could ask whether the tendency to assume an underlying common pathway was attenuated when anomalies were characterized by two different features.

Method

Materials
The six story problems used in experiment 11 were shortened for use in this study. Each story consisted of three (or four) parts. The first part described the problem to be solved, namely finding out whether a target factor could have produced a particular effect. The second part described the pattern of results (that when the target factor was present, there were two anomalous instances out of six in which the effect failed to obtain). And the third part provided information about the anomalous evidence. (The third part occurred in only the separate-features and the common-feature conditions.) The fourth part consisted of a series of questions and probes about the pattern of results.

Only the third part varied across conditions. In the control condition, subjects were told only that there were two anomalous instances (in which the target factor was present but the effect had not obtained). In the separate features condition, each anomaly was characterized by a different feature, while in the common feature condition, both anomalies were characterized by the same feature.

In the fourth part, the successive questions became increasingly specific.

Procedure
Each subject was interviewed individually. Both interviewer and subject loked at the story problem while the interviewer read it aloud and the subject read it silently.

Design
There were three between-subjects variables: age, sex, and condition (control versus separate features versus common features). The within-subject variable was story.

There were 48 subjects in each group, with 16 subjects (8 females and 8 males) in each of the three conditions. The separate-features condition involved two features, one for each of the anomalies. Therefore, in the common-feature condition, to avoid confounding story content with condition, for half the subjects, the common feature was one of the separate features, and for half the subjects, it was the other feature.

Results

Coding
Initially we attempted to code each response in terms of two variables: whether the subject assumed that the anomalies were characterized by either common or separate features and whether the subject assumed that the anomalies had been brought about by common or separate mechanisms. However, in almost all cases it did not prove possible to distinguish the two. In a response such as "Maybe these two books didn't sell because they were both boring," the distinction between boring as a characteristic feature and boring as the mechanism that accounts for low sales breaks down. Therefore, in coding subjects' responses, we did not try to distinguish the two.

For each story, each subject's response was coded into one of four mutually exclusive categories:

Common causal path In responses in this category the subject inferred that the two anomalies had resulted from a common causal pathway, for example, "Maybe advertising didn't work for these two books, because they're both just boring." Responses in this category made no mention of separate paths.

Distinct causal paths In responses in this category the subject inferred that the two anomalies had resulted from distinct causal pathways, for example, "Maybe these books didn't sell, because they're boring, and those ones because they're too expensive." Responses in this category made no mention of commonality.

Mixed response Responses in this category assumed some sort of common pathway that had two different realizations, for example, "Maybe they're both too expensive—these because they're too long, and these because they have too many drawings."

Other These responses included, for example, simple paraphrases of the story, denial of the story problem ("Advertising always works"), etc.

Analyses
Figure 9.3 summarizes the main finding, and it is a straightforward one: At all ages and in all conditions, the most likely response to anomalous data is to assume that the anomalies have something in common. Indeed, at all ages and in all conditions, this responses is more likely than the other two responses taken together. And perhaps most striking, even

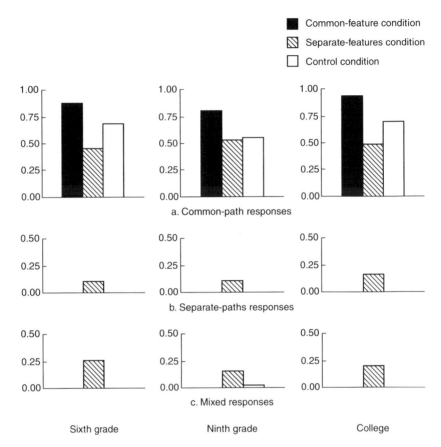

Figure 9.3
Response types as a function of grade and condition.

when subjects were explicitly told that the anomalies were characterized by separate features, an assumption of commonality was still the most frequent response. The statistics to support this conclusion follow.

Each of the first three response types was analyzed separately with an age × condition × story × sex analysis of variance.

Common-path responses

Age × condition   There were main effects for age, $F(2, 756) = 3.23$, $p = .04$, and for condition, $F(2, 756) = 58.04$, $p = .0001$, which must be qualified by the interaction of age and condition, $F(4, 756) = 2.43$, $p = .04$.[2]

As figure 9.3a illustrates, the interaction was *not* due to age differences in the way subjects responded to the control versus common-feature conditions: The control versus common-feature difference averaged across age groups was significant, $F(1, 756) = 40.02$, $p = .0001$. Furthermore, the difference in response rate between control and common-feature conditions was comparable for sixth-graders and college students, $F(1, 756) = .36$, $p = .55$, and the ninth-graders' response rate was comparable to the rates of the other two age groups averaged together, $F(1, 756) = .25$, $p = .62$. In short, at all ages, subjects were more likely to assume a common causal pathway in the common-features condition (where they were explicitly told that the anomalies shared a common feature) than they were in the control condition.

Rather, for assumed commonality responses, the age × condition interaction was due to age differences in the way subjects responded to the control versus separate-features conditions: for these responses, there was a difference between control and separate-features conditions averaged across age, $F(1, 756) = 19.99$, $p = .0001$. However, the control versus separate features difference was comparable for sixth-graders and college students, $F(1, 756) = .06$, $p = .81$, but was smaller for the ninth-graders than for the other two age groups averaged together, $F(1, 756) = 8.13$, $p = .004$. As figure 9.3a illustrates, ninth-graders gave fewer common-path responses in the control condition than did the other two age groups. An ad hoc hypothesis is that when there was no information about the anomalies (as was the case in the control condition), the ninth-graders' overgeneralization of uncertainty made them less likely than the other two age groups to attribute a common causal path to the anomalies.

In short, sixth-graders and college students, in contrast to ninth-graders, were more likely to assume a common causal pathway in the control condition than in the separate-features condition (where they were explicitly told that anomalies were characterized by different features), although, in both conditions, even ninth-graders were more likely to give a response that assumed commonality than to give either a response that assumed distinctness or a mixed response.

Age × sex   There was also a main effect for age, $F(2, 756) = 3.23$, $p = .04$, and for sex, $F(1, 756) = 6.63$, $p = .01$, and for the interaction of age and sex, $F(2, 756) = 4.54$, $p = .01$. For sixth- and ninth-graders, males gave slightly more common-path responses than did females, but there was no sex difference for college students.

Separate-path responses

Condition   There was a main effect for condition, $F(2, 756) = 46.6$, $p = .0001$.[3] As can be seen in figure 9.3b, at all ages the *only* condition in which subjects assumed separate causal pathways was in the separate-features condition, the condition in which subjects were explicitly told that the two anomalies were characterized by two different features. (And even in this condition, for all ages, a response that assumed commonality was more likely than the other two responses taken together.) Specifically, there was no difference in separate path responses between the control and the common-features condition, $F(1, 756) = 0$, $p = 1.0$, but there was a difference between the control and the separate-features condition, $F(1, 756) = 70$, $p = .0001$.

Mixed responses

Condition × age   The main effect of condition, $F(2, 756) = 71.98$, $p = .0001$, must be qualified by the interaction of condition and age, $F(4, 756) = 2.36$, $p = .05$.[4] As can be seen in figure 9.3c, the interaction was *not* due to age differences in the way subjects responded to the control versus common-feature conditions: this difference, averaged across age groups, was not significant, $F(1, 756) = .13$, $p = .72$.

Rather, for mixed responses, the age × condition interaction was due to age differences in subjects' responses to the control versus separate-features conditions: for these responses, there was a difference between control and separate-features conditions averaged across age, $F(1, 756) = 105$, $p = .0001$. However, the control versus separate-features difference was comparable for sixth-graders and college students, $F(1, 756) = 1.19$, $p = .27$, but was smaller for the ninth-graders than for the other two age groups averaged together, $F(1, 756) = 6.71$, $p = .009$. In short, sixth-graders and college students, in contrast to ninth-graders, were more likely to give a mixed response in the separate-features condition (where they were explicitly told that anomalies were characterized by different features). An obvious explanation for this age difference does not suggest itself.

To summarize, the results documented that, in general, learning that anomalies shared a common feature made subjects increasingly likely to assume that the anomalies had resulted from a common causal pathway, while learning that the anomalies were characterized by separate features made subjects increasingly likely to treat the anomalies as resulting from separate causal pathways. In a word, subjects' judgments about anomalies did take account of the information about the anomalies that they were presented with.

However, as figure 9.3 illustrates, a separate-path response can be relatively more likely in one condition than in others but still not be very likely, in an absolute sense, even in the condition in which it most frequently occurs and in which it was most strongly suggested. Therefore, we also examined response distributions within the three individual conditions (common feature, separate features, control).

Individual conditions

For each condition, we asked whether subjects were more likely to give common-path responses than to give separate-path responses.

Common-path responses were more likely than separate-path responses in both the common-features condition, $t(562) = 46.8$, $p = .0001$, and in the separate-features condition, $t(515) = 10.5$, $p = .0001$. That is, even when subjects were explicitly told that the anomalies were characterized by separate features, they were nevertheless more likely to treat the anomalies as having resulted from a common path rather than from two separate paths.

Common-path responses were also more likely than separate path responses in the control condition for each of the ages as well, $t(95) = 14.8$, $p = .0001$; $t(95) = 11.1$, $p = .0001$; $t(95) = 15.6$, $p = .0001$, for sixth-graders through college students, respectively. (In the control condition, we tested each age separately because of the age difference reported above.)

Discussion

We began this experiment with the question of whether, when people encounter anomalous data, they treat the anomalies as resulting from a common causal pathway or as having followed separate causal routes. We found, not surprisingly, that in making these judgments, subjects certainly did take account of the information they were presented with: subjects were more likely to treat anomalies as resulting from a common path when told that the anomalies were characterized by a common feature and were more likely to treat anomalies as resulting from separate causal paths when told that the anomalies were characterized by separate features. In short, information about a common feature or separate features did affect the way subjects treated the anomalous information that they encountered.

However, although information about separate features played a statistically significant role in subjects' judgments, what was striking was how small a role it played in an absolute sense. In the control condition, when there was no additional information about the anomalies, separate-path responses were *never* generated, but common-path responses were generated frequently. Moreover, even when subjects were explicitly told that the anomalies were characterized by separate features, common-path responses were nevertheless still much more likely than separate-path responses. In a word, when presented with anomalous information, subjects were disposed to treat the anomalies as resulting from a common causal path even when given information that made separate paths more likely.

As we noted earlier, part of our motivation for doing this experiment was to shed some light on the frequent conclusion that explanations are often preserved in spite of disconfirming or anomalous evidence that reduces the explanations' crediblity. And, as also noted earlier, one scientifically legitimate strategy for preserving an explanation in light of anomalous data is to modify the explanation so that it takes account of the data but to do so in a theoretically motivated way. Treating anomalous data as resulting from a common causal path makes theoretically motivated modifications especially feasible. It identifies the anomalies as forming a pattern, and it specifies a mechanism that might have brought the anomalies about. That is, it enables one to fine-tune the explanation in a theoretically motivated way because it enables one to indicate when the explanation does not apply, and this, in turn, enables one to specify more precisely when the explanation does apply.

In experiment 11, we documented that when deciding whether to modify an explanation in light of anomalous data, subjects do take account of whether the anomalies form a pattern and whether there are mechanisms to explain how the anomalies might have come about. I argued that such behavior is reasonable. The present results suggest that not only do subjects take account of such information when it is presented to them but they also have a tendency to assume the existence of patterns and explanatory mechanisms even when not explicitly told that they exist. That is, they have a tendency to make exactly the assumptions that make theoretically motivated modifications, which preserve explanations in light of anomalous data, especially warranted. Such assumptions are not necessarily reasonable and might shed some light on why anomalous evidence sometimes does little to reduce the credibility of an explanation.

A question that remains for future research is, Are subjects as inclined to make these assumptions when the explanations in question are not as initially plausible as they were in the present experiment, so that preserving the explanation seems less warranted?

Chapter 10

Disconfirming Mechanism and Covariation Components of a Theory

---

Experiment 13
Barbara Koslowski, Lynn Okagaki, Regina Cannon, Kimberley Sprague

The present experiment was, quite candidly, a long shot. I argued, in chapters 2 and 3 that beliefs about causal relations typically include two components: a belief that a certain factor covaries with a certain effect and a belief about what the mechanism is that explains why the covariation obtains. I further argued that this may have consequences for the sorts of evidence that people count as disconfirming a causal belief. Specifically, evidence that calls into question only the covariation component of the belief allows one to replace the belief in covariation with a belief in non-covariation. However, such data do nothing to replace the mechanism component of the belief. (And it is the mechanism component that renders the covariation component causal rather than coincidental.)

I suggested that this might have been one reason why, in D. Kuhn et al.'s (1988) research, subjects tried to maintain their beliefs about what covaried with colds in the light of disconfirming evidence. For example, when subjects held the belief that type of cake eaten covaried with colds, disconfirming evidence consisted of learning that type of cake was found not to covary with colds. That is, subjects were offered a chance to replace their belief about whether a factor covaried with colds. However, they were *not* offered a chance to replace their belief in the mechanism that explained *why* the covariation had been expected to obtain in the first place. This point becomes especially salient when one considers that many of the subjects in Kuhn et al.'s study did explicitly verbalize beliefs about mechanism, albeit not always the correct mechanism (for example, that chocolate cake has sugar and sugar increases blood pressure).

I suggested further that this analysis could also explain Kuhn et al.'s finding that the causal belief that x and y did covary was harder to disconfirm than the noncausal belief that x and y did not covary. When the belief was that covariation did obtain, there was a belief about mechanism that needed to be replaced. In contrast, when the belief was that covariation was absent, there was less likely to be a belief about mechanism that needed to be disconfirmed and discarded.[1]

In this experiment I refer to data that are "disconfirming" rather than "anomalous" because "disconfirming" is the term used by Kuhn et al. But recall that in Kuhn et al.'s study, the "disconfirming" data do not definitively call for the hypothesis to be rejected outright. The data are, in fact, merely anomalous; the hypothesis can be modified to take account of the data, and in fact subjects do this when they claim, roughly, that the hypothesis was not right with respect to certain instances. Kuhn et al. treat such modification as reflecting flawed reasoning. What I am arguing is that because modifications can reflect reasonable, rather than flawed, thinking, the real question is whether subjects choose modification when outright rejection would be more appropriate. And I am arguing that outright rejections would have been more likely to be warranted if the mechanism as well as the covariation component of the belief had been called into question—which we do in the present experiment.

We presented subjects with two types of disconfirming evidence: one offered a replacement for only the covariation component of their beliefs, while the other offered a replacement for the covariation component along with a replacement for the mechanism component as well. (We also presented subjects with analogous types of confirming evidence.) We wanted to see whether disconfirming evidence that included a mechanism would, in contrast to what Kuhn et al. had found, have a greater effect on a noncausal rather than a causal belief. We reasoned that because causal beliefs included beliefs about mechanism, disconfirming evidence that included information about mechanism would be more relevant to causal than to noncausal beliefs.

In this study we wanted to minimize information-processing demands. Therefore, in contrast to Kuhn et al.'s study, we asked subjects to evaluate hypotheses about two target variables rather than four, and we presented as evidence only one instance based on 20 children (rather than 8 instances, each based on 12 children).

However, like Kuhn et al., we also wanted to measure the subjects' initial commitment to their theories. Therefore, we asked subjects to rate the two hypotheses before the subjects were presented with evidence.

The hypotheses consisted of beliefs about what sorts of foods eaten before bedtime make it difficult for children to fall asleep. One hypothesis was that type of candy eaten (high-sugar versus low-sugar) affected children's ability to fall asleep. We included this hypothesis because pilot interviews made it clear that adolescents as well as adults hold the belief that amount of sugar does affect children's ability to sleep (that is, that eating a lot of sugar before bedtime makes it difficult for children to fall asleep). The other hypothesis was that type of milk consumed (high-fat versus low-fat) did *not* affect children's ability to fall asleep. We included this hypothesis because no one in pilot interviews expressed the belief that type of milk affects sleep. Therefore, one hypothesis identified a variable that subjects were likely to find causal, and the other identified a variable subjects were likely to find noncausal.

Finally, we presented each subject with confirming evidence for one target hypothesis and disconfirming evidence for the other. We were not aiming to replicate Kuhn et al.'s results regarding the effects of covariation (and noncovariation) evidence. Therefore, we did not include a condition in which no evidence was presented that we contrasted with a condition in which evidence about covariation (or noncovariation) alone was presented. Instead, we were interested in contrasting the effects of covariation evidence alone with the effects of evidence that included information about both covariation and mechanism. Hence our confirming (and disconfirming) evidence was of two sorts.

For some subjects, the evidence was restricted to covariation: subjects were told only that the target variable either did or did not covary with the effect. (Whether it did or did not covary depended on whether the subject's belief was being confirmed or disconfirmed.) For other subjects, the information included not only information about covariation but also information about causal mechanism: subjects were told whether the target variable did or did not covary with the effect and in addition were told about the causal mechanism that would explain the observed covariation or noncovariation.

We had several reasons for treating the present experiment as a long shot. The causal belief that we were aiming to disconfirm was widespread (held by roughly 75 percent of the subjects we interviewed), supported by parents' and teachers' statements, congruent with subjects' own personal experience, and accompanied by a mechanism to explain the effect ("Sugar revs you up"). In chapter 3, I argued that such beliefs should be difficult to disconfirm because, rather than existing in isolation, they are imbedded in a web of other beliefs and are widely shared. This experiment was a long shot because the effort we were expending on disconfirming the belief was small: the disconfirming evidence we were presenting was minimal and described during only a single experimental session. Nevertheless, we thought that if mechanism information were found to play a role even under these conditions, the finding would endorse examining this approach in more depth.

Method

There were some differences in the materials and procedures between our study and D. Kuhn et al.'s (1988). The differences and the rationale for them are described in the relevant sections.

Materials

Subjects were presented with a single story problem to be solved. The first part of the story problem described the story problem, namely that scientists wanted to know whether children's ability to fall asleep at night was affected by different bedtime snacks (high-sugar versus low-sugar candy or low-fat milk versus whole milk). In the problem, to study the effects of type of candy, the scientists gave one group of children a snack of high-sugar candy and another group a snack of low-sugar candy. To study the effects of type of milk, the scientists gave a third group of children a snack of whole milk and a fourth group a snack of low-fat milk.

In the second part of the story problem, for each of the two types of snacks (candy and milk) subjects rated on a scale of $+5$ to -5 whether both types of candy (or milk) had the same effect (-1 to -5) or whether one type of candy (or milk) was better than the other ($+1$ to $+5$) at inducing sleep or whether one could not tell (0). (This was slightly different from Kuhn et al.'s scale in which subjects rated whether the different foods "do or do not make a difference." We changed the wording because, in pilot testing, some children interpreted "does make a difference" to mean that both foods had *some* effect rather than that one food had more of an effect than the other food.)

Subjects were also asked why they held the particular belief that they did and were asked to describe the process by which the target variable might produce the effect that they had specified. The appendix to this experiment includes the story problems in the condition in which covariation evidence was coupled with information about mechanism and in the versions in which beliefs about milk were confirmed and disconfirmed and in which beliefs about candy were confirmed and disconfirmed. (In these versions, the belief about candy was that high-sugar candy is better than low-sugar candy at inducing sleep.)

Note that we included a subject in the final sample only if she gave milk a negative (noncausal) rating and candy a positive (causal) rating (see below).

In the third part of the story problem, subjects were given information about what some scientists had predicted and what they had in fact found. For both foods, the scientists' "predictions" were identical to those the subject had made. For one type of food (e.g., type of milk) the scientists' (and therefore the subject's) prediction was confirmed; for the other type of food (e.g., type of candy), the scientists' (and therefore the subject's) prediction was disconfirmed. For example, if the subject had stated that low-sugar candy made sleep easier than high-sugar candy, then in the disconfirming condition, she was told, "Children who ate high-sugar candy fell asleep *just as easily* as children who ate low-sugar candy." (We couched the information in terms of the scientists' predictions to make it more likely that we were measuring subjects' cognitive ability to deal with disconfirming evidence rather than their emotional reluctance to relinquish a belief to which they had already expressed a commitment.)

For half of the subjects, the confirming or disconfirming information presented in the third part of the story problem consisted only of information about covariation (the covariation-only condition). For half the subjects, the information consisted of information about covariation as well as information about causal mechanism (covariation and mechanism condition). When the information referred to causal mechanism, we were careful to mention that the subject's own mechanism (if she had mentioned one) had also been either confirmed or disconfirmed. (The protocol listed the subjects causal mechanism to remind the interviewer to do this.) For example, if a child in the covariation and mechanism condition said that high-sugar candy makes it hard to sleep because "all that sugar revs you up," she would not only be told the standard disconfirming-mechanism information but would also be told, "I know what you mean when you talk about being revved up and unable to sleep. But you know what? Scientists have found that the reason lots of kids get revved up when they eat a lot of candy is that they often eat *chocolate* candy, and chocolate has caffeine in it. So it's not the sugar that's revving them up; it's really the caffeine."

After subjects were presented with the confirming or disconfirming information, they were again asked to rate, for each variable, whether both values of the variable had the same effect or different effects and to justify their rating. If a subject's ratings had been extreme ($+5$ or -5) for the first rating and were also extreme for the second rating, then we asked her whether, if the scale had gone higher (or lower) than $+5$ (or -5), she would have chosen a different number the second time or would still have chosen the same number. If the subject would have chosen a higher (or lower) number, then her second rating was changed, conservatively, to a $+6$ or a -6.

Procedure

All subjects, including the college students, were individually interviewed. During each interview, interviewer and subject both looked at the same copy of the story problem while the interviewer read it aloud. However, to maintain the fiction that the scientists' prediction was the same as the subject's, the interviewer held the scientists' "predictions" about candy so that they could not be seen by the subject until the experimenter had chosen the prediction that corresponded to the subject's. (No such deception was necessary for the milk predictions, because we included only subjects who claimed that both types of milk had the same effect.) Subjects were allowed to reread the story problem if they wanted to. The interviewer wrote down the subject's responses.

Design

Between-subjects variables were age (sixth-graders versus ninth-graders versus college students), sex, and mechanism status (covariation only versus covariation and mechanism).

Within-subject variables were evidence type (disconfirming versus confirming) and causal status (causally relevant versus causally irrelevant). (Causal status corresponded to content, as we had expected subjects to believe that candy consumption did affect sleep, while milk consumption did not.) The design may be represented schematically as follows:

Group 1: covariation information alone
- Causal belief (candy) confirmed, noncausal belief (milk) disconfirmed
- Causal belief (candy) disconfirmed, noncausal belief (milk) confirmed

Group 2: covariation information plus information about mechanism
- Causal belief (candy) confirmed, noncausal belief (milk) disconfirmed
- Causal belief (candy) disconfirmed, noncausal belief (milk) confirmed

At each age (sixth-grade, ninth-grade, college), thirty-two subjects (16 females and 16 males) were interviewed. Half of each age × sex group was in the covariation-only condition; half was in the covariation plus mechanism condition.

Within each age × sex group, in the covariation-only condition and in the covariation plus mechanism condition, for half the subjects, the milk hypothesis (that type of milk did not matter) was confirmed, and the candy hypothesis (that type of candy did matter) was disconfirmed. For the other subjects, the milk hypothesis was disconfirmed, and the candy hypothesis confirmed. In addition, for half the subjects, evidence relevant to the milk hypothesis was presented first, and evidence relevant to the candy hypothesis second. For the other half of the subjects, order of presentation was reversed.

Finally, in the covariation plus mechanism condition, the mechanism for one of the target variables involved blood supply to the brain, and the mechanism for the other variable involved production of serotonin. For half of the subjects in each age × sex group, the blood-supply mechanism was paired with the type-of-milk variable, and the serotonin mechanism was paired with the type-of-candy variable. For the other subjects, the pairing was reversed. (And, of course, this was counterbalanced with which hypothesis was being confirmed or disconfirmed and with order of presentation.)

Results

Initial causal relevance of type of candy versus type of milk

As I already noted, we included subjects in the final sample only if they had given milk a negative rating and candy a positive rating. We replaced a total of 39 subjects: 11 sixth-graders (6 females and 5 males), 13 ninth-graders (7 females and 6 males), and 15 college students (7 females and 8 males).

Subjects' initial ratings were analyzed with an age × sex × confirmation status (confirm versus disconfirm) × evidence status (covariation versus mechanism) × type of cause (candy versus milk) analysis of variance. Not surprisingly, initial ratings for candy and for milk were significantly different from each other, $F(1, 72) = 1,934$, $p = .0001$, with the initial mean rating for candy being approximately $+3.28$ and for milk being approximately -3.02. Less obviously, there were no main effects for age, $F(2, 72) = .6$, $p = .55$, or for sex, $F(1, 72) = .19$, $p = .66$, and p values for each of the interactions were equal to or greater than .15. In a word, the only significant difference in the initial ratings was the difference that formed the basis for including subjects in the first place: we had wanted to include subjects for whom candy type was seen as causally relevant to sleep and milk type was seen as causally irrelevant, and we did.

Effects of evidence about mechanism

In analyzing their data, Kuhn et al. (1988) made the point that it did not make sense to ask about a belief that x was causal (or noncausal) whether that belief would be changed more by confirming or by disconfirming evidence. If someone believed already that, for example, type of candy was causally related to sleep, her causal rating would already be relatively high, and therefore there would be less room for movement if subsequent evidence were confirmatory rather than disconfirmatory.

However, as Kuhn et al. argued, it did make sense to look at confirmatory evidence and disconfirmatory evidence separately, and this we did. Following Kuhn et al., we asked whether confirming evidence that included a mechanism had a greater effect on a causal belief (that candy type did have an effect) than it did on a noncausal belief (that type of milk did not have an effect). Similarly, we asked whether disconfirming evidence that included a mechanism had a greater effect on a causal belief than it did on a noncausal belief.

Confirming evidence   Mechanism information did more to confirm a causal belief (about candy) than it did to confirm a noncausal belief (about milk). Specifically, the covariation alone versus covariation plus mechanism

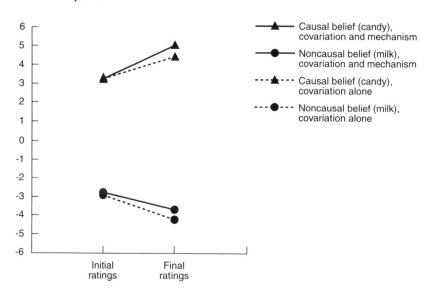

Figure 10.1
Initial and final ratings for confirming evidence.

difference for candy was not comparable to the covariation alone versus covariation plus mechanism difference for milk, $t(72) = 3.34$, $p = .0001$. As can be seen in figure 10.1, when the initial belief was that the factor (candy) was causal, information about covariation and mechanism made the belief even more causal than did information about covariation alone. In contrast, when the initial belief was that the factor (milk) was noncausal, then information about covariation and mechanism made the belief, if anything, less causal (the rating being closer to zero) than did information about covariation alone.

Recall Kuhn et al.'s finding regarding confirming covariation evidence: confirming (covariation) evidence had greater influence on a causal theory than on a noncausal theory (1988, chap. 6). This is parallel to our finding: when contrasted to evidence about covariation alone, covariation plus mechanism evidence had a greater effect on a causal theory than on a noncausal theory.

When the belief is that a factor (candy) is related to an effect, additional evidence that confirms the theory is, in a sense, unquestionable: it definitely has an effect (although in this case its effect was small). In contrast, when the belief is that a factor (milk) is *not* related to an effect, evidence that confirms the noncausal relation is a bit more questionable. Scientists may have found no relation, but the question always remains, Did they look hard enough?

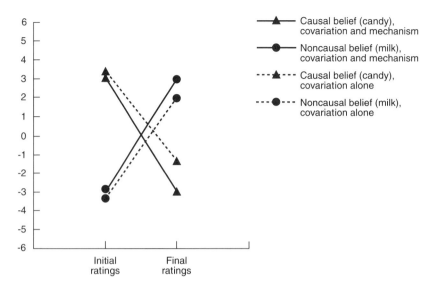

Figure 10.2
Initial and final ratings for disconfirming evidence.

Disconfirming evidence   The results regarding disconfirming evidence
were as we had expected and were parallel to the results for confirming
evidence: mechanism information did more to disconfirm a causal belief
(about candy) than it did to disconfirm a noncausal belief (about milk).
Specifically, the covariation alone versus covariation plus mechanism difference for candy was *not* comparable to the covariation alone versus
covariation plus mechanism difference for milk, $t(72) = 8.86$, $p = .0001$.
As figure 10.2 illustrates, when the initial belief was that the factor
(candy) was causal, the before and after change for covariation plus mechanism is roughly 1 1/3 points greater than the before and after change for
covariation alone. In contrast, for the noncausal milk ratings, the before
and after change for covariation plus mechanism is not even 1/2 point
greater than the before and after change for covariation alone.

Recall Kuhn et al.'s finding regarding disconfirming covariation evidence: disconfirming (covariation) evidence had greater influence on a
noncausal theory than on a causal theory. In contrast, the covariation plus
mechanism evidence in this study had a greater influence on the causal
theory than on the noncausal theory. That is, when the disconfirming evidence involved information about covariation and mechanism (rather than
covariation alone), we found the greater effect for precisely the sort of
(causal) theory that Kuhn et al. found to be the more resistant to disconfirming evidence.

General Discussion

To summarize the general findings, evidence that included a mechanism (in contrast to evidence that consisted of covariation alone) had a greater effect on causal (candy) ratings than it did on noncausal (milk) ratings. And this was true when the evidence was disconfirming as well as when it was confirming.

In line with the general thrust of this book, I suggest that causal beliefs involve more than beliefs about what covaries with what; they also involve beliefs about why the covariation obtains, either because the reasoner has some particular mechanism in mind or because she expects that there is one even if she does not know it. Therefore, when evidence, be it confirming or disconfirming, includes information about mechanism, the evidence is treated as more relevant to causal beliefs than to noncausal beliefs. Because noncausal beliefs involve the belief that covariation does *not* obtain, questions about mechanism do not arise in the first place, and so evidence that involves a mechanism is correspondingly less relevant.

Finally, regarding confirming evidence, though the present study asked questions that are not directly comparable to the questions asked in experiments 9 and 10, nevertheless it might appear at first glance that the present results are at odds with the results of experiments 9 and 10 regarding the effects of mechanism information. Recall that in those studies, when two factors were found to covary and the covariation was plausible, the presence of a mechanism that could explain how the covariation obtained did little to make the covariation seem more causal. In accounting for those results, I suggested that part of what it means for a covariation to be plausible is that there is a mechanism to explain it, so learning that a mechanism was present constituted redundant information. The present results might appear to conflict with the redundant-information suggestion because, in the present study, information about mechanism had a greater effect on the causal belief (which included a belief about mechanism) than on the noncausal belief. That is, information about mechanism was not treated as redundant. However, I suggest that, far from conflicting with my earlier suggestion, these results converge with it. In the present study, the most common mechanism cited for the belief that the type of candy affects sleep was that too much sugar revs children up or makes them hyper. However, the mechanism information that we presented to subjects dealt with blood supply to the brain or with serotonin production—particular mechanisms that, for our subjects, did not constitute redundant information.

There are two obvious limitations of the present study. Perhaps the more obvious is that it involved only one causal belief and only one noncausal belief. Considerations of external validity would require more instances. And in the ideal case, it would be useful to have one group of subjects who believed that, for example, the type of candy was causal and another group who believed that it was not. Another limitation involves the particular types of evidence used to disconfirm the causal beliefs. Our subjects believed that a large amount of sugar makes it hard to sleep because it revs people up. To disconfirm their belief, we presented "evidence" that the amount of sugar did not covary with sleep, and we described a mechanism that explained the noncovariation. That is, one way in which we disconfirmed the mechanism component of our subjects' belief was by substituting our result and its attendant mechanism for the ones the subjects had started with. It is an open question whether the mechanism component of the subjects' belief could have been disconfirmed more directly, without simply substituting an alternative mechanism for the one the subjects had initially cited. In addition, in disconfirming the causal belief, we also identified a confounding factor (the presence of caffeine in chocolate) that explained why eating a lot of candy often actually did make it difficult to sleep. It remains an open question whether disconfirming evidence would also have been effective if we had not explained why subjects' initial belief appeared to be correct.

I introduced this experiment frankly acknowledging that it had been a long shot. The causal belief that our subjects held was supported by parents' and teachers' advice and by the subjects' own personal experience, and was also accompanied by a mechanism to explain the effect. In chapter 3, I argued that beliefs of this sort should require a lot of effort to disconfirm because they are imbedded in a network of other beliefs. The present experiment was a long shot because the effort we expended on disconfirming the belief was small: the evidence that we described was minimal and was presented during the course of a single experimental session. In spite of this, however, the disconfirming-mechanism information did have an effect, granted, not a large one but one larger than the effect of covariation information alone. I conclude that, its limitations notwithstanding, this study legitimizes the suggestion that disconfirming evidence might be more effective (and confirmation bias more tractable) if the disconfirming evidence acknowledges information about mechanism as well as information about covariation.

Appendix to Experiment 13

First and second parts of the story problem

Problem Some scientists want to know whether certain kinds of bedtime snacks make a difference in how easy it is for children to fall asleep at night. The scientists do their study at a boarding school where the children live. This means that the children all eat the same food during the day. But at the end of the day the scientists divide the children into four groups.

Each group has 10 children in it. The groups are the same in terms of age, weight, gender, activity level, etc. The only difference among the groups is that each group is given a different bedtime snack:

• To see whether type of candy makes a difference, the scientists give the first group high-sugar candy and the second group low-sugar candy.
• To see whether type of milk makes a difference, the scientists give the third group ordinary whole milk and the fourth group low-fat milk.

Here are the four groups and their bedtime snacks.

Group 1: high-sugar candy
Group 2: low-sugar candy·
Group 3: whole milk
Group 4: low-fat milk

Think about type of candy and type of milk, and I'm going to ask you some questions about them.

[New page]

1. Is one type of candy better than the other at causing easy sleep? Or do they both have the same effect?

−5	−4	−3	−2	−1	0	+1	+2	+3	+4	+5
Both types definitely have the same effect		Both types probably have the same effect			Can't tell if both have same effect or if one is better			One type is probably better than the other		One type is definitely better than the other

2. How do you know that one type of candy is better than the other? Why do you think so?
3. How will type of candy work? What will be the process by which one type of candy is better than the other?

[New page]

1. Is one type of milk better than the other at causing easy sleep? Or do they both have the same effect?

−5	−4	−3	−2	−1	0	+1	+2	+3	+4	+5
Both types definitely have the same effect		Both types probably have the same effect			Can't tell if both have same effect or if one is better			One type is probably better than the other		One type is definitely better than the other

2. How do you know that one type of milk is better than the other? Why do you think so?
3. How will type of milk work? What will be the process by which one type of milk is better than the other?

Third part of the story problem in various conditions and versions

Condition: covariation and mechanism, noncausal (milk) belief confirmed   This is what the scientists predicted: the two types of milk will both have the same effect.

1. This is what the scientists found: children who drank whole milk fell asleep *just as easily* as children who drank low fat milk.

2. They also found out something about how this happens. They found that, when you eat fats, blood rushes to your stomach to digest them. This leaves less blood in other parts of your body, including the brain. The lower blood supply in the brain makes the brain sleepy. However, the brain needs only a slightly lower supply of blood to become sleepy. Eating even a small amount of fat reduces the blood supply to the brain enough to make the brain sleepy. So it doesn't matter whether children drink low-fat milk or hi-fat, whole milk.

3. [The subject's causal mechanism]

Now that you know what the scientists have found, do you think one type of milk is better than the other at causing easy sleep? Or do they both have the same effect?

−5	−4	−3	−2	−1	0	+1	+2	+3	+4	+5
Both types definitely have the same effect		Both types probably have the same effect			Can't tell if both have same effect or if one is better			One type is probably better than the other		One type is definitely better than the other

Condition: covariation and mechanism, causal (sugar) belief disconfirmed   This is what the scientists predicted: high-sugar candy is better than low-sugar candy at causing easy sleep.

1. However, this is what the scientists found: children who ate high-sugar candy fell asleep *just as easily* as children who ate low-sugar candy.

2. They also found out something about how this happens. They found that eating sugar causes the brain to produce something called serotonin, and serotonin causes the brain to sleep. However, the brain needs only a small amount of serotonin to become sleepy. Eating even a small amount of sugar produces enough serotonin to make the brain sleep. So it doesn't matter whether children eat high-sugar or low-sugar candy.

3. [Subject's causal mechanism]

Now that you know what the scientists have found, do you think one type of candy is better than the other at causing easy sleep? Or do they both have the same effect?

−5	−4	−3	−2	−1	0	+1	+2	+3	+4	+5
Both types definitely have the same effect		Both types probably have the same effect			Can't tell if both have same effect or if one is better			One type is probably better than the other		One type is definitely better than the other

Condition: covariation and mechanism, noncausal (milk) belief disconfirmed   This is what scientists predicted: the two types of milk will both have the same effect.

1. However, this is what the scientists found: children who drank *whole milk* fell asleep *more easily* than children who drank low-fat milk.

2. They also found out something about how thls happens. They found that eating fats causes the brain to produce something called serotonin, and serotonin causes the brain to sleep. The more fats you eat, the more serotonin your brain produces, and the sleepier you become. Therefore, whole milk makes you sleepier than low-fat milk.

3. [Subject's causal mechanism]

Now that you know what the scientists have found, do you think one type of milk is better than the other at causing easy sleep? Or do they both have the same effect?

−5	−4	−3	−2	−1	0	+1	+2	+3	+4	+5
Both types definitely have the same effect		Both types probably have the same effect			Can't tell if both have same effect or if one is better			One type is probably better than the other		One type is definitely better than the other

Condition: covariation and mechanism, causal (sugar) belief confirmed   This is what the scientists predicted: high-sugar candy is better than low-sugar candy at causing easy sleep.

1. This is what the scientists found: children who ate *high-sugar* candy fell asleep *more easily* than children who ate low-sugar candy.

2. They also found out something about how this happens. They found that when you eat a lot of sugar, blood rushes to your stomach to digest it. This leaves less blood in other parts of your body, including your brain. The lower blood supply in the brain makes the brain sleepy. The more sugar you eat, the more blood leaves your brain and goes to your stomach, and the sleepier you become. Therefore, high-sugar candy makes children sleepier than low-sugar candy.

3. [The subject's causal mechanism]

Now that you know what the scientists have found, do you think one type of sugar is better than the other at causing easy sleep? Or do you think they both have the same effect?

−5	−4	−3	−2	−1	0	+1	+2	+3	+4	+5
Both types definitely have the same effect		Both types probably have the same effect			Can't tell if both have same effect or if one is better			One type is probably better than the other		One type is definitely better than the other

General Summary

I began this chapter with the argument that causal beliefs often include two components: the belief that a certain factor does covary with a certain effect (lots of sugar causes sleeplessness) and the belief that there is some mechanism that can explain the covariation (sugar makes children hyper). I argued further that to disconfirm such a belief, one would need to call both components into question. This argument received some support from the present findings.

Using covariation evidence alone, Kuhn et al. found that causal theories are more resistant to disconfirmation than are noncausal theories. In our study, disconfirming evidence that involved covariation and mechanism had the greater effect for precisely those (causal) theories that Kuhn et al. found to be the more resistant to change. What the present findings suggest is that the effects of disconfirming evidence in Kuhn et al.'s work might have been greater if the disconfirming evidence had included information about mechanism as well as information about covariation.

Chapter 11

Confirmation, Disconfirmation, and Differing Views of Scientific Inquiry

In this chapter I summarize the results of two experiments that have already been published (Koslowski and Maqueda 1993) because they illustrate the general theme that conclusions about whether people reason scientifically depend, in part, on what one's view of scientific inquiry is. In addition, they also illustrate the more specific suggestion that conclusions about confirmation bias and hypothesis testing also depend on one's view of scientific inquiry.

Mynatt, Doherty, and Tweney's Study

Mynatt et al.'s Tasks

In our experiment, we replicated (with modifications) the Mynatt, Doherty, and Tweney (1977) study described briefly in chapter 3. Recall that in their task, subjects (college students) were shown two computer screens, one at a time. Each screen displayed triangles, disks, and squares each of which was either one brightness level or another. (I refer to the brightness levels as "black" versus "gray".) The first screen displayed a gray triangle, a black square, and a black disk. The second screen is reproduced in figure 11.1. On each screen, a particle could be fired from a fixed point at any of the figures. The subject's task was to generate a hypothesis to describe the motion of the particle.

In fact, all gray figures repelled the moving particle because a circular, nonvisible boundary extended 4.2 cm from the geometric center of the gray figures. However, the task was contrived to suggest, instead, that it was shape that mattered, by having a black triangle located within the boundary that surrounded the gray disk (see figure 11.1). Thus, the gray triangle and the black triangle both repelled the particle, but the gray triangle did so because it was gray, whereas the black triangle did so because it was within the boundary of the gray disk.[1]

After generating their hypotheses based on the two initial screens, subjects were presented with 10 pairs of screens, one pair at a time, and told to choose one member of each pair to have the particle fired at (see table 11.1). However, the particle was not actually fired. For some of the pairs,

Input particle direction?

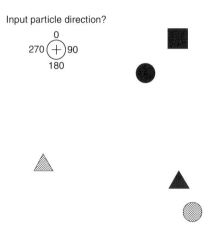

Figure 11.1
The second screen from Mynatt et al. 1977.

certain choices were identified as *confirmatory*, *disconfirmatory*, or *as providing evidence for an alternative* to a triangle hypothesis. I stress that the three types of choices (confirmatory, disconfirmatory, and suggestive of an alternative) were treated by Mynatt et al. as mutually exclusive. And one screen, 5B (black triangle), was designated as providing "absolute, unambiguous disconfirmation of a triangle hypothesis."

After the paired-screen tasks, subjects were allowed to fire the particles on either chosen or nonchosen screens, but only at one member of each pair (*a restriction some subjects ignored*). After firing as many particles as they wished, subjects were told to write down their final hypothesis.

Mynatt et al.'s Conclusions

The data of interest consist of the screen choices made by the 20 subjects who generated an initial triangle hypothesis that included no mention of brightness. Mynatt et al. concluded the following: "The tendency to choose confirmatory screens was present from the very first pair of screens: Fifteen of the twenty subjects choose screen B (a confirmatory choice) on pair 1" (1977, 91). Furthermore, subjects with triangle hypotheses preferentially chose screens that could only confirm the hypothesis (that is, screens that displayed gray triangles or black triangles within the boundary of a gray figure) rather than screens that would allow them to disconfirm the hypothesis or to test alternatives (such as screens that displayed a black triangle or a gray disk or square). In addition, Mynatt et al. also concluded that subjects do not appear to look for and test alternative hypotheses.

Table 11.1
Paired-screen descriptions

Pair no.	Screen A	Screen B
1	Gray disk, black square[b]	Gray triangle, black square[a]
2	Gray triangle[a]	Gray square[b]
3	Black square, black disk	Black square, black square
4	Gray disk, gray disk[b]	Gray disk, gray triangle[a]
5	Gray triangle	Black triangle[c]
6	Black square	Black disk
7	Black triangle, gray square[a]	Black disk, gray square[b]
8	Black square	Black disk, black disk
9	Gray triangle[a]	Gray disk[b]
10	Black disk, gray disk[b]	Gray triangle, black disk[a]

a. Confirmatory choices for subjects with triangle hypotheses.
b. A particle fired at the figures on this screen would stop, providing evidence for an alternative to a triangle hypothesis.
c. A particle fired at the triangle on this screen would not stop, logically disconfirming a triangle hypothesis.

The free-response data indicated that subjects could use falsifying data once they got it: Nearly all of the subjects who had an initial triangle hypothesis but who obtained "unambiguous falsifying evidence" changed to a correct or partially correct hypothesis (in contrast to those subjects who did not obtain falsifying data). That is, if confronted with unambiguous falsification, subjects can take it into account.

In a subsequent study (Mynatt, Doherty, and Tweney 1978), subjects were shown 27 objects, only some of which repelled the particle. The angle of deflection was determined by the angle of incidence, brightness, and size. Subjects reasoned outloud. Mynatt et al. (1978) concluded that subjects almost always seemed to be seeking confirmation (for example, "My pet hypothesis is ..., so I'm going to start trying to figure out if that's feasible"). Furthermore, when tests yielded disconfirming data, the hypothesis was rejected only 30 percent of the time but modified 37 percent of the time. Mynatt et al. treated the small number of hypothesis rejections as additional evidence of confirmation bias.

In summary, Mynatt et al. concluded that "confirmation bias ... may be a general cognitive process" but that subjects can use falsifying data once they obtain it (1977, 93).

Problematic Assumptions and Conclusions

I argue that in Mynatt et al.'s task, claims about what constitutes correct performance are both unclear and based on faulty tacit premises. The result is that it is impossible to tell what the subjects are actually doing; their behavior is compatible with alternative interpretations.

Some of the problems involve a lack of clarity in the task itself, while others involve the view of scientific inquiry that the task is based on. The problematic assumptions and conclusions include the following:

The hypothesis is that triangles and only triangles always repel
Although Mynatt et al. (1977) do not make this explicit, for their argument to be consistent, the triangularity hypothesis must be understood as "All and only triangles repel" rather than as "All triangles repel." Treating the hypothesis as "All triangles repel" is neutral about whether disks and squares also repel; treating the hypothesis as "All and only triangles repel" implies that disks and squares do not repel. The distinction is important because it determines which tests are appropriate. To test an "all triangles" hypothesis, one would simply test more and more triangles. However, to test an "all and only triangles" hypothesis, one would need to test a triangle and a *non*triangle. (Just as to test whether only wood floats, one would test nonwood as well as wood.) I assume the authors had in mind an "all and only triangles" hypothesis because of the task structure: the initial screens were contrived to suggest, misleadingly, that triangles repelled but disks and squares did not, and the task was arranged to make it true that gray figures repelled but black ones did not. Therefore, I stress, the appropriate test of the "all and only triangles" hypothesis is to examine a triangle as well as a nontriangle. I will refer to this as the "appropriate triangle test."

A test of the triangle hypothesis that consisted of examining only a triangle (and that did not include an examination of a nontriangle) would not be an adequate test. It would be what Klayman and Ha (1987) call a "biased, positive test." (However, as Klayman and Ha note, even a positive-test strategy can yield disconfirming data; testing a triangle can disconfirm the hypothesis that triangles repel if the triangle chosen is the black one.)

The fact that the appropriate triangle test requires at least two instances (a triangle and a nontriangle) makes it difficult to understand what subjects in Mynatt et al.'s task are doing. When subjects choose a screen such as the "confirmatory" 2A (gray triangle), it is certainly possible that they are merely carrying out a biased positive-test strategy. However, it is equally possible that they are simply carrying out one part of the *appropriate* triangle test, namely the part that consists of examining a triangle. Because of the way the task is designed, there is no way to decide between the two possibilities, because subjects are allowed to choose only one screen, and an appropriate test would require two. Nevertheless, Mynatt et al. treat such choices as confirming instances.

Similarly, when subjects examine screens 6A (black square), 8A (black square), or 6B (black disk), they could be carrying out the other part of the appropriate triangle test, namely the part that consists of examining a nontriangle. However, Mynatt et al. do not describe these three screens as being *any* of the three choices (confirmatory, disconfirmatory, suggestive of an alternative).

Tests to confirm, tests to disconfirm, and tests to suggest an alternative are treated as distinct

Furthermore, treating confirming choices, disconfirming choices, and choices that suggest an alternative as mutually exclusive of one another raises additional problems, as does the corollary assumption that it was the particular tests themselves, rather than the results of the tests, that confirmed or disconfirmed.

Recall my argument in chapter 3: The test strategies to confirm a hypothesis are the same as the tests to disconfirm a hypothesis because both involve considering alternative hypotheses. Furthermore, it is the results of tests, not the tests themselves, that disconfirm. If one tests the triangle hypothesis by testing a gray triangle (which Mynatt et al. treat as a confirming choice), the results could nevertheless *disconfirm* the hypothesis: one could learn that, contrary to one's hypothesis, a particular gray triangle did *not* repel the particle.

However, one could argue that testing a gray triangle such as 2A does constitute a confirmatory test in the sense that it is redundant: It tells the subject no more than what she had already learned in the second screen of the initial set, a screen that also displayed a gray triangle (see figure 11.1). But it is not clear that this argument would be warranted because of the third point:

The role of the initial screens is not clear

In Mynatt et al.'s task, it is not clear whether correct performance was to consist of treating the two initial screens as part of the subject's actual "data set" or as "pilot data" that merely suggested a hypothesis that was actually to be tested with the paired screens. As we will see below, many subjects do treat the two initial screens as not providing part of the actual test data. Even more problematic, if correct performance did consist of treating the initial screens as test data, this presents as many problems for the coding system as if correct performance had consisted of treating the initial screens as pilot data—a point to which I return shortly.

The alternative hypotheses are not clear

In addition, the tacit assumption behind the task was that shade was the only alternative hypothesis that subjects were considering. But in fact, the correct hypothesis was more complicated than that: it involved positing not only that shade was relevant but also that the repelling boundary extended beyond the gray figures, which enabled other figures within the boundary to appear to be repelling. That is, even the correct hypothesis involved more than just the variable of shade. Therefore, subjects might (and, as we will see below, did) generate hypotheses that involved variables other than shape, shade, and boundaries, such as whether the target figure was in close proximity to another, whether the two proximal figures were both of the same shade and/or shape, whether figures repelled if they were both gray and angled (gray triangles and gray squares), etc.

Now in light of the above points, consider the "disconfirming" black triangle (5B). If the initial screens were to be treated as actual test data, then it made sense to choose the "disconfirmatory" black triangle (5B) *only* if the triangle hypothesis in fact took account of both variables: shape and the fact that the repelling boundary extended beyond the figures. If the initial screens were to be treated as actual data but the hypothesis did not acknowledge the boundary variable, then testing 5B would have been redundant (providing, if anything, confirmatory rather than disconfirmatory data) because a black triangle had already been tested on the second of the initial screens.

However, perhaps correct performance consisted of treating the two initial screens as pilot data. In this case, the black triangle (5B) would not have been redundant, but there would have been a problem with some of the other paired-screen choices. For example, consider again the gray triangle (2A), classified as confirmatory. If one treats the initial screens as pilot data, then testing a gray triangle need not have been redundant, "confirming" data; it could instead have been simply one part of a two-part triangle test (a triangle and a nontriangle) that was actually testing the hypothesis that had merely been suggested by the two initial screens.

Hypotheses are treated as specific rather than as "working"
An additional, tacit assumption is that subjects were generating hypotheses that were both circumscribed and specific. However, as we will see below, laymen, like scientists, often start out with a general working hypothesis ("It depends on shape") that they then refine and try to specify the limits of as additional data come in. (As noted earlier, I am using the term "disconfirming data" rather than the term "anomalous data" because that is the term Mynatt et al. [1977] used. But note that if the subject's initial hypothesis is a nonspecific working hypothesis, then the data are merely anomalous because they provide the occasion for modifying the hypothesis rather than rejecting it outright. Furthermore, note also that in a strictly logical sense, even a revised hypothesis disconfirms a working hypothesis because, from a logical point of view, the modified hypothesis

is incompatible with the working hypothesis. From a strictly logical point of view, a subject who modifies her working hypothesis in the face of noncongruent data can be construed as rejecting her working hypothesis, that is, as not exhibiting a confirmation bias.)

For example, consider the "confirmatory" screen of a gray triangle and a black square (1B). It is possible that in choosing this screen, subjects were not seeking redundant, and therefore confirmatory, information about a (gray) triangle but were rather trying to specify the limits of an initial working hypothesis about shape that was not very specific, for example, "I wonder whether triangles repel if they're near another figure" (if the second initial screen, which also has a triangle near another figure, is only considered pilot data), or "I wonder whether triangles repel if they're near another figure that is black" (if the second initial screen, which showed a triangle near a gray figure, is treated as actual data). (Analogous arguments can be made for other "confirmatory" screens, such as 4B and 7A).

The disconfirming test is misdescribed

To return to my earlier point, if the triangle hypothesis is "Only triangles repel," then the appropriate test consists of a triangle and a nontriangle. Whether the test confirms or disconfirms the hypothesis depends on the results, not on the test itself. If the triangle does not repel, this would disconfirm the triangle hypothesis and suggest an alternative. But if a disk or square were to repel, then this too would simultaneously disconfirm the triangle hypothesis and suggest an alternative.

Therefore, if the subject testing the triangle hypothesis had chosen, as the nontriangle part of the appropriate test, a nontriangle that was gray, namely a gray disk (9B) or a gray square (2B), then either nontriangle would have disconfirmed the hypothesis that only triangles repel because each would have been an example of a nontriangle that did repel. Furthermore, while disconfirming the triangle hypothesis, each figure would have simultaneously suggested (or provided data that corroborated) the alternative hypothesis that it was really shade that mattered. That is, the "disconfirming" black triangle (5B) was not the only figure that could have disconfirmed the triangle hypothesis.

In light of the above points, what do we make of the finding that those subjects who chose the "disconfirming" black triangle (5B) were more likely than those who did not to achieve a correct or partially correct final hypothesis, that is, one that involved shade. The obvious question to ask is whether subjects would have done just as well if they had chosen a gray square (2B) or a gray disk (9B). As just noted, both of these too would have disconfirmed the triangle hypothesis and suggested the alternative of shade because they too would have repelled the dot. I suggest that the black triangle was useful not because it involved a special kind of "disconfirming test" that was different from a confirming test. Rather, it was useful because for those subjects who had not thought of the shade alternative (but who were astute observers), the black triangle suggested that alternative. And for those subjects who had already been considering shade as well as triangularity, the black triangle provided disconfirming results (not a disconfirming *test*) for the triangle hypothesis and confirming results (not a confirming *test*) for the shade hypothesis. This demonstrates that subjects who had already been considering the shade alternative and who tested the black triangle were able to take account of data that confirmed their alternative. That is, this finding demonstrates that subjects do take account of data. However, this finding does not demonstrate that there is a special kind of disconfirming test, nor does it demonstrate that it is this kind of *test* (rather than the results of the test) that propels a subject toward the correct hypothesis. (By way of underlining the distinction between tests and results, note that the *test* that consisted of examining the black triangle provided confirming *results* only if the shade alternative was being considered. If the altrnative being considered was something other than shade, then the black triangle might or might not have confirmed the alternative.)

The subject's motivation is inferred from the test

Finally, to return to an earlier point, because the tests to confirm are the same as the tests to disconfirm, one cannot infer a subject's motivation from the kind of test that she carries out. One can make judgments about whether the test was the correct one, but this is a separate issue. Thus it was inappropriate to conclude that a confirmation bias was reflected by statements such as, "My pet hypothesis is . . . , so I'm going to start trying to figure out if this is feasible." To return to one of the distinctions invoked in chapter 3, this statement may have reflected the hope that the hypothesis would be confirmed, but the subject voicing such a hope could still have generated a fair test and, if the results had been anomalous or disconfirming, could still have modified or rejected her hypothesis in light of the results. Note that conducting a fair test and acknowledging anomalous or disconfirming evidence would have constituted two senses in which the subject did not have a confirmation bias. Figuring out if a hypothesis is feasible is a far cry from either hoping that it is confirmed and from making sure that the test is limited enough to ensure that anomalous or disconfirming data will not be detected.

Experiment 14
Barbara Koslowski and Mariano Maqueda

In our first experiment, we replicated the Mynatt et al. (1977) paired-screen study with 20 undergraduates and 20 college-bound ninth-graders.

However, we added a modification: we asked our subjects to verbalize their motivation for each paired-screen choice. (An additional difference between our task and Mynatt et al.'s task was that we presented the initial screens and figures on posterboard and moved the particle manually when subjects told us where to "fire" it.)

Motivations to Confirm

We found that a verbalized motivation to confirm was rare. Fifteen subjects generated a triangle hypothesis. Of these, seven subjects (three college students and four ninth-graders) chose screen B on the first pair. For all seven students, their stated motivation was to specify more precisely what the data set was. For example, "It seemed (on the initial screens) to get a little bit closer to that black triangle, but I'm not sure it did, so I want to try it again" or "I just want to check on what that black triangle does" or "Does it stop the dot on my screen as well as yours?" That is, in terms of what they verbalized, subjects were motivated not to confirm a hypothesis but to specify the data set more accurately. Furthermore, the data from the entire sample also provide little evidence for a motivation to confirm. The number of reasons that involved an attempt to confirm (for example, "I know how the dot will move") came from only three ninth-graders, two of whom gave this response only once.

Alternative Hypotheses

The modal response was to consider alternative hypotheses. The college students did this an average of seven times, and the ninth-graders an average of five times. In addition, all of the college students and 19 of the ninth-graders did this at least once. That is, subjects were not using the tunnel vision of confirmation bias to focus only on their own initial hypotheses.

Working Hypotheses

Furthermore, in each age group, 17 of the 20 subjects said, at least once, that they wanted to test an alternative hypothesis based neither on triangularity alone nor on shade alone. In doing this, subjects were not restricting themselves to the two particular hypotheses (one based on shape and the other based on shade) that Mynatt et al. (1977) had tacitly anticipated would be the only contenders. Sometimes their hypotheses involved wondering whether shape and shade might interact; sometimes they involved other variables (for example, wondering whether the triangle would repel when it was near another figure, whether it would do so when the nearby figure was the same shade or shape as the triangle, etc.).

That is, these data illustrated another point relevant to the question of confirmation bias: When these nonanticipated hypotheses occurred, they occurred as modifications of existing hypotheses. In short, subjects were treating their existing hypotheses as working hypotheses and were trying to refine them by generating the unanticipated hypotheses.[2]

Relevance to Confirmation Bias

In short, in what subjects actually said they were doing, we found little evidence for a confirmation bias. In addition, subjects were keenly aware that they were testing alternative hypotheses, and the alternative hypotheses they generated were not restricted to the anticipated hypotheses of shade alone or of triangularity alone. Furthermore, most subjects, at least once, treated an existing hypothesis as a working hypothesis to be further refined. That is, what subjects actually said they were doing was not congruent with some of the assumptions that characterized Mynatt et al.'s task and some of the conclusions that were drawn from it.

Age Differences

Finally, there were no age differences in the total number of responses generated. However, college students were more likely than ninth-graders to verbalize the aim of testing or ruling out alternative hypotheses and less likely than ninth-graders to verbalize the aim of merely gathering information. Gathering information included such things as: testing a figure, like a gray square, because there had been no gray square on the initial screens; double-checking a result, which frequently happened because the subject could not remember what a particular figure had done; checking whether a figure did the same thing consistently; etc. The age difference made intuitive sense. One would expect younger subjects to be more concerned than older ones with verifying what the facts were that they had to work with.

Experiment 15
Barbara Koslowski and Mariano Maqueda

In our second experiment, we allowed subjects (who included sixth-graders as well as ninth-graders and college students) to design their own displays to test their hypotheses. In addition, we gave them feedback on their tests. We did this because verbalizing an intention to test an alternative hypothesis (as subjects did in the first experiment) does not guarantee the wherewithal to be able to do so. Therefore, in the first experiment, when subjects said that they were testing a hypothesis and then chose a particular screen, they could have been doing one of two things: They could have been choosing the screen because it constituted one part of an appropriate test (the other part of which they would have completed had the task been structured differently). For example, if choosing a triangle screen to test the triangle hypothesis, they could have been treating the screen as one part of an appropriate test that, under different circumstances, would have included a triangle and a nontriangle. Alternatively, subjects could have been choosing the screen because they mistakenly believed that choosing a single screen would constitute an adequate test. To distinguish these two possibilities, in our second experiment we allowed subjects to design their own screens to test.

We interviewed 20 subjects in each of three age-groups: college students and college-bound ninth- and sixth-graders. As in the first experiment, subjects were first presented with the same two initial screens as in that experiment, allowed to fire the particle at whatever they wanted, and asked to write their hypothesis. Then subjects were given a blank screen, 12 loose figures (two of each of the three shapes in each of the two shades) and were told that they could design any screens they wanted and have the experimenter "fire" the particle at any figure that they chose.

Appropriate or Contrastive Tests

One bit of evidence against a confirmation bias was that, except for three ninth-graders, all of the subjects carried out at least one appropriate test (for example, contrasting one black figure and one gray figure in order to test the shade hypothesis). Specifically, sixth-graders, ninth-graders, and college students, respectively, carried out an average of 2.9, 2.4, and 4.3 appropriate tests.

Even more striking with regard to confirmation bias was the fact that when subjects carried out appropriate tests, 11, and 13 of the sixth-graders, ninth-graders, and college students, respectively, carried out tests that were exhaustive. This is noteworthy because exhaustive testing maximizes the likelihood of finding disconfirming instances.

Alternative Hypotheses

Additional evidence against a confirmation bias was that in each of the age groups, 18 of the 20 subjects tested at least one alternative hypothesis other than the obvious alternative hypotheses about shape alone or shade alone. That is, as in the first experiment, there was little evidence that a confirmation bias was restricting subjects to focus only on their initial hypothesis or, indeed, only on the obvious hypotheses.

Working Hypotheses and Confirmation Bias

Also, as in the first experiment, subjects did not restrict themselves to testing only the hypotheses that Mynatt et al. had anticipated: The same 18 subjects in each of the age groups tested at least one hypothesis other than the hypothesis about shape alone or shade alone, and most of the subjects at each age tested at least two such hypotheses. That is, Mynatt et al. had deemed some tests to be disconfirming on the basis of an assumption of a single alternative hypothesis (shade), but subjects were not restricting themselves to that single alternative.

And as in the first experiment, when the 18 subjects in each age group generated the nonanticipated hypotheses, they treated the hypotheses as further refinements or modifications of existing hypotheses. That is, as in the first experiment, most of the subjects in each age group generated at least one hypothesis that they treated as a working hypothesis, and this argues against the presence of a confirmation bias: subjects were quite willing to revise their initial hypothesis. (Recall, also, the point made early in chapter 2: If the initial hypothesis—be it working or specific—is that triangles repel and if the subsequently refined hypothesis asks whether triangles repel even when they are close to a square, then, in a strictly logical sense, the refined hypothesis does disconfirm the initial hypothesis. The hypothesis that triangles repel is, from the point of view of logic, incompatible with the hypothesis that triangles repel even when they are close to a square.)

This finding is congruent with Klahr and Dunbar's (1988) point that subjects in Mynatt et al.'s (1977, 1978) studies were not clinging to a hypothesis in the face of disconfirming data but rather were modifying what Klahr and Dunbar call a "frame" (and what I am calling a "working hypothesis") and were then testing the modified frame before switching to another frame.

With regard to hypothesis testing, there was also another sense in which few subjects in any of the age groups gave evidence of a confirmation bias: Eight (of the 60) subjects generated a screen that tested only one part of an appropriate hypothesis. That is, they generated a biased, positive-test strategy. However, for four of the subjects, this came near the very end of the session, when subjects were verifying hypotheses that they had already (correctly) tested against several alternatives.

In summary, subjects of all ages considered alternative hypotheses; the alternative hypotheses were not restricted to shade alone or to shape alone; subjects often treated hypotheses as working hypotheses to be revised; the tests were appropriate and therefore had the potential for confirming the alternative hypothesis and disconfirming the original hypothesis; and many of the tests were exhaustive, which maximized the probability of uncovering disconfirming data. That is, we did not find a confirmation bias, in part because we took into account the following facts: tests that have the potential for disconfirming the initial hypothesis and tests that have the potential for confirming an alternative hypothesis are not mutually exclusive tests; depending on what the results are, testing one triangle and one nontriangle can simultaneously disconfirm the triangle hypothesis and confirm an alternative; and it is scientifically legitimate to revise as well as to reject hypotheses.

Age Differences

Although subjects in all three age groups arranged appropriate tests of hypotheses, the younger subjects arranged a smaller number than did the college students. (This did not reflect age differences in the average totals of responses generated.) In addition, younger subjects were more likely than college students to carry out, at least once, an appropriate test that was redundant (for example, testing black squares versus grey squares after having already tested all black figures and all gray figures) or an appropriate test that involved only a subportion of the data (for example, testing whether shape matters but using only gray figures to test the hypothesis).

We conclude that the younger subjects' behavior reflects primarily information-processing limitations. This is why, even though they were presented with the same stimulus display as the college students, they generated fewer alternative hypotheses. This is also why they carried out tests that were redundant or that considered only subportions of the data. Both strategies minimized the information-processing load.

General Summary

I argued that the strategies for confirming a hypothesis, for disconfirming a hypothesis, and for testing an alternative all involve the same tests. The tests are not mutually exclusive. It is the results of the tests, not the tests themselves, that either confirm or disconfirm. For example, an appropriate test of a triangle hypothesis (whether the intent is to confirm or to disconfirm it) consists of examining nontriangles as well as triangles, and this test has the potential for uncovering confirming as well as disconfirming results.

At all ages, the overwhelming majority of the tests that subjects carried out were appropriate. We found very little evidence of inappropriate, positive-test strategies (testing only triangles). That is, we found very little evidence for a confirmation bias. Furthermore, we found that subjects tested alternative hypotheses and carried out exhaustive tests (which maximize the likelihood of uncovering disconfirming data). Both findings also argue against a confirmation bias. We also found that subjects often treated their initial hypotheses as working hypotheses to be refined rather than as circumscribed hypotheses to be either confirmed or disconfirmed. In a word, whether subjects are seen as having a confirmation bias depends in part on whether one acknowledges that confirmation, disconfirmation, and testing an alternative do not involve mutually exclusive tests and also depends on whether one views it as scientifically legitimate to treat hypotheses as working hypotheses to be revised rather than as circumscribed hypotheses to be rejected in the face of noncongruent evidence.

Younger subjects tested fewer alternatives (although when they did, they did so appropriately), and they tested redundant hypotheses or hypotheses that concerned only a subportion of the data. I argued that age differences reflected differences in information-processing capacity.

Chapter 12

Spontaneous Generation of Appropriate Tests, Causal Mechanisms, and Alternative Hypotheses

Experiment 16
Barbara Koslowski, Renee Goodwin, Eileen Gravani,
Margaret Adams

In this study we had two aims. One was to examine the psychological validity of some of the types of information we had been asking subjects to reason about. The second, related but more specific aim was to examine, in a different task situation, some of the issues concerning confirmation, disconfirmation, and alternative hypotheses that were also addressed in experiments 14 and 15.

Regarding psychological validity, in many of the previous experiments our aim had been to present subjects with different types of information (for example, about causal mechanisms, alternative accounts, internal and external validity, etc.) and to see whether subjects would take account of the information when reasoning about causal explanations. And we found that to varying degrees, subjects did take account of such information. This suggested that some sorts of information that have been identified as playing a role in scientific inquiry can also play a role in the thinking of individual subjects.

In the present study we had a somewhat different but converging aim. We wanted to see whether, in evaluating a causal explanation, subjects would seek these sorts of information on their own, even if it was not presented to them.

Regarding our second, more specific aim, recall the argument that motivated experiments 14 and 15: in a certain sense, the test to confirm a hypothesis is the same as the test to disconfirm it, because aiming to find confirming results and aiming to find disconfirming results both involve taking account of alternative hypotheses—either to rule them out or to demonstrate that it is in fact an alternative factor rather than the target factor that is causing the effect. Therefore, in terms of assessing confirmation bias, the real question is whether people take account of the relevant alternatives.

One way of taking account of relevant alternatives is to consider, for example, whether alternative hypotheses have been ruled out (see experiments 7 and 8). However, another way of taking account of alternatives is to propose tests that would discover results supporting an alternative hypothesis and calling the target hypothesis into question. That is, one way of taking account of alternatives is to propose tests that will uncover disconfirming evidence if it exists. We examined this question in experiments 14 and 15 but in those experiments, the tasks were highly artificial. Therefore, we decided to examine it again in the less artificial context of the present experiment. In line with the discussion in chapter 3, we coded the tests that subjects proposed, in the present experiment, in terms of whether they involved an appropriate contrast as well as whether they explicitly took account of alternative hypotheses.

We presented each subject with two problems. One problem asked whether allowing parents to stay overnight with their hospitalized children improves the children's recovery rate. The other asked whether having a small number of sales clerks increases shoplifting. For each problem, we asked the subject to describe whatever information she felt would be useful to solve the problem.

Because our question was whether subjects would request various sorts of information, we had the following concern: We thought it quite conceivable that the path of least resistance would involve proposing a straightforward experimental intervention designed to acquire information about covariation and would stop there. (For example, have some parents stay overnight and others not and see whether the children in the first group recover faster than the children in the second group.) That is, we thought that an interview that permitted direct experimental intervention would decrease the liklihood that subjects would show an interest in information other than information about covariation. Therefore, for half the subjects, the story problems were presented in an unrestricted way: the subject could use whatever strategy she wanted, including direct experimental intervention, to solve the problem. However, for the other subjects, the story problems made it clear that because of practical considerations, direct experimental intervention was not an option.

Method

Materials
Two story problems were constructed: one about whether having parents stay overnight with their hospitalized children would improve recovery rates, the other about whether having a small number of sales clerks in a store results in higher rates of shoplifting.

Each story appeared in one of two conditions. Both stories in each of the two conditions are in the appendix to this experiment. In the direct-intervention condition, subjects were not restricted in the sorts of information they could request. In the natural-occurrence condition, subjects were restricted to using naturally occuring or correlational information because, given practical considerations, direct intervention was not an option. (For example, in the natural-occurrence condition, the hospital head wants to learn the likely answer to his question before he allows parents to stay overnight, because arranging for parents to do so is expensive.) For both problems in both conditions, subjects were asked, "What sorts of information/evidence would you consider" to answer this question?

Because one of our concerns was whether subjects would spontaneously consider the need for controls, both stories were written in a way that avoided any suggestion of a treatment-group versus control-group paradigm. For example, the hospital story asked "whether having parents stay overnight probably causes high rates of recovery in the children," with no mention of whether the rates would be higher than among comparable children whose parents had not stayed overnight.

Procedure

Each subject was interviewed individually. Both interviewer and subject looked at a written version of the story problem while the interviewer read it aloud and the subject read it silently. During the interview, the written version of the story problem was left in front of the subject for her to look at whenever she wanted to.

For each story problem, the interview consisted of two parts. In the first part, the subject was asked simply to think out loud while the interviewer made brief notes about (and simultaneously tape-recorded) what the subject was suggesting. In the second part, the interviewer relied on her notes to remind the subject of each of the points the subject had made in the spontaneous section and asked, about each point, whether the subject could amplify it. The requests for amplification were all very general, for example: "Remember when you said ...? Could you tell me a bit more about that?" or "You suggested that.... Can you tell me a little about why you made that suggestion?" or "You mentioned that.... Is there anything more you can tell me about this?" We included the probe section to elicit information from subjects who might be less inclined than others to elaborate their statements.

Design

Each subject was interviewed about each of the two stories and, for each subject, one story was presented in the direct-intervention condition and the other was presented in the natural-occurrence condition. At each age, the story-condition pairings and the order of presentation of stories were counterbalanced across subjects. At each age, we aimed for four subjects (two males and two females) in each of the four story-order × story-condition groups. For the sixth-graders, our final yield included 19 subjects (1 additional male in the direct-intervention condition and 2 additional males in the natural-occurrence condition). For the ninth-graders, our final sample included 7 females and 7 males in each of the two conditions. Our final college sample included 15 subjects (8 females and 7 males). (Missing subjects resulted from defective tape storage. Additional subjects reflected students' requests to be interviewed.)

Results and Discussion

Coding categories
We coded subjects' protocols in terms of whether they included mention of the following types of responses:

Appropriate contrastive tests   When a subject proposed an appropriate contrast, she proposed one condition in which the target possible cause was present and one in which it was absent. For example, "You'd need one kid with his parents and one kid without his parents" or "You'd need to find some children who were recovering and find out how fast and then have their parents start to stay and see if they started to recover faster."

   Coding was conservative; to be counted as having proposed a contrast, the subject had to mention explicitly both conditions (target present and target absent).

Specific expectations   To shed additional light on subjects' willingness to propose designs that allowed the discovery of disconfirming results, we also counted the total number of subjects who proposed a specific expectation about the target factor. For example, "Having parents there isn't going to do anything, because kids in a hospital are too sick to care" or "A child with their parents will get better faster."

Alternative hypotheses   This was a lenient measure that included any mention of a factor other than the target factor that might have brought about the target results. For example, "Maybe it (the recovery rate) has something to do with different illnesses."

Controlled alternative hypotheses   Subjects mentioned some alternative hypotheses in the context of control, and this constituted a more conservative measure of concern for alternative hypotheses. A subject was counted as having generated a controlled alternative hypothesis only if she mentioned another factor (other than the target factor) that could also produce the effect *and* she also gave some indication that the alternative would have to be controlled for or ruled out. For example, "You'd have to make sure they (the children whose parents stayed) didn't just have better doctors" or "You'd have to make sure the children had the same illnesses."

Coding was conservative: the subject had to give some indication that the alternative would have to be ruled out or controlled for (although, obviously, we did not require that subjects use these words). Thus, for example, a statement such as "If you've got something like a broken leg, it's not going to heal faster if your mom is there" would *not* have been coded as a controlled alternative hypothesis.

Treatment-control designs   In line with my discussion of scientific thinking in the first three chapters, we required a subject to propose two things in order to be credited with having proposed a complete treatment-control design: an appropriate contrastive test and some alternative hypothesis that was specifically mentioned as a factor to be controlled for. For example, "You'd need some kids with their parents and some kids without their parents," along with "You'd have to make sure the children had the same illnesses."

External validity   A subject showed a concern for external validity when she mentioned a factor that might limit the extent to which any results would generalize to other contexts. For example, "If you did the study at Cornell Med, it might not work at Harlem Hospital because those kids might be sicker" or "The results would be tailored to the type of child who would use this hospital. The hospital might specialize in certain diseases."

Nontarget causes   To help shed light on some of the results, we also counted the total number of subjects who, at least once during a problem story, made some mention of another causally relevant factor besides the target factor. Specifically, a subject was coded as having mentioned a nontarget cause if she made any mention of an alternative hypothesis (irrespective of whether or not it was mentioned as a controlled alternative hypothesis) or if she mentioned a factor that might limit external validity.

Causal mechanisms   A subject was coded as having considered information about causal mechanism if she explicitly mentioned the process or means by which the target or the alternative might have operated or if she mentioned the process by which external validity might fail to obtain.

For example, "You could have some parents stay overnight and some not, because parents might help their kids by telling the doctors if there were problems" or "You'd have to make sure you didn't have the overnight kids have cancer and the other kids have broken legs, because you can die from cancer so you might be sad and your parents could help you get better by comforting you but a broken leg doesn't affect you emotionally" or "If you did it with kids, it might not work with teenagers, because a lot of teenagers don't get along with their parents and having a parent around would just stress them out."

Note that the coding of alternative hypotheses, external validity, and causal mechanisms was conservative. For example, if a subject said, "It might not work for all kids, because different kids feel differently about their parents," it is not clear whether the parental-child relationship was being cited as an alternative hypothesis that would have to be controlled for in the experimental sample or as a variable that might limit the external validity of the experiment or as a mechanism to explain why the target factor would not have an effect or simply as a variable that was thought to be relevant to the question but the nature of whose relevance was not clear in the subject's own mind. Because of the lack of clarity, the parent-child relationship was coded in this protocol neither as an alternative hypothesis nor as a variable that would limit external validity nor as a causal mechanism.

Age and condition differences
The results are easy to summarize: Virtually all of the subjects showed a spontaneous concern for causal mechanism and proposed appropriate contrasts even when they had specific expectations about how the target factor would operate. Age differences in concern for alternative hypotheses, limits on external validity, and proposals of complete treatment-control designs seemed to reflect the fact that with decreasing age, there was a decreasing concern with nontarget causal factors.

Table 12.1 presents the percentage of subjects in each age × condition group who gave a response type at least once during the interview. (Recall that in each age × condition group, each subject completed both story problems, one in each condition.) We analyzed each of the response types with an age × condition analysis of variance. Table 12.1 presents the percentage of subjects who produced the various response types in each age × condition.

Appropriate contrastive tests
Except for one of the sixth-graders in one of the story problems, all of the subjects in each of the conditions spontaneously proposed an appropriate contrastive test as a way of gathering

Table 12.1
Percentage of subjects who produced various response types in each age × condition in experimeent 16

Response type	Sixth grade		Ninth grade		College	
	DI	NO	DI	NO	DI	NO
Contrasts	100	94	100	100	100	100
Causal mechanisms	95	94	100	100	94	94
Specific expectations	50	67	43	57	19	19
External validity	35	33	21	43	44	75
Alternative hypotheses	35	44	57	86	88	88
Althernatives as factors to be controlled	35	33	29	86	81	88
Nontarget causes	45	67	57	86	88	88
Treatment-control designs	35	33	29	86	81	88

Conditions are abbreviated as follows: DI = direct intervention, NO = natural occurrence.

evidence. (Recall that coding was conservative: both groups—control as well as treatment—had to be explicitly mentioned for a subject to be coded as having proposed a contrast.)

Thus the results support the suggestion made in experiments 14 and 15 that in Mynatt et al.'s (1977) task, subjects failed to test appropriate contrasts in part because the structure of the task precluded their doing so: on each trial in their study, subjects were allowed to choose only one screen, and an appropriate contrast would have required two screens. In our present study, when subjects were allowed to identify two groups (the analogue of two screens), they did indeed choose to test both a treatment and a control group. That is, when allowed to do so, subjects did test an appropriate contrast.

In addition, these results extend the findings of experiments 14 and 15 and the findings of Bullock (1991). In experiment 15 we found that when presented with various instances to choose among (in that experiment, discs, triangles, and squares of different shades), even sixth-graders chose the sorts of instances that allowed them to generate an appropriate contrast (for example, a triangle and a nontriangle to test whether triangularity had an effect). Similarly, in the Bullock study, subjects who were presented with instances of different sorts of lanterns were also able to choose the sorts of instances that enabled them to arrange an appropriate contrast. (For example, they were able to choose to test one lantern with a roof and one without in order to determine whether presence of a roof affects how well a lantern burns.)

The present results extend these findings by demonstrating that even when subjects are not explicitly presented with specific instances to choose among, they can nevertheless generate on their own the instances required for an appropriate contrast. (The Bullock study also examined subjects' ability to control for alternative hypotheses, and I will discuss related results below.)

Specific expectations The fact that virtually all of the subjects proposed appropriate contrasts is especially striking when one considers that in the various age × condition groups, subjects verbalized a total of 42 specific expectations (see table 12.1). That is, even when subjects had a personal expectation that the target factor would operate in a certain way, they nevertheless proposed an appropriate contrast designed to uncover disconfirming evidence if it existed. For example, if a subject hypothesized that parental presence would affect recovery rate, the subject would nevertheless propose examining both a group of children whose parents stayed and a group whose parents did not. By arranging to examine both groups, subjects increased the liklihood that they would detect a situation in which the children whose parents did not stay recovered faster than those whose parents did. That is, they proposed a strategy that increased the liklihood of detecting disconfirming results.

Causal mechanisms Except for two college students and two sixth-graders, all of the subjects relied, at least once, on information about causal mechanism. The percentage of subjects who explicitly mentioned causal-mechanism information did not vary with age, $F(2, 92) = .82$, $p = .4$, or condition, $F(1, 92) = .00$, $p = .96$, nor was there an interaction of the two, $F(2, 92) = .00$, $p = .99$.

That is, the present results extend the findings of experiments 9 and 10. In those experiments we found that information about mechanism is one of the things that subjects take account of in deciding whether a particular factor is likely to be causal. In the present experiment we found that subjects also spontaneously consider mechanism information when reasoning about how to design an experiment to test a causal claim.

Limits on external validity With increasing age, there was an increasing number of subjects who explicitly mentioned a nontarget factor that might limit external validity, $F(2, 92) = 3.18$, $p = .05$. There were fewer sixth-graders who did this than there were college students, $F(1, 92) = 4.77$, $p = .03$, and the number of ninth-graders who mentioned a limit on external validity was not significantly different from the average number in the other two age groups, $F(1, 92) = 1.85$, $p = .18$.

There was also a trend for subjects to raise questions about external validity when they were restricted to using naturally occuring data than when direct intervention was possible, $F(1, 92) = 2.61$, $p = .10$, but there were no significant age differences in subjects' tendency to do this, $F(1, 92) = 1.09$, $p = .34$ (see table 12.1).

With regard to the trend for the condition to have an effect, I suggest that when subjects are prevented from using direct intervention to collect data, they have to consider possible sources of naturally occurring data. However, such sources are often different enough from the target situation that the differences suggest precisely the sorts of factors that might constrain external validity.

The age difference in the proportion of subjects who mention external validity are parallel to the age differences in the proportion of subjects who mention alternative hypotheses, to which I now turn.

Alternative hypotheses   Among the college students, almost all of the subjects generated some sort of alternative hypothesis (whether or not the alternative was couched in the context of something that had to be controlled for). However, subjects were less likely to generate an alternative hypothesis with decreasing age $F(2, 92) = 10.97$, $p = .0001$, with fewer sixth-graders generating alternatives than college students, $F(1, 92) = 20.66$, $p = .0001$, and with ninth-graders being comparable to the average of the other two groups, $F(1, 92) = .64$, $p = .43$ (see table 12.1).

Controlled alternative hypotheses   Furthermore, when we considered only those alternative hypotheses couched in the context of control, most of the college subjects generated such a hypothesis in each of the two conditions. However, there were differences in age, $F(2, 92) = 11.62$, $p = .001$, in condition, $F(1, 92) = 4.09$, $p = .05$, and in the interaction of the two, $F(2, 92) = 4.12$, $p = .02$. As can be seen in table 12.1, the age differences reflected the fact that fewer sixth-graders than college students generated alternatives in the context of control, $F(1, 92) = 23.25$, $p = .0001$, while ninth-graders were comparable to the other two age groups averaged together, $F(1, 92) = .05$, $p = .83$. The condition differences did not result from differences between sixth-graders and college students, $F(1, 92) = .14$, $p = .7$, but from the fact that in the direct intervention condition, many fewer ninth-graders suggested alternatives to be controlled for than did the other age × condition groups, $F(1, 92) = 7.98$, $p = .006$.

To shed additional light on age differences regarding external validity and alternative hypotheses, we turn to the next measure.

Nontarget causes   Recall that with decreasing age, there were fewer subjects who mentioned alternative hypotheses (controlled as well as noncontrolled), and there were also fewer subjects who mentioned factors limiting external validity. Both of these involved factors that were non-target causes. One possibility was that at younger ages, most of the subjects did mention nontarget causes, but some of the subjects did so by mentioning an alternative hypothesis and others by mentioning a limit on external validity, while among college students, most of the subjects mentioned both types. Another possibility was that at younger ages, there were fewer subjects who mentioned any nontarget cause, either an alternative hypothesis or a limit on external validity.

To address this issue, we counted a subject as having mentioned a non-target cause if she mentioned any kind of nontarget cause (either an alternative hypothesis—whether controlled or not—or a limit on external validity). As table 12.1 indicates, with decreasing age, there was a smaller proportion of subjects who mentioned any kind of nontarget cause, $F(2, 92) = 4.73$, $p = .01$, with sixth-graders being different from college students, $F(1, 92) = 9.10$, $p = .003$, and ninth-graders being comparable to the average of the other two groups, $F(1, 92) = 0.0$, $p = .9$.

That is, the decrease, with age, in total number of subjects who mentioned alternative hypotheses and who mentioned limits on external validity reflects the fact that with decreasing age, there are fewer subjects who mention any sort of nontarget cause. And this finding is in turn compatible with either a limited knowledge base among younger subjects or a limited ability to generate, during the course of a single experimental session, the various additional causal factors that might affect the anticipated result.

Treatment-control designs   Recall that to be credited with having proposed a complete treatment-control design, a subject had to do two things: propose an appropriate contrast and propose an alternative hypothesis as something to be controlled for. All of the subjects who proposed a controlled alternative hypothesis also proposed a contrast. Therefore, the age and condition differences in proposals of treatment-control designs are equivalent to the age and condition differences, reported above, in proposals of controlled alternative hypotheses. That is, most of the college students proposed a complete treatment-control design (because most college students mentioned a controlled alternative hypothesis), but the tendency to do so decreased with decreasing age.

In summary, in all age × condition groups, virtually all of the subjects proposed an appropriate contrastive test (even though almost half of the subjects voiced specific expectations about what the results would be), and almost all of the subjects explicitly mentioned, at least once, considerations that involved causal mechanisms.

Almost all of the college students also generated at least one alternative hypothesis, and most of the college students in each condition mentioned at least one alternative hypothesis along with a strategy for controlling for it. However, with decreasing age, there were fewer subjects who mentioned any sort of causally relevant factor other than the target factor. As a result, with decreasing age, there were fewer subjects who mentioned an alternative hypothesis (controlled or otherwise) and fewer subjects who mentioned a limit on external validity. In addition, since one aspect of a treatment-control design consisted of an alternative hypothesis to be controlled for, with decreasing age there were also fewer subjects who proposed a complete treatment-control design.

General Discussion

Psychological validity

One of the aims of this study was to examine the psychological validity of some of the types of information (such as information about causal mechanisms and alternative accounts) that we had been asking subjects to reason about in the earlier experiments. Our question was whether, in evaluating a causal explanation, subjects would spontaneously consider or request this information on their own, even if it was not presented to them.

We found that at all ages and in both conditions, virtually all of the subjects did propose an appropriate contrast to answer the question (even when they had a specific expectation about the target result) and did spontaneously mention at least one causal mechanism relevant to solving the problem. That is, the information about mechanism and appropriate contrasts that subjects took account of when it was presented to them in the earlier experiments was, indeed, information that subjects in the present experiment consider on their own.

Lack of confirmation bias

In terms of confirmation bias, the results of this experiment extend the results of experiment 15. Even when subjects made it clear that they expected the target factor to have a specific effect, they nevertheless proposed the sort of contrast that would have detected results that disconfirmed their expectations. In voicing their expectations, subjects made it clear that they found the two hypotheses that we had asked them to test to be quite plausible. Nevertheless, this did not blind them to the need for a contrast group that would assess whether the effect would have occurred anyway, even without the presence of the target possible cause (parental presence or an increased number of clerks).

Age differences in knowledge base and/or information processing
With decreasing age, there were fewer subjects who mentioned alternative causes and limits on external validity. One possibility is that the younger subjects simply knew about fewer alternatives than the college students did. Another possibility is that the younger subjects had more difficulty switching their attention, during the course of a single interview session, from the target cause to other causal factors. That is, it is possible that if the subjects had been interviewed during a second session, they would have given more consideration to the question of alternatives, just as Klahr and Dunbar's (1988) subjects explored the limits of one hypothesis (or "frame" in their terminology) before switching to another one.

Limitations
The only data we had from the present study were subjects' verbal descriptions of what they would do. This resulted in two obvious limitations. One, already noted, is that some verbalizations were ambiguous. Specifically, when subjects mentioned an additional possible causal factor, it was not always clear whether the additional factor was being cited as an alternative hypothesis that would have to be controlled for, a limit on the external validity of the results, or a possibility to be pursued in subsequent work in case the proposed experiment did not work. Indeed, the subject could simply have been citing a variable that she knew was relevant without even considering in more detail exactly what the relevance was.

The second limitation is twofold: One aspect of it is that the only data we had from subjects was what they spontaneously verbalized. The other is that, even when the subjects' verbalizations were not ambiguous, the relevance of their suggestions was typically verbalized in conceptual rather than technical terms (Koslowski, Susman, and Serling 1991). For example, a point about internal validity might consist of noting, "You'd have to make sure the kids who had parents staying with them weren't just more attached than the other kids." Although the verbal responses often indicated an appropriate conceptual consideration, they did not indicate whether the subject had the technical wherewithal to translate conceptual awareness into a concrete research strategy. To pursue the preceding example, we do not know whether the subject understood what sort of design would control for level of attachment. Did she have in mind that patients would be matched on attachment level or that only patients who were securely attached would be included? Similarly, when a subject proposed a treatment-control contrast ("You'd have to have some kids have their parents stay and some kids not"), it was not clear whether the subjects understood that one would have to contrast proportions rather than absolute numbers in the two groups. In a word, we do not know whether the subjects understood various sorts of technical issues and simply did not verbalize them or whether they did not verbalize them because they did not have this sort of expertise.

An obvious question that remains is why it is that subjects in this experiment gave evidence of quite sophisticated scientific reasoning when in many studies, adults as well as children are judged to be poor scientists. I have already argued that one answer is that what are in fact legitimate aspects of scientific inquiry (such as relying on information about causal mechanism) are instead often treated as examples of flawed reasoning. Another possibility is that many studies of scientific reasoning require that the subject make sense of some fairly complicated information (for example, the necessity and sufficiency relations in Siegler's [1975] task), and this was something that our subjects were not asked to do. Furthermore, they did not spontaneously suggest how the causal variable would be related to the effect, whether it would be a necessary cause, a sufficient cause, neither, or both. If the focus of the present study had been on this sort of technical knowledge, then, like Siegler's subjects, the subjects in this study might also have been found to be deficient in scientific reasoning. We do not know whether subjects were aware of technical aspects of experimental design but did not verbalize them or whether they did not verbalize them because they were not aware of them.

Appendix to Experiment 16

Direct-intervention condition

Hospital story problem   The head of a new hospital wants to find out whether high recovery rates among children are probably caused by allowing parents to stay in the hospital overnight with their children. The head of the hospital asks for your help. How would you decide whether having parents stay overnight probably causes high rates of recovery in the children? What sorts of information/evidence would you consider?

Shoplifting story problem   The manager of a new department store wants to find out whether high rates of shoplifting are probably caused by having a small number of sales clerks. The manager asks for your help. How would you decide whether high levels of shoplifting are probably caused by having a small number of sales clerks? What sorts of information/evidence would you consider?

Natural-occurrence condition

Hospital story problem   The head of a new hospital wants to find out whether high recovery rates among children are probably caused by allowing parents to stay in the hospital overnight with their children. The head of the hospital does not want to allow parents to stay overnight unless there is a good chance that this would work, because it is an expensive thing to do. (For example, it costs money to buy the additional beds.) The head of the hospital asks for your help. How would you decide whether high recovery rates are probably caused by allowing parents to stay in the hospital overnight with their children? What sorts of information/evidence would you consider? Remember that the hospital head wants you to find this out *before* he starts allowing parents to do this.

Shoplifting story problem   The manager of a new department store wants to find out whether high rates of shoplifting are probably caused by having a small number of sales clerks. The manager does not want to hire more clerks unless there is a good chance that this would work, because it takes a lot of time to interview and to train new sales clerks. The manager asks for your help. How would you decide whether high levels of shoplifting are probably caused by having a small number of sales clerks? What sorts of information/ evidence would you consider? Remember that the manager wants you to find this out *before* he hires more sales clerks.

General Summary

In all of the age groups in both conditions, virtually all of the subjects spontaneously proposed an appropriate contrastive test (even when they had specific expectations about the target factor) and relied, at least once, on a causal mechanism in explaining one of their proposals. In addition, at the college level, most of the subjects spontaneously proposed an alternative hypothesis that would have to be controlled for or ruled out and also proposed a complete treatment-control design.

Age differences in concern for alternative hypotheses, limits on external validity, and complete treatment-control designs seemed to reflect the fact that with decreasing age, there was a decreasing tendency to mention nontarget causal factors. At all ages, statements that reflected technical expertise were rare.

The results of this study suggest that the sorts of information we had asked subjects to reason about in some of our earlier studies are what subjects will spontaneously request when solving a problem that involves trying to identify the cause of an event. In a word, subjects on their own consider some of the sorts of information that we had been presenting them with in our other experiments. That is, the earlier experiments documented that subjects *could* use these sorts of information if it was given to them. This experiment documents that subjects also request these sorts of information when they are asked to generate what they would need to solve a causal problem. These sorts of information have psychological validity in that they play a role in the thinking of individual subjects.

General Summary and Conclusions

One's Vew of Scientific Inquiry Determines One's Assessment of Scientific Reasoning

This book began with the following argument: One's view about whether people are adept at scientific reasoning depends heavily on what one's view of scientific inquiry is. I argued that in the psychological literature, the prevailing view of scientific inquiry is continuous with the tradition of logical positivism. The result is that in the psychological literature, the study of scientific reasoning is characterized by an emphasis on covariation and a corresponding neglect of the role of theory or mechanism. One consequence of this approach is that people are portrayed as reasoning in a way that deviates quite significantly from a scientific ideal. For example, according to the received view, when asked to convince someone of an argument, subjects rely not on gathering evidence based on covariation but rather on weaving a causal scenario about how the phenomenon being defended might happen (D. Kuhn 1991); subjects ignore confounding in the sense that they do not treat confounded data as causally indeterminate (Kuhn, Amsel, and O'Loughlin 1988); subjects cling to their theories in the face of disconfirming evidence and do not search for disconfirming evidence when trying to test a theory (Wason 1960, Mynatt et al. 1977); when asked to make predictions, subjects ignore base-rate data and rely instead on causal theories (Tversky and Kahneman 1974, 1980); indeed, subjects rely on theories to such an extent that they sometimes see correlations that are only illusory (Chapman and Chapman 1967, 1969).

I have argued that this approach paints a picture of people's ability to reason scientifically that is often either incomplete or distorted. When the picture is incomplete, it is because people are asked to reason about situations that are theoretically impoverished. Such situations might enable us to study how people reason when plausible hypotheses to explain a phenomenon have been ruled out and not even a vague theory exists to guide further investigation. However, many of the most exciting aspects of scientific reasoning occur when people should and do rely on considerations of theory or mechanism. Therefore, studying scientific reasoning by asking subjects to reason about theoretically impoverished situations provides a picture of scientific reasoning that is incomplete.

When the picture is distorted, it is because people are asked to reason about situations that are theoretically rich but in which correct performance is defined operationally to consist of overriding or ignoring considerations of theory or mechanism and relying instead only on covariation information. In such situations, subjects rely on theoretical considerations as well as covariation information, and it is sound scientific practice to do so. Therefore, in such situations, people are treated as reasoning nonscientifically when in fact their reasoning is scientifically legitimate. One aim of this book, then, was to examine the scientific reasoning of college students and college-bound adolescents in light of some aspects of scientific inquiry and practice that are often either ignored or treated as examples of flawed reasoning.

I have also argued that neither theory nor data alone is sufficient to achieve scientific success; each must be evaluated in the context of, and constrained by, the other. That is, science involves bootstrapping. Therefore, I have argued, to support the claim that subjects rely on considerations of theory or mechanism in a way that is scientifically reasonable, it is not sufficient simply to demonstrate that subjects rely on theory when evaluating data; one must demonstrate as well that subjects are relying on theoretical considerations in a way that is judicious and methodologically legitimate.

What follows in the next section is a summary of the results of the experiments presented in this book with special attention to results that would be ignored or treated as a reflection of faulty reasoning by an approach that focuses on the importance of covariation to the exclusion of other information and with special attention to results that illustrate the interdependence of theory and data that constitutes bootstrapping.

Subjects Take into Account Information Often Neglected in Studies of Scientific Inquiry

In view of one of the aims of this book, perhaps the most basic finding is that when engaging in causal reasoning, subjects, like scientists, do not rely exclusively on covariation but also take account of information about mechanism and alternative explanations.

Information about Mechanism or Theory Is Treated as Evidential

One of the central activities in scientific reasoning consists of deciding whether a factor is likely to be causal. In doing this, subjects at all ages certainly do realize that the Humean index of covariation plays a crucial role (experiments 1 and 2). However, an emphasis on covariation that ignores the role of mechanism does not account for why it is that some covariations are taken seriously as plausible possible causes, while others are dismissed. (Even when covariations occur numerous times, they are not always causal.) This is a critical omission because, as was noted in chapters 2 and 8, the world is rife with correlations. Taking seriously all implausible possible causes would result in traveling along many dead ends.

We found in experiments 9 and 10 that when there is a mechanism present that can explain how a possible cause might have brought about the effect, then the presence of the mechanism can render plausible a possible cause that seems initially to be implausible. The presence of a mechanism that constitutes a process by which the factor could have operated is treated as some evidence that the factor might indeed have been causal.

Furthermore, when mechanisms have been ruled out, subjects treat the factor as decreasingly likely to be causal (experiment 3).

Subjects also show a concern for questions of causal mechanism even when the subjects themselves (and not the experimenters) decide what sorts of information would be relevant to solving a causal problem (experiment 16).

In a word, the extent to which a factor is seen as a plausible cause is not static; it depends on, among other things, information about explanation or mechanism. That is, information about mechanism or explanation is treated as evidential. Approaches to scientific reasoning that focus exclusively on the importance of covariation ignore the important role played by considerations of mechanism.

It is worth noting that there is a sense in which subjects appear to restrict the extent to which they treat the presence of a mechanism as an index of causation: when the correlation involves a possible cause that is plausible at the outset, being informed that a mechanism is present has only a negligeable effect. However, I argued that one of the things it means for a factor to be a plausible cause is that a possible mechanism is known to exist that can mediate between the factor and the effect. Therefore, I argued, when a factor is a plausible cause to begin with, being informed that a mechanism is present has a negligeable effect not because it is ignored but because it constitutes redundant information (experiments 9 and 10).

Reliance on mechanism information is (appropriately) tempered

Although subjects do rely on mechanism information, they do so judiciously by tempering their reliance with other considerations and doing so in a scientifically legitimate way. One consideration consists of realizing that known mechanisms are not the only index of causation. Even when there is no known mechanism that could have mediated between a factor and an effect, it is possible that factor and effect are nevertheless causally related but that the mediating mechanism has not yet been discovered. As mentioned, taking seriously all implausible possible causes runs the risk of traveling along many dead ends, but ignoring all *implausible* possible causes carries the risk of overlooking some genuine, though unexpected, discoveries. And we found, in experiments 9 and 10, that subjects do take account of this possibility: in navigating between these two strategies, subjects take account of whether there is a known mechanism that might have mediated between factor and effect. But they also take seriously implausible possible causes when no mediating mechanism is known provided that the association of factor and effect is systematic rather than one-time only. In addition, subjects also take account of whether the association of factor and effect is systematic when they evaluate plausible (as well as implausible) possible causes. In short, subjects' reliance on mechanism does not blind them to the fact that the absence of a known mechanism does not always indicate the absence of a causal relation. I argued that for an implausible factor, a large number of covariations is seen as indicating that the implausible factor should perhaps be moved to the class of plausible possible causes. For factors judged to be plausible causes to begin with, a large number of covariations is seen as improving the ranking of the factor relative to competing plausible causes.

Another restriction on reliance on mechanism information, one that develops with age, consists of realizing that not all possible mechanisms are plausible. We found, in experiments 3, 4, and 5, that so long as subjects are asked to explain plausible covariations, all age groups are comparable in proposing plausible mechanisms. However, our results suggested that young adolescents have an inflated notion of the range of possible mechanisms that can be operating in a situation. The age difference became apparent in two ways: One is that when presented with possible mechanisms to evaluate, young adolescents treated as quite reasonable mechanisms that college students found dubious. The other is that when asked to explain implausible covariations, college students were reluctant to propose dubious mechanisms. In contrast, young adolescents' explanations were not restricted to the same extent. Because they know less about the world, young adolescents are more likely than college students to propose dubious mechanisms to explain implausible covariations. Because they know less about the world, such mechanisms are not dubious to them.

In a word, information about mechanism (like information about covariation) is treated as one of several rules of thumb that makes correct identification of a causal relation more likely but whose application is tempered by other rules of thumb, rather than as the sole algorithm that guarantees success—a point that illustrates the bootstrapping nature of scientific reasoning, and which I will amplify in a later section.

Information about Alternative Accounts Is Treated as Evidential

In addition to taking account of mechanism information, subjects, like scientists, also take into consideration the context of rival alternative accounts. That is, they take seriously the principle of scientific inquiry that stresses the importance of control groups and ruling out alternatives.

For example, a target account is treated as increasingly likely to be causal if plausible alternative explanations have been controlled for, whereas causation is more likely to be treated as indeterminate when plausible alternative accounts are confounded with the target account (experiment 6). Furthermore, ruling out alternative accounts increases the credibility of the target account, irrespective of whether the target account explains a single event or multiple instances and irrespective of whether the fact that alternatives have been controlled for is explicit or merely implicit (experiments 1, 6, 7, 8). In addition, when alternatives are ruled out, the effects are comparable for plausible causes (experiments 7 and 8) as well as for nonstandard causes (experiment 1): subjects treat both types of possible causes as increasingly likely to be actual causes when alternative accounts are ruled out. In line with the earlier suggestion regarding frequency of covariation, I suggested that when the possible cause is plausible to begin with, then ruling out alternatives means that the target cause has fewer competitors in the set of standard causes. When the possible cause is nonstandard, then ruling out standard alternatives indicates that subjects may need to go beyond the set of standard causes and consider the possible cause that is nonstandard.

Most convincingly, subjects show a spontaneous concern for generating and ruling out alternative possible causes when they are asked to solve a problem themselves (experiments 14, 15, 16), and they do so even when the hypotheses being evaluated are ones that the subjects themselves have generated (experiments 14 and 15) and even when the subjects have specific expectations about the results (experiment 16). The fact that subjects do this is also relevant to the question of confirmation bias and of how subjects evaluate explanations in the light of disconfrming or anomalous evidence—a topic that I will discuss in a later section.

In summary, when subjects assess information about covariation, their assessments are tempered by two types of information often ignored by studies of scientific reasoning that focus on the importance of covariation: information about mechanism and information about alternative accounts. In addition, both types of information are themselves tempered by considerations of plausibility, so that, like covariation, they function not as algorithms but rather as heuristics or rules of thumb.

Emphasizing Covariation While Ignoring Mechanism Underestimates the Situations in Which Scientific Reasoning Is Taking Place

The preceding section made the point that approaches to scientific thinking that ignore the role of mechanism provide an incomplete picture of scientific reasoning. However, this could simply be the claim that a certain aspect of scientific reasoning has not yet been adequately examined and, of course, no study of a phenomenon examines everything. This section makes the stronger claim that a study of scientific reasoning that ignores the role of mechanism provides a picture of reasoning that may actually be distorted as well as incomplete. Ignoring mechanism does not merely leave a certain aspect of scientific reasoning unexamined; rather, it may lead one to treat as flawed, reasoning that is in fact scientifically legitimate.

Viewed from a different angle, the present section addresses the following question: if subjects are able, at least in the tasks examined in this book, to deploy various principles of scientific inquiry, then why is it that many studies conclude that people in general and adolescents in particular are poor scientists? This question is addressed with respect to four content areas: confounded data, disconfirming or anomalous evidence, working hypotheses, and confirmation bias.

Confounding

One of the canons of scientific inquiry is that explanations are evaluated in the context of rival alternatives. One consequence is that when the target possible cause is confounded with an alternative possible cause, causation is indeterminate. However, just as it would be impractical to take account of all possible covariations, so too would it be impractical to take account of all possible confounded alternatives. To decide whether to take a confounding factor seriously, subjects take account of plausibility, a plausible factor being one for which a mechanism exists that could have mediated between the factor and the effect. When the confounding factor has been antecedently judged to be an implausible possible cause, subjects treat the target factor as causal and ignore the confounding (D. Kuhn et al. 1988). In contrast, when the confounding factor is a plausible possible cause, then subjects do take it seriously and treat confounded data as more likely than controlled data to be indeterminate (experiment 6). That is, subjects do treat confounding as problematic but they rely on considerations of plausibility to decide when to do so, and considerations of plausibility involve (in part) considerations of mechanism. Tasks that use only confounding factors that are implausible causes give the misleading impression that subjects do not view confounding as problematic.

However, the fact that subjects ignore some confounding factors as implausible does not mean that they never take implausible possible causes seriously. As already noted, even when no mediating mechanism is known, subjects do take seriously implausible possible causes if the association of factor and effect is systematic rather than one-time only (experiment 10).

Disconfirming or Anomalous Evidence

Ignoring the importance of mechanism information also underestimates the situations in which subjects treat disconfirming or anomalous information as decreasing the credibility of a causal belief. For example, D. Kuhn et al. (1988) found that it was more difficult to disconfirm a causal than a noncausal belief. The task was one in which the "disconfirming" evidence consisted of the information that the assumed causal factor and the effect did not covary. However, although a causal belief does include the belief that a target possible cause covaries with an effect, it also often includes some belief (however rudimentary) about the mechanism by which the covariation obtains. Therefore, evidence that consists only of the information that target factor and effect do not covary does call into question the covariation component of the belief but leaves the mechanism component of the belief intact. This leaves the possibility that the belief ought not to be rejected, that the mechanism does bring about the expected covariation but, for whatever reason, not in the situation at hand. On a model that acknowledges the importance of mechanism, evidence that called into question the mechanism as well as the covariation component of a belief might be more effective than evidence that called into question the covariation component alone. And in line with this, we found, in experiment 13, that anomalous evidence that includes an explanatory mechanism has a greater effect on causal than on noncausal beliefs, that is, on precisely the sorts of beliefs that D. Kuhn et al. (1988) found to be the more resistant to change. In short, ignoring mechanism information might underestimate the extent to which subjects take account of disconfirming or anomalous evidence because it would focus on evidence that called into question only the covariation component of the belief but left the mechanism component intact.

Working Hypotheses

Ignoring the role of mechanism can also lead one to treat as unwarranted or flawed the sort of modification of working hypotheses that is, in fact, scientifically legitimate.

As I argued in the first three chapters, not all hypotheses ought to be rejected in the face of anomalous evidence; some hypotheses are basically correct formulations that ought, instead, to be informed by, and refined to accommodate, noncongruent data. However, in principle, a hypothesis can invariably be revised to take account of noncongruent data. It is considerations of theory or mechanism that help us decide which revisions are scientifically legitimate modifications or refinements and which revisions are instead unwarranted ad hoc patch-ups. Therefore, a research approach that pays little attention to the role of mechanism is ill equipped to examine the way in which subjects modify working hypotheses in response to anomalous data. And, in fact, research approaches that focus on covariation to the exclusion of theory or mechanism tend to operationalize tasks so that hypothesis modification is not one of the options. Such tasks are often designed so that anomalous data are to be treated as yielding all-or-none decisions (either the theory is wrong or, in some cases, the evidence is wrong). That is, within such a framework, experimental tasks are operationalized so that data not congruent with a theory are to be treated as disconfirming data that call for the theory to be rejected outright, rather than as merely anomalous data that call for the theory to be modified or revised. Therefore, subjects who do engage in theory modification are often treated as engaging in flawed reasoning when, in fact, their behavior may be scientifically legitimate.

We found that adolescents as well as college students use considerations of mechanism to decide which anomalies are more problematic for an explanation than others (experiment 11). When anomalies are characterized by a common feature, the anomalies form a pattern, and subjects are quite content to modify the explanation even if explanatory mechanisms are absent. I argued that the presence of a common feature, because it reflects a pattern in the anomalies, itself suggests an underlying causal mechanism that could have brought the anomalies about. Thus, learning that a causal mechanism is in fact present amounts to receiving redundant information (just as, in experiments 9 and 10, learning that a mechanism is present constituted receiving redundant information when the possible target cause was a likely cause to begin with). In contrast, when anomalies are characterized by separate features and therefore do not form a pattern, subjects are nevertheless more likely to treat the hypothesis as warranting modification (as opposed to rejection) if explanatory mechanisms are also present that can account for how the anomalies came to be. I argued that even anomalies that do not form a pattern are not very troublesome for an explanation if individual or common explanatory mechanisms exist that can account for how the anomalies came to be. By specifying situations in which the target cause fails to operate, such mechanisms refine our understanding of how it does operate.

In a word, at all ages, subjects treat hypothesis revision as theory-dependent in a scientifically reasonable way: causal mechanisms and common features make anomalies less problematic for an explanation because they embellish our understanding of why a target cause does operate by shedding light on when and why it fails to operate. The result is that when mechanisms and common features are present, subjects treat hypotheses as working hypotheses and modify them in ways that are theoretically motivated rather than ad hoc.

Related to the notion of modifying working hypotheses is the finding that subjects are attuned to considerations of external validity. Subjects realize that there are some contexts to which a result cannot be generalized (experiment 6). That is, they have the wherewithal to realize that hypotheses may need to be modified by being restricted to only certain contexts. Indeed, subjects show some concern for questions of external validity even when they are identifying, on their own, the sorts of information that would be required to solve a causal problem (experiment 16).

Nevertheless, although subjects typically modify hypotheses in theory-dependent, scientifically legitimate ways, they tend also to have theory-dependent expectations that may be less defensible. Specifically, when subjects were given no additional information about the anomalies, they never assumed that the anomalies resulted from separate causal paths and frequently assumed that the anomalies resulted from a common causal path (experiment 12). Indeed, even when subjects were explicitly told that the anomalies were characterized by separate features, their assuming a common path was nevertheless still much more likely than their assuming a separate path. In short, subjects assumed patterns in the anomalies, and patterns suggest a specific way that a hypothesis can be modified. Thus subjects made the kinds of assumptions most congenial to treating the explanations as working hypotheses to be modified to accommodate, rather than rejected in light of, anomalous data. (More about this in the section on confirmation bias.) It may be that when the theory is a plausible one based on strong evidence, assuming that anomalies reflect a pattern is a reasonable stance. It is less defensible to make this assumption when the anomalies are characterized by separate features.

In short, it is sometimes legitimate to treat hypotheses as working hypotheses to be modified rather than rejected in light of anomalous data. However, it is considerations of mechanism that help decide when modification is warranted. Studies that ignore the role of mechanism may therefore be limited to operationalizing tasks so that only rejection is treated as an appropriate response to anomalous data (D. Kuhn et al. 1988; Mynatt, Doherty, and Tweney 1977, 1978). The result is that subjects who modify hypotheses instead of rejecting them might be portrayed as engaging in flawed reasoning when their behavior is in fact scientifically legitimate (Klahr and Dunbar 1988). However, the tendency to modify a hypothesis is not without its pitfalls: when subjects assume that anomalous data reflect the sort of pattern that calls for hypothesis modification rather than rejection, their assumption may not be warranted.

Confirmation Bias

Even when the data actually do call for rejection rather than modification of a hypothesis, ignoring the importance of mechanism can also underestimate subjects' willingness to reject hypotheses when rejection would be appropriate. For example, as already noted, the finding that it is more difficult to disconfirm causal than noncausal beliefs may reflect not a confirmation bias but rather the fact that the evidence called into question the covariation component, but not the mechanism component, of the belief.

When combined with Popper's work, the emphasis on covariation has lead to a distinction between confirmatory tests and disconfirmatory tests and to a distinction between both of these tests and tests that suggest an alternative (Mynatt et al. 1977, 1978). Such an emphasis focuses on theory-independent strategies for testing a hypothesis, that is, in terms of our framework, strategies independent of considerations of mechanism. Furthermore, Popperian and positivist approaches, as already noted, also put a premium on treating hypotheses as circumscribed statements to be either rejected or not rejected, rather than as working hypotheses to be modified, in the light of problematic data. Therefore, an emphasis on theory-independent tests along with a corresponding neglect of the role of mechanism can lead to a tendency to treat, as examples of confirmation bias, behaviors that are in fact legitimate hypothesis testing or legitimate modification of a working hypothesis.

As noted earlier, criticisms of the confirmation/disconfirmation distinction note that in fact, the distinction between confirming and disconfirming *strategies* is a false one because both strategies require taking account of alternative hypotheses. It is the results of the tests, not the tests themselves, that either confirm or disconfirm. Therefore, the real measure of whether someone is open to having her hypothesis disconfirmed is not whether she chooses a disconfirming test, as opposed to a confirming test, but whether she takes into account plausible alternative hypotheses.

When subjects were given a problem to solve but were not presented with alternative hypotheses, they spontaneously generated specific alternatives (experiments 14, 15, and 16) (although the tendency to do so increased with age). More important, they did so even when evaluating hypotheses they themselves had generated (experiments 14 and 15) and even when they had specific expectations about the results (experiment 16).

There was also evidence that subjects took more specific other-generated alternative hypotheses into account, as well. For example, subjects also took account of specific confounding factors and did so when the confounding was made explicit (experiment 6) as well as when the confounding was only presented implicitly (experiments 1, 7, and 8).

Of course, the most rigorous way to take account of alternative hypotheses is to use appropriate tests rather than what Klayman and Ha (1987) call "positive test strategies." An appropriate test consists of testing a condition in which the target possible cause is absent as well as one in which it is present. An appropriate strategy tests the general alternative hypothesis that maybe the effect would have obtained anyway, even if the target cause had not been operating, and this strategy increases the likelihood of detecting anomalous instances.

In our experiments, subjects certainly proposed appropriate, rather than positive, test strategies, even for hypotheses that they themselves had generated (experiments 14, 15, and 16). As I suggested in experiments 14 and 15, because subjects in Mynatt et al.'s task were restricted to choosing only one member of a pair of test screens, it is not clear whether, in choosing a single screen, subjects were using a positive test strategy or were simply choosing the first half of an appropriate test that they could not complete because of the constraints of the task.

Thus, insofar as a confirmation bias consists of ignoring alternative accounts (especially those that conflict with one's own theory or expectation), the subjects in our experiments provided ample evidence that they did not have a confirmation bias. (This is not to say that they would also show a lack of this sort of confirmation bias if the beliefs in question were emotion-laden or imbedded in a broader web of beliefs. It is merely to point out that even among adolescents, the tendency to exhibit a confirmation bias is not an across-the-board phenomenon.)

There was also evidence that subjects took the plausibility of alternative hypotheses into account. As already noted, when evaluating a confounded design, subjects were likely to ignore a confounding factor that they had antecedently judged to be an implausible possible cause (D. Kuhn et al. 1988). However, when the confounding factor was a plausible cause, then subjects treated confounded data as more likely than controlled data to be indeterminate (experiment 6).

As I noted in experiment 6, one could, of course, argue that subjects who dismiss implausible confounding factors are, in fact, showing a confirmation bias because they are not adequately questioning whether their beliefs about plausibility are accurate. However, to mention Murphy and Medin's (1985) point yet again, it is not feasible to take all correlations seriously. Our subjects were generalizing to experiment 6 a strategy that is not only legitimate but actually necessary outside of the laboratory.

Additional data relevant to the question of confirmation bias is that subjects also gave evidence of treating hypotheses as working hypotheses to be refined rather than rejected in light of anomalous data and they did this when the hypotheses were ones that they had been presented with (experiment 12) as well as when the hypotheses were ones that the subjects had generated on their own (experiments 14 and 15). Earlier I argued that the notion of confirmation bias could refer to several different things. To the extent that "confirmation bias" means filtering out data not congruent with one's hypothesis, the fact that subjects refined their hypotheses to take account of anomalous data indicates that at least in this sense, they were not operating with a confirmation bias; the anomalous data had not been filtered out but had been used as a basis for modifying the explanation.

Nevertheless, subjects' behavior could indicate a confirmation bias in the sense that in light of the anomalous data, subjects did maintain the explanation (albeit it in modified form) rather than reject it. However, in our evaluation of this possibility, it is worth noting that in modifying their hypotheses, subjects were judicious: when deciding whether to refine hypotheses so as to accommodate anomalous data, subjects took account of whether there was a mechanism that could explain how the anomalies were brought about and whether the anomalies shared common characteristics, which may indicate an underlying mechanism (experiment 11). That is, subjects did not maintain explanations in an indiscriminate way that suggests a confirmation bias; rather, they modified explanations in order to maintain them when the evidence indicated that modification would be theoretically warranted.

Neglecting the legitimate function served by modifying working hypotheses may explain why subjects have sometimes been treated as being poor scientists. For example, as Klahr and Dunbar (1988) point out, subjects in the Mynatt et al.'s (1977) study and in Wason's (1960) tasks may have been not clinging to a hypothesis in the face of disconfirming data but rather modifying what I have been calling a working hypothesis (and what Klahr and Dunbar [1988] call a "frame") to take account of anomalous data and then testing the modified version before switching to another hypothesis (or frame). Furthermore, identifying a single positive instance also enables one to specify more precisely exactly what the relevant alternatives are likely to be. And, as Klayman and Ha (1987) remind us, Bruner et al. (1956) found that the strategy of trying to isolate a single positive instance is one way of reducing information-processing demands when the number of potentially relevant variables is large (as it was in Mynatt et al.'s [1977] task).

This is not to argue that there is no such thing as a confirmation bias. A confirmation bias can be the motivational hope that a test will yield confirmatory rather than anomalous results, or it can be the filter that makes one ignore or distort anomalous results. It can also consist of considering alternative hypotheses that are, in fact, not plausible competitors or of being so wedded to the target hypothesis that competing hypotheses simply do not occur to one. Finally, a confirmation bias can also consist of refining a hypothesis in the light of disconfirming or anomalous data even when an alternative hypothesis can explain not only the data that suggested the initial hypothesis but also the data that are anomalous to it. Clearly, a confirmation bias can exist.

However, what I am arguing is that some situations are thought to reflect a confirmation bias that may not. As noted in chapter 3, clinging to a hypothesis rather than rejecting it in favor of an alternative could reflect not having the wherewithal to generate an alternative or else a merely temporary strategy of holding a hypothesis in abeyance in order to see whether the pattern of anomalous data suggests some alternative in particular. More relevant to the experiments in this book, confirmation bias does not consist of using a particular kind of test, a confirming test, because tests to confirm and to disconfirm both involve taking account of alternative hypotheses. Nor is a confirmation bias necessarily reflected in attempts to modify a hypothesis in light of anomalous data. Such attempts could reflect methodologically legitimate and efficient refinements of a basically correct working hypothesis to make the hypothesis appropriately responsive to new data. Analogously, they could reflect the strategy of trying to identify a positive instance in order to identify more precisely the likely alternative hypotheses.

That is, in terms of the main thesis of this book, if the view of scientific inquiry that one adopts acknowledges that the real measure of being open to having one's hypothesis disconfirmed is a willingness to consider alternative hypotheses and if the view one adopts acknowledges that in some circumstances, refining a theory rather than rejecting it is warranted, then the extent to which people can be said to have a confirmation bias may well be less than one might infer from the psychological literature. Put more generally, whether people are seen as relying on the principles of scientific inquiry depends heavily on what one's view of scientific inquiry is.

Science as Bootstrapping

At several points in this book, the view of scientific inquiry that motivated the experiments was that science is a bootstrapping operation. This view reflected two aspects of scientific inquiry: the fact that background information and the principles of scientific inquiry are interdependent and the fact that much of scientific inquiry consists of generating and modifying working hypotheses. (See Schauble 1990 for an additional discussion of bootstrapping.)

The Interdependence of Scientific Principles and Background Information

The principles of scientific inquiry function as rules of thumb because their success depends on the accuracy of background information

One of the themes running through this book is that the various principles of scientific inquiry do not guarantee success; they simply make it increasingly likely. That is, they function as rules of thumb rather than algorithms. In this regard, the approach in this book contrasts with approaches to scientific inquiry that accord a central role to covariation. When covariation is accorded a primary role, there is an algorithm for guaranteeing that the cause of an event will be correctly identified: One examines which factors have covaried with an event. Either a factor does covary with the event (in which case it is a cause) or else it does not covary (in which case it is not a cause). Furthermore, even when an approach does not explicitly maintain that covariation guarantees success, the claim is often implicit in the way the tasks are operationalized: the tasks are designed so that, operationally, the actual cause of an event is the factor that covaries with it (witness, for example, tasks for assessing formal operations).

In contrast, the approach taken in this book is that there are no principles that guarantee success. Another way of making this point is to note why there is no guarantee: The principles of scientific inquiry are used in conjunction with background information. What this means is that the success of the principles depends on the extent to which the background information is approximately correct, and there is no guarantee that background information is always correct. It may be, at worst, incorrect and is, at best, incomplete.

The obvious example of a rule of thumb versus an algorithm is that the principle of identifying causes of events by looking for factors that covary with the events will occasionally lead one to identify correlational artifacts rather than genuine causes and to overlook genuinely causal correlations because the relevant covariates have not been noticed.

But other principles as well function as rules of thumb. For example, consider the principle that covariation is more likely to reflect causation to the extent that there is a possible mechanism that can explain how the target factor could have brought about the effect and is less likely to reflect causation if possible mediating mechanisms have been ruled out. Our subjects relied on this principle (experiments 3, 9, 10).

However, although I am claiming that in doing this, our subjects were indeed relying on an important principle of scientific inquiry, my approach (in contrast to a covariation-centered approach) does not allow one to conclude that the subjects would definitely have been successful: the possible mechanisms assumed to be present might have been incorrect, and the mechanisms ruled out might not have included some that were relevant but had not yet been discovered.

Similarly, consider the role of rival alternative accounts: a target account is increasingly likely to be causal if plausible alternative explanations have been ruled out, while causation is more likely to be indeterminate when alternative accounts are still viable. Our subjects relied on this principle as well (experiments 6). However, again, although I claim that in doing this, the subjects were relying on an important principle of scientific inquiry, one cannot conclude that the subjects would definitely have been successful: subjects could have been mistaken in their antecedent beliefs that the alternative in question was implausible and should therefore be ignored, and the alternative that was considered might not have been the only competitor because other alternatives might not yet have been discovered.

In summary, then, on the approach I take in this book (and in contrast to approaches in which covariation is accorded the primary role), the principles of scientific inquiry do not guarantee success, because the principles are used in conjunction with background information. And when one relies on background information, there is no guarantee that the background information is accurate or that all of the relevant background information has already been discovered.

This point takes care of only one side of the interdependence of the principles of scientific inquiry and background information.

The principles of scientific inquiry help ensure the accuracy of background beliefs

The other side is that principles of scientific inquiry can help ensure that the background information being relied on is approximately accurate and can help in the discovery of relevant background information not now known. For example, one cannot take seriously every implausible possible cause. However, a strategy that ignores implausible possible causes runs the risk of overlooking an actual cause not yet identified. Relying on other principles of scientific inquiry is one strategy for identifying those possible causes that appear to be implausible but that might be worth a second look. For example, consider the principles, which our subjects followed (experiments 9 and 10), to the effect that implausible causes should be taken seriously if there is a possible mechanism that can account for how the implausible cause might operate and if the implausible cause covaries with the target effect a sufficient number of times. Similarly, a possible cause that initially appears to be nonstandard will merit a second look if most of the alternative accounts have been ruled out (experiment 1). And even when the target cause is standard and plausible, following the principle of ruling out alternative causes, which our subjects also did (experiments 6, 7, and 8), helps to ensure that the actual cause is accurately identified and is not a factor merely confounded with the actual cause.

In short, the success of the principles of scientific inquiry depends on the accuracy of the background information that the principles are used in conjunction with, and in turn, the principles of scientific inquiry help identify background information not yet discovered and help ensure the accuracy of background information already being considered. That is, one sense in which science involves bootstrapping is that the principles of scientific inquiry and the background information they are used in conjunction with are interdependent.

Science as the Generation and Modification of Working Hypotheses

The second, related sense in which science involves bootstrapping is that very often when explanations are first generated, they are neither complete nor perfectly accurate but rather are working hypotheses to be refined and augmented as additional data become available.

The problem is that bootstrapping suggests progress, and not all refinements are methodologically legitimate; sometimes hypotheses ought, in fact, to be rejected when anomalous data come to light. Therefore, treating hypotheses as working hypotheses is successful to the extent that the resulting modifications are theoretically motivated, which is something that our subjects took into account (experiment 11). To come full circle to the interdependence of scientific principles and background information, the principle of modifying rather than rejecting a working hypothesis when there seems to be a known mechanism to account for the anomalies or when the anomalies form a pattern that suggests a mechanism to be discovered is successful only to the extent that the assumed mechanisms are, in fact, accurate and only to the extent that the pattern in the anomalies actually does reflect an underlying mechanism rather than an artifact. And in turn, the principle of considering patterns and explanatory mechanisms can help uncover new information about the variables that restrict the generalizability of the working hypothesis.

(The point about bootstrapping might be seen as analogous to the difference between general knowledge and domain-specific knowledge. The strategy that one ought to take account of, for example, information about mechanism or information about alternative explanations might be construed as a general strategy to be applied across content areas. In contrast, it is domain-specific knowledge that informs us about which particular mechanisms and which particular alternative explanations ought to be treated as relevant.)

Age Differences

Absence of Age Differences

In terms of age differences, perhaps the most striking finding in the present experiments was the large number of instances in which age differences did *not* obtain. Like college students, adolescents used information about mechanism to decide which implausible possible causes might be worth pursuing. They used considerations of mechanism to navigate between taking seriously all implausible possible causes (and therefore traveling along many dead ends) and ignoring all implausible possible causes (and therefore possibly overlooking some unexpected discoveries). That is, even adolescents treated information about mechanism as evidential (experiments 9 and 10).

Adolescents also treated information about mechanism as evidential when they used mechanism information to decide when revising an explanation to take account of anomalous data is likely to be methodologically legitimate (experiment 11) and when it is likely to result in rejection (experiment 13).

And like college students, adolescents also showed an awareness of the importance of considering and ruling out alternative accounts, not only in the context of assessing data already collected (experiments 6, 7, 8, and 11) but also in the context of generating alternative hypotheses to be tested in the future—even when the target hypothesis is one that they themselves come to the experimental situation already believing (experiment 13) or propose during the task (experiments 14, 15, and 16).

In addition to an awareness of the importance of alternative accounts, adolescents, like college students, also showed a willingness to be open to anomalous evidence, which argues against an across-the-board confirmation bias. And even when adolescents, like college students, displayed what might have been a confirmation bias (by treating hypotheses as working hypotheses to be revised), they relied on considerations of mechanism to decide which revisions were warranted (experiment 11).

Formal versus informal aspects of scientific reasoning

Since students were able, in several of the experiments in this book, to rely on various principles of scientific inquiry, the obvious question to ask is what accounts for the frequent conclusion in the literature that people in general and adolescents in particular are poor scientists. One answer, which has been a theme running through this book, is that when scientific reasoning is construed as a process in which covariation plays a central role but in which considerations of theory or mechanism are to be either ignored or overridden, people in fact reason in a way deemed to be "nonscientific" precisely because their reasoning is theory-based, because they take into account information about mechanism as well as about covariation. Specifically, they rely on theory to decide which covariations to take seriously, when to ignore confounding and when to take it into account, when to refine rather than relinquish a conclusion in the face of anomalous data, etc. In contrast, when the importance of theory or mechanism in scientific reasoning is acknowledged, that is, when theory-based reasoning is deemed appropriate, subjects' reasoning in many situations can be seen to be more in line with the scientific ideal. In short, one answer to the question of what accounts for the frequent conclusion that people are poor scientists is that people make use of considerations of theory or mechanism (and do so in a methodologically legitimate way), while in many studies of scientific reasoning, considerations of theory or mechanism are, at least operationally, either ignored or treated as something to be overcome. This point was amplified in several earlier sections.

In this section I want to suggest that another reason why subjects' reasoning in many tasks may appear to be nonscientific has to do with a distinction between what might be called the "formal" or "technical" aspects versus the "informal" or "conceptual" aspects of scientific reasoning (Koslowski, Susman, and Serling 1991). Briefly, by formal (or technical) aspects of scientific reasoning, I mean those aspects that involve the sorts of considerations relevant to proposing an actual design for collecting data—whether the design involves using direct experimental intervention or relying on naturally occurring correlational data. In contrast, informal (or conceptual) aspects of scientific reasoning involve the sorts of issues relevant to scientific reasoning even before the stage of proposing an actual design for data collection. Put differently, a conceptual understanding of scientific reasoning would include an awareness of *what* needs to be done, while a technical understanding would include knowledge of *how to design* the actual data collection so that what needs to be done can get done. For example, consider the problem from experiment 16 concerning whether having parents stay with their hospitalized children causes improved recovery rates. For this problem, a conceptual understanding of what was needed would include an awareness that one would have to see whether parental presence was associated with faster recovery rates. A technical understanding would include an awareness that to do this, one would have to contrast the recovery rates of children whose parents stayed with those whose parents did not. A technical understanding would also include the awareness that one would have to consider the proportion (rather than the absolute number) of children in each of the two groups. Similarly, it is one thing to have the conceptual understanding that one would have to make sure that the children whose parents stayed were not just less ill to begin with. It is quite another to have the technical skill to design a study in which both groups would either have illnesses of the same severity or in which each child with one illness in the treatment group would be matched with a child who had the same illness in the control group. The difference between conceptual and technical (or formal and informal) knowledge could explain, for example, why subjects at all ages in experiment 16 had a solid grasp of the importance of contrasts but rarely proposed an actual experimental design.

An additional possibility for why subjects' reasoning often seems nonscientific is that in many studies of scientific reasoning, subjects must make sense of some quite complicated information (for example, the necessity and sufficiency relations in Siegler's [1975] task). This is something the subjects in our experiments were not asked to do. Nor did the subjects spontaneously suggest how the causal variable would be related to the effect: if it were a necessary cause, a sufficient cause, neither, or both. If we had asked our subjects to reason about this sort of technical knowledge, then like Siegler's subjects, our subjects might also have been found to be deficient in scientific reasoning, but their deficiency might have reflected limited capacity for processing information or a lack of strategies to enable them to perform the task with the processing capacity that they did have.

Age Differences That Are Present

The kinds of age differences we did find were of two general sorts. The first were those that showed an essentially linear change from sixth-graders to college students. Figure 5.4 in experiment 4 is a good example of this sort of change: with increasing age, ratings of implausible mechanisms decrease. A variant of this sort of change occurred when ninth-graders were comparable to one of the other two age groups, indicating either that ninth-graders' behavior had not yet begun to be different from that of the sixth-graders or else that it had already changed sufficiently to be comparable to that of the college students. Figure 8.4 in experiment 10 is an example of this sort of change.

One of the linear developmental differences emerged in experiments 3, 4, and 5 in which subjects were asked to evaluate plausible as well as implausible mechanisms and to generate and evaluate mechanisms to explain plausible and implausible covariations.

Recall that assessments of covariation were comparable across ages, with subjects treating implausible covariations as less likely to be causal than plausible covariations and partial covariation as less likely to be causal than perfect covariation. Age groups were also comparable in explaining covariations, so long as the covariations were plausible rather than implausible: when explaining plausible covariations, adolescents and college students were similar in generating reasonable mechanisms and in rating them as reasonable.

However, when asked to explain implausible covariations, sixth-graders were more likely than the older subjects to generate dubious mechanisms. Implausible covariations call up implausible explanatory mechanisms, which college students are unwilling to propose. In contrast, sixth-graders have an inflated belief in the range of possible mechanisms that can be operating in a situation and so were not restricted in the same way. In the same vein, although sixth-graders were able to propose reasonable mechanisms to explain plausible covariations, they were nevertheless more likely than older subjects to rate as reasonable a dubious mechanism proposed by someone else. Again, if a wide range of possible mechanism is likely, then perhaps dubious mechanisms proposed by others are likely.

We treated the age differences in the range of mechanisms that subjects found plausible as a straightforward result of their differential background information about various aspects of the world. Without very much information about an area, there is little basis for judging an explanation to be implausible, especially (as was the case in these experiments) when there is definitely a covariation to be explained.

There were also other age differences that seemed to reflect differential background information. For example, the adolescents were less likely to generate alternative hypotheses than were the college students when they were testing a hypothesis that they had generated themselves (experiment 16).

One other age difference seemed to reflect not so much differential background information as a difference in the interpretation of causal questions. Recall that in experiment 6 adolescents, but not college students, treated the presence of external validity as enhancing the liklihood of causation so long as internal validity was present to begin with. I suggested that the college students were concerned with whether the target factor played a causal role in the particular sample studied, whereas the adolescents were concerned with the general causal picture, that is, with whether the target factor is an important cause beyond the confines of the target experiment or is merely a minor one. And when an adolescent subject learns that external validity is present, she treats this as evidence that the target cause is important enough to operate across many situations.

There were also essentially linear age differences that seemed to reflect information-processing limitations. For example, in experiment 15, although there were no age differences in the number of responses generated, the younger age groups were more likely than college students to carry out an appropriate test that was redundant or an appropriate test that involved only a subportion of the data. I suggested that redundant information and focusing on only a subportion of the data both minimized information-processing demands.

Another example of age differences reflecting information-processing limitations is that when subjects were presented with general alternatives that had been ruled out, younger subjects often speculated that another alternative might have been operating even though the other alternative was merely a specific instance of one of the general alternatives that had already been ruled out (experiments 7 and 8). I suggested that this reflected a more limited ability to engage in deep levels of processing. With decreasing age, subjects were less likely to consider their specific hypotheses in sufficient depth to be able to infer that ruling out a general alternative meant ruling out specific instances of that alternative (including theirs). Another reason for suggesting that this age difference was due to information-processing limitations was that the difference was eliminated when we interviewed subjects individually, that is, when we made it explicit that the alternative suggested by the subject was a specific instance of the one that had been ruled out. Thus this age difference did not seem to reflect a different belief about the effects of ruling out alternatives.

Ninth-Graders

Another sort of age difference occurred when the ninth-graders' ratings were neither an average of the ratings of the other two age groups nor comparable to the ratings of either one of the other two age groups. This sort of difference suggested not a linear developmental difference but rather something specific to ninth-graders.

For example, in experiment 3, when told that several possible mechanisms have been ruled out, ninth-graders were more likely than the other two age groups to assume that there are other mechanisms that nevertheless exist and are waiting to be discovered (experiment 3, figure 5.3). In experiment 5, when covariations were implausible, ninth-graders' ratings were closer than the ratings of the other two age groups to the indeterminate rating of 5: there "might or might not be another way" that experts might discover that could explain how x caused y. That is, they were more likely than the other two age groups to be uncertain. In experiment 6, when external validity was absent, ninth-graders were less likely than the other two age groups to agree with statements about generalizability (experiment 6, figure 6.4). And in experiment 12, when subjects were presented with two anomalies and no information about the anomalies, ninth-graders were less likely than the other two age groups to infer that the anomalies had resulted from a common causal path.

Formal-operational reasoning

One answer might be that the ninth-graders' deviation from a linear developmental progression has something to do with the development of formal operations, which brings with it hypothetical thinking about the possible as well as the concrete. For example, one might argue that a growing awareness of hypothetical possibilities makes ninth-graders especially likely to assume that there are other mechanisms waiting to be discovered. However, it is less clear how a growing awareness of the possible could cause ninth-graders to be less likely than the other two age groups to rate an implausible covariation as causal or less likely to infer that anomalies resulted from a common causal path. If one construes formal-operational thought to refer to a general ability to consider hypothetical possibilities, then ninth-graders could equally well be more likely (or at least as likely as college students) to rate an implausible covariation as causal or to infer that anomalies resulted from a common causal path; both outcomes are certainly possible. That is, the notion of what it means to consider the hypothetical or the possible is not very precisely spelled out in the work on formal operations beyond what it means in the actual formal-operational tasks. The "what if" questions of preschoolers ("What if we had pizza every day for breakfast?" "What if we gave my baby sister to somebody else?") makes it clear that in some contexts, even very young children can consider the possible. Therefore, in general, the ability to consider hypothetical possibilities is not something that emerges for the first time around the ninth-grade. Clearly, for formal operations to be seen as something characteristic of ninth-graders but not of other age groups, one would have to specify what sorts of hypothetical possibilities become salient for ninth-graders and what the connection of such possibilities is to formal-operations.

Alternatively, one might construe formal-operational reasoning to refer to a more restricted ability: the abilitiy to consider the possible in those particular contexts in which formal-operational reasoning has been operationalized, namely, in tasks such as the chemicals task. However, even on this construal, the answer to why ninth-graders deviate from a linear developmental progression is not satisfying. For a subject to be counted as formal-operational, it is not sufficient for the subject merely to generate all possible combinations; in addition, the combinations must be generated in a systematic way. That is, formal-operational performance puts a premium on applying the formula for generating all possible combinations in a set. (In the chemicals task, for example, this would consist of generating the combinations $1 + 2, 1 + 3, \ldots, 1 + 5, 2 + 3, 2 + 4$, etc.)

There is no question that this is a useful skill to have in general and for purposes of doing research. Once the likely causes have been narrowed down to a small set of possibilities and when there are no theoretical considerations that favor one or some more than others, a formal-operational strategy will ensure that all possible combinations are generated so that they can be tested. However, as I noted in chapter 2, this strategy would seem to have very little bearing on the sorts of situations in which theoretical considerations play a role, such as how it is that the factors come to be included in the set of possible causes in the first place, when it is that anomalous results call for hypothesis modification rather than rejection, etc. More specifically, it is not at all clear how formal operations, as it is operationalized, could explain the ninth-graders' deviations in our experiments.

Overgeneralization of uncertainty
Another possible explanation for the ninth-graders' behavior is Keating's idea that in making the transition to more mature thinking, "early adolescents seem to reject the possibility that *any* reliable conclusions can be drawn." This might be termed an "overgeneralization of uncertainty." For example, "When early adolescents first begin correctly to give a 'can't tell' response to logical syllogisms, they also give such an answer when, indeed, there *is* a valid conclusion—and one that young children state quite readily" (Keating 1990, 67). The question then becomes, Why is the overgeneralization of uncertainty occurring in the ninth grade?

Integration of informal rules of evidence and formal teaching about science
I would suggest an alternative that builds on Keating's notion of overgeneralization of uncertainty: When adolescents are sixth-graders, they already possess considerable informal knowledge about scientific rules of evidence that they rely on when they reason about causal judgments. For example, even sixth-graders are aware of the importance of ruling out alternative accounts; they know that confounded data are suspect; they treat information about mechanism as evidential and use it in deciding which causes are plausible; they are judicious in the way they deal with anomalous evidence; etc. But in the ninth-grade, adolescents begin to be exposed to more formal instruction about science. They begin to be explicitly taught about the importance of science as a vehicle for discovery. And they begin to be taught about the method itself, that is, about testing hypotheses, using control groups, etc. I suggest that it is the

juxtaposition of their existing informal rules of evidence and their formal exposure to scientific method that accounts for some of the ninth-graders' uncertainty. For example, when ninth-graders are sensitized to all the problems that can occur in scientific research, the resulting skepticism, if overgeneralized, might well make them more likely than the other two age groups to dismiss implausible covariations (experiment 5), less likely to agree with statements about generalizability (experiment 6), and less likely to infer that anomalies resulted from a common causal path (experiment 12). If one is being very skeptical and if uncertainty looms large, then there is every reason not to take implausible covariations seriously, not to generalize, and not to infer a common causal path.

Of course, this explanation cannot be treated as operating across the board. The ninth-graders' behavior does not deviate from a linear developmental progression in all situations. Nor, on this account, would one expect it to. If the juxtaposition of informal rules of evidence and formal training in science is, in fact, part of the problem, there is no reason to expect that the resulting overgeneralization of uncertainty would always predominate; one would expect that existing informal rules of evidence would certainly be relied on in at least some situations. But this leaves us with a possible explanation that is only an incomplete working hypothesis. For it to be more compelling, it would need to be refined in a way that would specify what some of the situations are in which sensitivity to formal teaching about science (and the resulting overgeneralization of uncertainty) predominates over existing informal rules of evidence.

Sex Differences

Sex differences were not at all what we had expected to find. In consequence, the possible explanations for them (especially when they resulted from three-way interactions) that I offered in the text I openly acknowledge to have been ad hoc. However, in this chapter I would like to draw attention to three of the sex differences because they illustrate the general point that whenever two populations are contrasted, it is very difficult to avoid comparisons that are invidious to one of the groups.

In experiment 9, females rated a factor as more likely to be causal when there were more rather than fewer instances of covariation, while males rated it as less likely to be causal when there were more rather than fewer instances of covariation. That is, females' ratings were congruent with the principles of scientific inquiry: the more times a factor and an effect covary, the more likely the factor is to be causal.

Similarly, in experiment 10, in terms of ratings of how likely a factor was to be causal, the presence of a mechanism produced a greater effect for females than for males. In addition, in experiment 11, with increasing age, females were increasingly likely (while males were decreasingly likely) to reject an explanation when anomalies to the explanation were in the control condition than when the anomalies were accounted for by common explanatory mechanisms. Again, in both cases the ratings of the females were in line with what one would have expected on an account of scientific inquiry that acknowledged the importance of mechanism. In all three cases, then, the females' ratings were more in line with the principles of scientific inquiry than were those of the males. Whether, after the fact, one views this as evidence that females are better equipped (for whatever reason) to engage in scientific inquiry, or instead as evidence that the reasoning of males is unfettered by the kinds of rules of evidence that might constrain creativity, is, I suspect, largely a matter of how feminist one's general orientation is.

What Constitutes Rational Reasoning?

One of the themes running through this book is that a theory- or mechanism-based view of scientific reasoning suggests that deviations from rational or sound thinking may be less extreme or of a different nature than is often supposed. From a different perspective, this is the argument that a view of scientific inquiry that accords a central role to covariation and a view that acknowledges the importance of theory or mechanism make different statements about what sorts of behaviors are rational (or at least sensible or appropriate). I have drawn attention to two points about scientific inquiry that are often ignored in theory-independent, covariation-based models of scientific reasoning. First, a reliance on theory or mechanism is a legitimate (indeed, necessary) aspect of scientific thinking because information about mechanism is evidential. Second, because science is cumulative, considerations of causal mechanism sometimes lead us, appropriately, to treat hypotheses as working hypotheses that can be informed by, and revised (rather than rejected) in the light of, anomalous evidence.

These points carry with them several implicit suggestions about what sorts of reasoning is rational. In this section I would like to make the suggestions explicit and to do so by discussing them with respect to the educational question of what students ought to be taught in order to teach them to reason scientifically.

The theory-independent view of scientific reasoning criticized in this book is one in which, at least in terms of how tasks are operationalized, the rules of rational thinking are treated as a set of formal rules that are content-free. The core of this approach is that the presence of covariation is the primary index of causation and that if covariation is absent, then belief in a causal relation ought to be relinquished. On this view, pushed to its extreme, one need not know anything about a subject area in order to be able to engage in sound scientific reasoning about the area. One need only to apply the covariation rule and the causal relations will be identified.

However, pushing this view to its extreme throws into relief what its shortcomings are. If simply applying the covariation rule were sufficient (along with, for example, the principle that one ought to rule out alternative hypotheses), then we would all be able to contribute to cancer research. The fact that we are not all able to do so illustrates the most basic suggestion about what is rational and important to communicate to students, namely, that rules of scientific reasoning (an important one of which involves covariation) and existing information about a content area are interdependent: we need to rely on information about the area to decide which covariations to look for in the first place, which ones to take seriously when they occur, and which alternative hypotheses to treat as plausible.

This approach has several concrete implications. One is that principles, such as the principle of covariation, cannot be taught as content-free algorithms that, by themselves, guarantee success. Rather, they are heuristics that make success increasingly likely only to the extent that the existing information base or knowledge about the phenomenon in question (including information about theory or mechanism) is approximately correct. Conversely, it makes sense to treat existing knowledge (including existing theories) about a phenomenon as something that can be tested, refined, and augmented by relying on principles such as the principle of covariation. Viewed from a different perspective, another concrete implication of the interdependence of scientific principles and background information is that one ought to be skeptical when evaluating covariation as well as when evaluating one's existing knowledge base, because the former does not guarantee success and the latter might be, at best, merely incomplete and approximately accurate. However, one's skepticism should be constrained and informed. Skepticism about covariation should be constrained and informed by the existing knowledge base, and confidence in one's existing information should be constrained and informed by knowledge about covariation. In a word, the interdependence of scientific principles and background information suggests that scientific reasoning ought to be treated as a bootstrapping operation whose end result is cumulative. Finally, the suggestion that the results of scientific reasoning are cumulative leads to the additional suggestion that many hypotheses ought to be treated as approximately correct working hypotheses that may need to be refined and augmented, rather than necessarily rejected, in light of anomalous evidence. However, to come full circle to the original point, decisions about when to reject and when to modify ought to be based on existing background information as well as on the principle of covariation. Again, skepticism about working hypotheses ought to be constrained.

Practically, what this means is that teaching people to reason scientifically ought to be presented as something that requires at least two things: attention to covariation, to be sure, but, in addition, a solid grasp of content—theoretical as well as observational knowledge. As a concrete example, this means that it is important to teach students that it is not rational to treat all instances of covariation as equally indicative of causation. This is done by drawing students' attention to the distinction between causation and coincidence by way of indicating that some skepticism about covariation is warranted. What my approach suggests in addition is to tell students that one strategy for deciding which covariates to pursue (that is, for distinguishing correlations that are causal from those that are coincidental) is to rely on background information, including information about theory or mechanism. Such a strategy would make it explicit that relying on covariation alone will not mechanically churn out the correct answer; that it is rational to rely on information about theory or mechanism in order to decide which implausible covariations merit a second look (and which correlations ought to be searched for in the first place) because to do otherwise would, at the very least, not be pragmatically feasible.

But again, it is also important to teach students that just as relying on covariation does not guarantee success, neither does relying on information about theory or mechanism: we might well dismiss an implausible correlation that is, in fact, causal simply because the relevant mechanism has not yet been discovered. And one clue that a mechanism exists that has not yet been discovered is repeated and systematic covariation (especially if alternative causal factors can be ruled out). Once again, the point is not that relying on information about mechanism assures success; the point is that it would not be rational to rely on information about covariation in a way that did not take information about mechanism into account.

Analogous considerations arise with respect to the related point that theories are evaluated not in isolation but with respect to plausible alternative accounts. Plausibility depends in part on whether there is a mechanism that can account for how the alternative might have brought about the observed data. Therefore, students need to be explicitly taught that no experiment ever controls for all logically possible alternatives and that one must rely on knowledge about various areas (including knowledge about theory or mechanism) in order to decide which alternatives are plausible and ought actually to be controlled for. For example, making sure that a phenomenon is observed under conditions of standard temperature and pressure might be crucial in chemistry but would be less important in a study of psychological attachment precisely because there are known mechanisms that explain how it is that chemical reactions are affected by changes in these variables but there are no corresponding theories suggesting that these factors affect quality of attachment. Of course, to point up again the interdependence of principles and knowledge base about an area, the strategy of relying on knowledge about an area to decide which alternatives to control for is successful only to the extent that the knowledge base is approximately correct.

In Tversky and Kahnemann's (1974) approach, it is the principles of statistical inference rather than covariation that constitute the rational ideal, but the conclusion is the same: people's reasoning deviates from the rational ideal, and the deviation results from a reliance on theory-dependent causal beliefs rather than on content-free principles of (in this case, statistical) inference. Thus, for example, subjects rely on naive theories of personality rather than on base-rate data to decide that a tidy, orderly person is probably a librarian rather than a farmer even though farmers comprise a full 70 percent of the population. On the theory-dependent view, however, the problem with ignoring base-rate data is not that causal or theory-based reasoning is used as a substitute; rather, the problem is that since the theory being relied on is a naive theory, the theory has probably not been examined and therefore the subject probably does not know to what extent the theory is valid. Similarly, it makes sense to rely on (and would be medically irresponsible to ignore) theory-based knowledge about the way AIDS is transmitted in order to decide that a drug user who shares needles and works as a male prostitute is more likely than the population average to have AIDS, because knowledge about AIDS transmission is anything but naive. Of course, if the theory of AIDS transmission is wrong (or if tidy, orderly people choose farming as a way of bringing order to the earth), then having one's conclusion informed by this particular theory would lead one astray. But this just demonstrates that when one relies on theory-based information, the theory should be as accurate as possible. It also demonstrates that because theories can be either incomplete or inaccurate, it is important to be judiciously skeptical about one's theory and willing to reject or modify it in the face of anomalous information, including information about covariation. It does not demonstrate that theory-based judgements per se should (or can) be avoided.

The difference between the view that one ought to minimize (or eliminate) reliance on theory-based beliefs and the view that one ought, instead, to try to make one's theory-based beliefs as complete and accurate as possible is not trivial, because it also has implications for teaching people how to engage in scientific reasoning. If one construes the problem as one of relying on theory-based knowledge rather than on, for example, base-rate data, then the appropriate educational strategy is to try to convince people to ignore information about theory or mechanism and to teach them instead to place more emphasis on the principles of statistical inference. If, on the other hand, one sees the problem as involving reliance on theories that may not be valid, then the appropriate educational strategy is to encourage people to be suitably skeptical of the theories that they hold and to give them the sophistication and data with which to evaluate them, especially with respect to competing theories.

The approach being argued for in this book also has concrete implications for how one teaches students to deal with anomalous evidence. For example, if one acknowledges the interdependence of covariation and existing explanatory knowledge about an area, and especially if one takes a cumulative view of science according to which many hypotheses are working hypotheses to be refined as new data and theories become available, then it makes sense to teach students that not all hypotheses or theories ought immediately to be rejected in the face of anomalous evidence. It makes sense to teach students that some anomalous data provide additional information about how a working hypothesis that is approximately correct needs to be refined. This is a different way of making the earlier point that science is cumulative. It means teaching students that few theories can be stated in complete form before all of the data are in. And this, in turn, means teaching students that as new data become available, it is often appropriate to treat the existing theory as a working hypothesis that can and should be informed by, and modified in light of, the new data.

For example, if a theory is based on sound initial evidence but an expected covariation fails to obtain in a particular context, this need not mean that the theory that predicted the covariation should be jettisoned. If may mean, instead, that the theory should be maintained in broad outline but that it should be refined so as to qualify the extent to which it operates in the situation in question (especially if plausible competing explanations have been ruled out or are nonexistent). If, on the other hand, the expected covariation fails to obtain (especially across a variety of contexts) and there is also evidence that calls into question the theoretical explanation (or mechanism) that predicted the covariation, then it probably makes sense to teach students that the initial theory should be treated with an increasingly jaundiced eye.

The approach in this book would also suggest that students should be taught to look for patterns in anomalous data. One reason is that if there is no discernable pattern, then this might suggest that the theory is mistaken about so many different contexts that rejecting it is, indeed, in order. Conversely, the presence of a pattern might suggest that the theory needs to be restricted so that it does not apply to certain contexts, and the pattern might suggest what these contexts are.

On a theory-based view of scientific reasoning, then, we should teach students that it is sometimes reasonable to modify a theory in light of anomalous data. It is unreasonable to modify rather that reject a theory when the anomalies can be accommodated only by ad hoc, rather than methodologically legitimate, theorizing.

Finally, in terms of educational practice, we should keep in mind the extent to which adolescents can be said to be relying on various principles of scientific reasoning, because if it is not clear what students *are* doing when they reason, then it is not clear what they need to be taught.

What the data in this book suggest is that in at least some situations, adolescents have many strengths that can be built on in teaching them to think with scientific rigor. When reasoning about causation, adolescents take into consideration information about mechanism, alternative accounts, confounding, external validity, anomalous evidence, the plausibility of possible causal factors, whether the possible causal factor is standard or nonstandard, whether the data occur systematically or one time only, and whether the target hypothesis ought to be treated as a working hypothesis to be modified rather than rejected in the face of anomalous data. This is not at all to claim that subjects can rely on this information in all situations. It is merely to point out that when we teach students to reason scientifically, we do not have to start from scratch, because in at least some situations, they are already able, when engaging in causal reasoning, to rely on various principles of scientific inquiry.

General Conclusions

The empiricist aim in the philosophy of science has been to describe the principles of scientific inquiry in a way that is theory-independent. Historically, this has meant rationally reconstructing scientific inquiry in terms of the Humean indices of causation, the most prominent of which is covariation. The idea was that covariation (and priority and contiguity) would constitute methodological principles that were "objective," that is, uncontaminated by theoretical biases.

In the philosophy of science, the empiricist aim of identifying a set of theory-independent principles that underlie scientific inquiry has been criticized for some time. Critics have pointed out that theoretical considerations determine which of the many covariations in the world are taken seriously and which are dismissed as specious, and that existing background theories determine which of the many possible alternative hypotheses are actually controlled for in scientific investigation.

Nevertheless, among many psychologists studying scientific reasoning in lay subjects, research has continued to be based on an empiricist approach. This is reflected in two sorts of tasks. One sort consists of studying scientific reasoning by asking subjects about situations that are theoretically impoverished (such as the formal-operations task). There is no question that during certain steps in the scientific process, an exclusive reliance on covariation information might be the only option available. If, for example, all of the plausible hypotheses to explain a phenomenon have been ruled out and one is left with not even a vague theory to guide further investigation, then one's only option might be to rely on covariation to decide on the next step. This is exactly the case in the formal-operations task in which any clues about causal mechanisms are carefully eliminated. However, many of the most exciting aspects of scientific reasoning involve using information about theory or mechanism to evaluate covariation information. Tasks designed to be theoretically impoverished provide no opportunity to study the many aspects of scientific inquiry in which theoretical considerations play an important (and legitimate) role. One of the aims of this book has been to argue that studying how subjects behave in theoretically impoverished tasks allows us to study, at best, only a very circumscribed aspect of scientific reasoning.

The other sort of psychological task that reflects an empiricist approach involves asking subjects to reason about a theoretically rich situation but operationally stipulating that correct performance consists of ignoring (or at least overriding) theoretical considerations. In such tasks, subjects are counted as performing correctly when they base their decisions only on the covariation information presented in the task. Another aim of this book has been to suggest a reinterpretation of such research. I have argued that research approaches that treat scientific reasoning as consisting of an exclusive reliance on covariation seriously underestimate the extent to which subjects engage in scientific reasoning, because they treat a reliance on theory or mechanism as reflecting defective reasoning, when in fact such a reliance can be scientifically legitimate. When subjects rely on theory to determine which covariations to take seriously and which alternative hypotheses should be controlled for, they are reasoning in a way that is scientifically reasonable rather than flawed.

Although I have argued that theoretical considerations play a crucial and legitimate role in scientific reasoning, I have also argued that theory and data are interdependent; just as covariation information alone does not guarantee scientific success, neither does theory alone. Rather, sound scientific reasoning involves bootstrapping: using theory to constrain data and using data in turn to constrain, refine, and elaborate theory. Scientific progress often consists of a repeated cycle of using a working hypothesis as a guideline for searching for particular covariations and then using the resulting covariations (including those that were not anticipated by the working hypothesis) to refine and elaborate the working hypothesis.

Therefore, to demonstrate that subjects are reasoning scientifically, it is not sufficient simply to document that they rely on causal theories when they evaluate covariation information. As already noted, this has been amply demonstrated in many situations involving theory-rich tasks. Nor is it sufficient to demonstrate that subjects sometimes rely on covariation information without regard to theory, because people almost never should. Rather, to demonstrate that subjects are reasoning scientifically, one must demonstrate that subjects are relying on covariation information and on information about theory or mechanism in reasonable, methodologically legitimate ways. To this end, a third aim of this book has been to present some preliminary data documenting that subjects rely on theory and data in a judicious way.

Specifically, the experiments reported here have documented that, although subjects rely on mechanism information to decide which covariations to take seriously, they do not let theoretical considerations blind them to the utility of covariation information: subjects realize that a covariation that seems, on theoretical grounds, to be implausible should be given a second look if it occurs systematically, because it may indicate a genuinely causal relation for which the relevant mechanism has not yet been discovered (although the range of dubious mechanisms judged by the subject to be plausible increases with decreasing age). Subjects are also judicious when deciding whether anomalous data call for rejecting, rather than simply modifying, a hypothesis; in making this decision, they take account of whether the anomalies occur systematically as well as whether there are mechanisms to explain them. And when evaluating and testing a hypothesis, even one that they themselves have generated, subjects rely on theoretical considerations, even when doing so holds the possibility of disconfirming their own theory: they arrange to test the target hypotheses in an appropriate way rather than relying only on a positive-test strategy, they generate and take account of alternative hypotheses, and they rely on considerations of mechanism to decide whether hypotheses that were controlled for are theoretically plausible or implausible.

In short, the research presented in this book suggests the working hypothesis that at least in some situations, subjects reason in a scientifically legitimate way to a greater extent than one might infer from the existing literature: they treat data and theory as interdependent, and they do so judiciously, relying on theory to decide which covariations to pursue and relying on covariation to test, refine, and elaborate theory. If, as I have argued, this working hypothesis is approximately correct, it will point the way to additional data that will enable it to be refined and augmented, and we will have bootstrapped ourselves up to a better theory.

Notes

Chapter 1

1. Siegler has also examined whether children rely on priority and contiguity in assessing cause, but I focus on covariation because it is the most frequently studied of the Humean indices, which formed the basis of the positivist approach.

Chapter 3

1. I thank Richard Boyd for suggesting the term "straw-person confirmation."

Chapter 4

1. In the published version of this study, when covariation was absent, we inferred that for the sixth-graders as well as for the college students, ratings were lower when mechanisms were absent rather than present. We inferred this from the lack of a significant interaction of age × covariation status × mechanism status. We have since tested this directly. When covariation is absent, the sixth-graders' ratings are in fact lower when mechanisms are absent rather than present, t(two-tailed) = 3.66, p = .0003.

2. This type of justification was not mentioned in the published report of this study, because at the time we did not realize its possible significance and therefore treated it as "noise."

Chapter 5

1. For the question 1 ratings, the main effect for story was significant, $F(3, 360) = 12.10$, $p = .0001$, as was the interaction of story and mechanism status, $F(3, 360) = 3.01, p = .03$. However, since neither the main effect nor the interaction seemed to reflect any discernible pattern, I do not discuss the effects of story further.

2. What can also be seen in figure 5.1 is what we interpret to be a result of sampling error. For both question 1 ratings and question 2 ratings, respectively, there was a borderline interaction of covariation type and mechanism status, $F(1, 360) = 3.6, p = .06; F(1, 359) = 4.16, p = .04$. Furthermore, the interaction of covariation type and mechanism status for the difference between question 1 and question 2 ratings was not at all significant, $F(1, 359) = .03, p = .85$. The statistics reflect the fact that for subjects in the mechanisms-rule-out condition, the difference between perfect and partial covariation was greater than for subjects in the control condition. Question 1 ratings occurred before subjects had received any information about mechanisms. Therefore, this information could not have played a role in the question 1 ratings. Recall that mechanism status was a between-subjects variable. It would appear that by chance, the subjects assigned to the mechanisms-ruled-out condition distinguished the two covariation types more at the outset than

did the subjects in the control condition. And these subjects continued to exhibit the same difference in their question 2 ratings.

3. Subjects' initial ratings of how likely it was that x had caused y were analyzed with an age × sex × plausibility type × story analysis of variance, with plausibility nested in story. There was a main effect for story, $F(10, 288) = 6.16$, $p = .0001$, although none of the interactions involving story were significant at even the .3 level.

4. There was a main effect for story, $F(5, 288) = 8.3$, $p = .0001$, but none of the interactions involving story reached the .05 level of significance.

5. Again, there was a main effect for Story, $F(5, 288) = 4.23$, $p = .0001$.

6. There was a main effect for Story, $F(10, 162) = 2.01$, $p = .04$.

Chapter 6

1. The results of experiment 6 were presented at the meetings of the Society for Research in Child Development in 1991.

2. Recall that this type of justification was not mentioned in the published report of experiment 2 because at the time we did not realize its possible significance and therefore treated it as "noise."

3. Not surprisingly, for question 1 ratings, there was a main effect for story, $F(5, 216) = 3.81$, $p = .0025$, and an interaction of story × condition, $F(5, 216) = 6.10$, $p = .0001$. However, this interaction reflected merely quantitative differences; across stories, the differences in ratings between the controlled and the confounded conditions varied in magnitude but were all in the same direction (with controlled ratings higher that confounded ratings).

4. For the question 3 ratings, there was a main effect for story, $F(5, 216) = 3.23$, $p = .0078$, an interaction of story × age, $F(10, 216) = 2.33$, $p = .01$, and an interaction of story × age × condition, $F(10, 216) = 2.18$, $p = .02$. For college students, for each story, confounded ratings were higher than controlled rating. For the two younger groups, for each story (with one exception), controlled ratings were higher than confounded ratings. Therefore, as in question 1, the effects of story reflect, for the most part, differences in magnitude and do not substantively affect the results.

5. For the question 2 ratings, neither the main effect for story nor any of the interactions involving story reached significance at the .05 level.

6. For the question 4 ratings, there was a main effect for story, $F(5, 216) = 3.10$, $p = .01$, but none of the interactions involving story reached the .2 level of significance. Therefore, the effects of story did not substantively affect the results.

Chapter 7

1. There was a main effect for age, $F(2, 408) = 6.73$, $p = .001$. Causal ratings increased as subjects' age decreased. Specifically, sixth-graders' ratings were higher than those of college students, $F(1, 408) = 13.27$, $p = .0001$, and ninth-graders' ratings were comparable to the average of the other two groups, $F(1, 408) = .183$, $p = .669$. This is parallel to findings from other studies.

2. The information in the later report also included, for example, "There has just not been time to find out whether there could be some other reason why John was sitting near one of the top students." This information was included to coordinate this experiment with another experiment not reported here. This particular piece of information was constant across conditions and therefore cannot have accounted for any of the differences between conditions.

3. There were main effects for story for both initial target ratings, $F(5, 144) = 10$, $p = .0001$, and for initial alternatives ratings, $F(5, 144) = 5.71$, $p = .0001$. However, none of the

interactions involving story reached the .05 level of significance, which indicates that the story does not substantively affect the results.

Initial target ratings were affected by the interaction of sex and interview type, $F(1, 60) = 4.72$, $p = .034$, as well as by the interaction of sex, interview type, and age, $F(2, 60) = 4.30$, $p = .023$. Note that both interactions involved interview type, which did not come into play until after initial ratings had been made. Therefore, we attribute the two interactions to sampling error.

Chapter 9

1. For the modify explanations, there were a main effect for story, $F(5, 342) = 5.49$, $p = .0001$, and a significant interaction involving story and age, $F(10, 342) = 2.07$, $p = .03$. This interaction appeared primarily with the story that involved the vaccine, on which the sixth-graders provided somewhat higher modify ratings that would have been expected if there were no interaction. However, the sixth-graders also gave higher average ratings than the college students on the other five stories. Thus, ignoring the interaction does not affect the ordering of the average modify ratings for each age, and thus does not substantively affect the conclusions.

   Reject ratings did not differ among stories, $F(5, 342) = 1.72$, $p = .13$, and no interactions with story were significant.

2. There was a main effect for story, $F(5, 756) = 7.07$, $p = .0001$, and an interaction of story and condition, $F(10, 756) = 3.3$, $p = .0003$. However, because the interaction reflected no discernible pattern, it will be ignored.

3. Again, there was a main effect for story, $F(5, 756) = 3.83$, $p = .002$, and there was an interaction of condition and story, $F(10, 756) = 3.73$, $p = .0001$, as well as an interaction of age and condition and story, $F(20, 756) = 1.61$, $p = .04$. But again, the results reflected no discernible pattern.

4. There were a main effect for story, $F(5, 756) = 5.39$, $p = .0001$, and an interaction of story and condition, $F(10, 756) = 5.13$, $p = .0001$. But these again reflected no obvious pattern.

Chapter 10

1. As I already noted in chapter 3, Kuhn et al. also mentioned subjects' beliefs about mechanisms when assessing causal theories. However, their disconfirming evidence was restricted to evidence about covariation and did not focus on beliefs about mechanism.

Chapter 11

1. For those who are interested in rereading the Mynatt et al. (1977) report, it is important to point out that the reproduction of the second screen in the original article is different from the reproduction in the condensed version of the article that appears in the Johnson-Laird and Wason volume. In the condensed version, the gray disk (within whose boundary the black triangle appears) is mistakenly reproduced as a black disc.

2. Strictly speaking, of course, these were not working hypotheses, because they were not modified in the light of disconfirming evidence, since subjects were given no feedback, either disconfirming or confirming. However, they were generated as hypotheses that might lead to *possible* refinements of existing hypotheses.

References

Baron, J. (1985). *Rationality and intelligence*. Cambridge: Cambridge University Press.

Beattie, J., and Baron, J. (1988). Confirmation and matching biases in hypothesis testing. *Quarterly Journal of Experimental Psychology* 40A (2): 269–297.

Boyd, R. N. (1982). Scientific realism and naturalistic epistemology. In P. D. Asquith and R. N. Giere, (eds.), *PSA 1980: proceedings of the 1980 biennial meeting of the Philosophy of Science Association*, vol. 2. E. Lansing: Philosophy of Science Association.

Boyd, R. N. (1983). On the current status of the issue of scientific realism. *Erkenntnis* 19:45–90.

Boyd, R. N. (1985). Lex orendi est lex credendi. In Paul M. Churchland and C. A. Hooker (eds.), *Images of science: scientific realism versus constructive empiricism*. Chicago: University of Chicago Press.

Boyd, R. N. (1989). What realism implies and what it does not. *Dialectica* 43 (1–2): 5–29.

Boyd, R. N. (1990). Realism, approximate truth, and philosophical method. In W. Savage (ed.), *Scientific theories*, Minnesota Studies in the Philosophy of Science, no. 14. Minneapolis: University of Minnesota Press.

Boyd, R. N., Gaspar, P., and Trout, J. D. (eds.) (1990). *The philosophy of science*. Cambridge: MIT Press.

Brown, A. L. (1989). Analogical learning and transfer: what develops? In S. Vosniadou and A. Ortony (eds.), *Similarity and analogical reasoning*. New York: Cambridge University Press.

Bruner, J. S., Goodnow, J. J., and Austin, G. A. (1956). *A study of thinking*. New York: Wiley.

Bullock, M. (1991). Scientific reasoning in elementary school: developmental and individual differences. Paper presented at the Biennial Meetings of the Society for Research in Child Development, Seattle, Washington.

Bullock, M., Gelman, R., and Baillargeon, R. (1982). The development of causal reasoning. In W. F. Friedman (ed.), *The developmental psychology of time* (pp. 209–245). London: Academic Press.

Carey, S. (1985). *Conceptual change in childhood*. Cambridge: MIT Press.

Chapman, L., and Chapman, J. (1967). Genesis of popular but erroneous diagnostic observations. *Journal of Abnormal Psychology* 72:193–204.

Chapman, L., and Chapman, J. (1969). Illusory correlation as an obstacle to the use of valid psychodiagnostic signs. *Journal of Abnormal Psychology* 74:271–280.

Chi, M. T. H. (1992). Conceptual change within and across ontological categories: Examples from learning and discovery in science. In R. N. Giere (ed.), *Cognitive models of science*, Minnesota Studies in the Philosophy of Science, no. 15. Minneapolis: University of Minnesota Press.

Chi, M. T. H., Feltovich, P., and Glaser, R. (1981). Categorization and representation of physics problems by experts and novices. *Cognitive Science* 5:121–152.

Chi, M. T. H., and Koeske, R. (1983). Network representation of a child's dinosaur knowledge. *Developmental Psychology* 19:29–39.

Dunbar, K., and Klahr, D. (1989). Developmental differences in scientific discovery processes. In D. Klahr and K. Kotovsky (eds.), *Complex information processing: the impact of Herbert A. Simon.* Hillsdale, N.J.: Lawrence Erlbaum Associates.

Evans, J. St. B. T. (1982). *The psychology of deductive reasoning.* London: Routledge & Kegan Paul.

Gilhooly, K. J. (1982). Thinking: directed, undirected, and creative. New York: Academic Press.

Gleitman, H. (1983). *Basic psychology.* New York: W. W. Norton & Co.

Goodman, N. (1973). *Fact, fiction, and forecast.* 3rd ed. Indianapolis: Bobbs-Merrill.

Hanson, N. R. (1958). *Patterns of discovery.* Cambridge: Cambridge University Press.

Inhelder, B., and Piaget, J. (1958). *The growth of logical thinking from childhood to adolescence.* New York: Basic Books.

Johnson-Laird, P. N., Legrenzi, P., and Legrenzi, M. (1972). Reasoning and a sense of reality. *British Journal of Psychology* 63:395–400.

Johnson-Laird, P. N., and Wason, P. C. (1977). *Thinking: readings in cognitive science.* Cambridge University Press.

Karmiloff-Smith, A. (1984). Children's problem solving. In M. E. Lamb, A. L. Brown, and B. Rogoff (eds.), *Advances in developmental psychology* (vol. 3, pp. 39–90). Hillsdale, N.J.: Lawrence Erlbaum Associates.

Karmiloff-Smith, A., and Inhelder, B. (1974/1975). If you want to get ahead, get a theory. *Cognition* 3:195–212.

Keating, D. P. (1990). Adolescent thinking. In S. S. Feldman and G. R. Elliott (eds.), *At the threshold: the developing adolescent* (pp. 54–89). Cambridge: Harvard University Press.

Kitcher, P. (1993). *The advancement of science.* New York: Oxford University Press.

Klahr, D., and Dunbar, K. (1988). Dual space search during scientific reasoning. *Cognitive Science* 12:1–48.

Klahr, D., Dunbar, K., and Fay, A. L. (1990). Designing good experiments to test bad hypotheses. In J. Shrager and P. Langley (eds.), *Computational models of discovery and theory formation.* Hillsdale, N.J.: Lawrence Erlbaum Associates.

Klahr, D., Fay, A. L., and Dunbar, K. (1993). Heuristics for scientific experimentation: a developmental study. *Cognitive Psychology* 25:111–146.

Klayman, J., and Ha, Y. (1987). Confirmation, disconfirmation, and information in hypothesis testing. *Psychological Review* 94:211–228.

Klayman, J., and Ha, Y. (1989). Hypothesis testing in rule discovery: strategy, structure, and content. *Journal of Experimental Psychology: Learning, Memory, and Cognition* 15 (4): 596–604.

Koslowski, B., and Maqueda, M. (1993). What is confirmation bias and when do people have it? *Merrill-Palmer Quarterly* 39 (1): 104–130. Invitational issue entitled *The development of rationality and critical thinking.*

Koslowski, B., and Okagaki, L. (1986). Non-Humean indices of causation in problem-solving situations: causal mechanism, analogous effects, and the status of rival alternative accounts. *Child Development* 57:1100–1108.

Koslowski, B., Okagaki, L., Lorenz, C., and Umbach, D. (1989). When covariation isn't enough: the role of causal mechanism, sampling method, and sample size in causal reasoning. *Child Development* 60:1316–1327.

Koslowski, B., Spilton, D., and Snipper, A. (1981). Children's beliefs about instances of mechanical and electrical causation. *Journal of Applied Developmental Psychology* 2:189–210.

Koslowski, B., Susman, A., and Serling, J. (1991). Conceptual vs. technical understanding of evidence in scientific reasoning. Paper presented at the Biennial Meetings of the Society for Research in Child Development, Seattle, Washington.

Kuhn, D. (1989) Children and adults as intuitive scientists. *Psychological Review* 96 (4): 674–689.

Kuhn, D. (1991). *The skills of argument.* New York: Cambridge University Press.

Kuhn, D., Amsel, E., and O'Loughlin, M. (1988). *The development of scientific thinking skills.* Orlando, Fla.: Academic Press.

Kuhn, T. S. (1970). *The structure of scientific revolutions.* 2nd ed., enl. Chicago: University of Chicago Press.

Mackworth, N. H., and Bruner, J. S. (1966). Selecting visual information during recognition by adults and children. Unpublished manuscript, Harvard Center for Cognitive Studies.

McCloskey, M. (1983a). Intuitive physics. *Scientific American* 248 (4): 122–130.

McCloskey, M. (1983b). Naive theories of motion. In D. Gentner and A. L. Stevens (eds.), *Mental models.* Hillsdale, N.J.: Erlbaum.

Mendelson, R., and Shultz, T. R. (1976). Covariation and temporal contiguity as principles of causal inference in young children. *Journal of Experimental Child Psychology* 22:408–412.

Murphy, G., and Medin, D. (1985). The role of theories in conceptual coherence. *Psychological Review* 92 (3): 289–316.

Mynatt, C. R., Doherty, M. E., and Tweney, R. D. (1977). Confirmation bias in a simulated research environment: an experimental study of scientific inference. *Quarterly Journal of Experimental Psychology* 29:85–95. Excerpts reprinted in P. N. Johnson-Laird and P. C. Wason (eds.), *Thinking: readings in cognitive science* (pp. 315–325). Cambridge: Cambridge University Press.

Mynatt, C. R., Doherty, M. E., and Tweney, R. D. (1978). Consequences of information and disconfirmation in a simulated research environment. *Quarterly Journal of Experimental Psychology* 30:395–406.

Nisbett, R., and Ross, L. (1980). *Human inference: strategies and shortcomings of social judgment.* Englewood Cliffs, N.J.: Prentice-Hall.

Piaget, J. (1972). *The child's conception of physical causality.* Totowa, N.J.: Littlefield, Adams and Co. First published in English by Routledge & Kegan Paul, London, 1930.

Popper, K. R. (1959). *The logic of scientific discovery.* London: Hutchinson.

Putnam, H. (1962). The analytic and the synthetic. In H. Feigl and G. Maxwell (eds.), *Scientific explanation, space, and time,* Minnesota Studies in the Philosophy of Science, no. 3. Minneapolis: University of Minnesota Press.

Putnam, H. (1972). Explanation and reference. In G. Pearce, and P. Maynard (eds.), *Conceptual change.* Dordrecht: Reidel.

Putnam, H. (1974). The "corroboration" of theories. In P. A. Schilpp (ed.), *The philosophy of Karl Popper.* LaSalle, Ill.: Open Court.

Putnam, H. (1975a). The meaning of "meaning." In his *Mind, language, and reality.* Cambridge: Cambridge University Press.

Putnam, H. (1975b). Language and reality. In his *Mind, language, and reality.* Cambridge: Cambridge University Press.

Quine, W. V. (1969). Natural kinds. In W. V. Quine, *Ontological relativity and other essays.* New York: Columbia University Press.

Schauble, L. (1990). Belief revision in children: the role of prior knowledge and strategies for generating evidence. *Journal of Experimental Child Psychology* 49:31–57.

Schunn, C. D., and Klahr, D. (1992). Complexity management in a discovery task. *Cognitive Science.*

Schunn, C. D., and Klahr, D. (1993). Self- vs. other-generated hypotheses in scientific discovery. *Cognitive Science.*

Shultz, T. R. (1982). *Rules of causal attribution.* Monographs of the Society for Research in Child Development, vol. 47, no. 1 = serial no. 194. Chicago: University of Chicago Press.

Shultz, T. R., and Mendelson, R. (1975). The use of covariation as a principle of causal analysis. *Child Development* 46:394–399.

Siegler, R. (1975). Defining the locus of developmental differences in children's causal reasoning. *Journal of Experimental Child Psychology* 20:512–525.

Siegler, R. (1976). The effects of simple necessity and sufficiency relationships on children's causal inferences. *Child Development* 47:1058–1063.

Siegler, R., & Liebert, R. M. (1974). Effects of contiguity, regularity, and age on children's causal inferences. *Developmental Psychology* 10:574–579.

Sodian, B., Zaitchick, D., and Carey, S. (1991). Young children's differentiation of hypothetical beliefs from evidence. *Child Development* 62:753–766.

Stevenson, H. W. (1972). *Children's learning.* Englewood Cliffs, N.J.: Prentice-Hall.

Tversky, A., and Kahneman, D. (1974). Judgment under uncertainty: heuristics and biases. *Science* 185:1124–1131.

Tversky, A., and Kahneman, D. (1980). Causal schemata in judgments under uncertainty. In M. Fishbein (ed.), *Progress in social psychology.* Hillsdale, N.J.: Lawrence Erlbaum Associates.

Van Fraassen, B. (1980). *The scientific image.* Oxford: Oxford University Press.

Wason, P. C. (1960). On the failure to eliminate hypotheses in a conceptual task. *Quarterly Journal of Experimental Psychology* 12:129–140.

Wason, P. C. (1966). Reasoning. In B. Foss (ed.), *New horizons in psychology.* Harmondsworth: Penguin Books.

Wason, P. C. (1977). Introduction to hypotheses and theories. In P. N. Johnson-Laird and P. C. Wason (eds.), *Thinking: readings in cognitive science.* Cambridge: Cambridge University Press.

Wason, P. C., and Shapiro, D. (1971). Natural and contrived experience in a reasoning problem. *Quarterly Journal of Experimental Psychology* 23:63–71.

Wiser, M. (1987). The differentiation of heat and temperature: history of science and novice-expert shift. In S. Strauss (ed.), *Ontogeny, phylogeny, and historical development.* Norwood, N.J.: Ablex.

Index